ASSURED
DESTRUCTION

TITLES IN THE SERIES

The Other Space Race: Eisenhower and the Quest for Aerospace Security

An Untaken Road: Strategy, Technology, and the Mobile Intercontinental Ballistic Missile

Strategy: Context and Adaptation from Archidamus to Airpower

Cassandra in Oz: Counterinsurgency and Future War

Cyberspace in Peace and War

Limiting Risk in America's Wars: Airpower, Asymmetrics, and a New Strategic Paradigm

Always at War: Organizational Culture in Strategic Air Command, 1946–62

How the Few Became the Proud: Crafting the Marine Corps Mystique, 1874–1918

TRANSFORMING WAR

Paul J. Springer, editor

To ensure success, the conduct of war requires rapid and effective adaptation to changing circumstances. While every conflict involves a degree of flexibility and innovation, there are certain changes that have occurred throughout history that stand out because they fundamentally altered the conduct of warfare. The most prominent of these changes have been labeled "Revolutions in Military Affairs" (RMAs). These so-called revolutions include technological innovations as well as entirely new approaches to strategy. Revolutionary ideas in military theory, doctrine, and operations have also permanently changed the methods, means, and objectives of warfare.

This series examines fundamental transformations that have occurred in warfare. It places particular emphasis upon RMAs to examine how the development of a new idea or device can alter not only the conduct of wars but their effect upon participants, supporters, and uninvolved parties. The unifying concept of the series is not geographical or temporal; rather, it is the notion of change in conflict and its subsequent impact. This has allowed the incorporation of a wide variety of scholars, approaches, disciplines, and conclusions to be brought under the umbrella of the series. The works include biographies, examinations of transformative events, and analyses of key technological innovations that provide a greater understanding of how and why modern conflict is carried out, and how it may change the battlefields of the future.

ASSURED DESTRUCTION

BUILDING THE BALLISTIC MISSILE CULTURE OF THE U.S. AIR FORCE

DAVID W. BATH

NAVAL INSTITUTE PRESS • ANNAPOLIS, MARYLAND

Naval Institute Press
291 Wood Road
Annapolis, MD 21402

Library of Congress Cataloging-in-Publication Data

Names: Bath, David W., date, author.
Title: Assured destruction : building the ballistic missile culture of the
    U.S. Air Force / David W. Bath.
Other titles: Building the ballistic missile culture of the U.S. Air Force
Description: Annapolis, Maryland : Naval Institute Press, [2020] | Series:
    Transforming war | Includes bibliographical references and index.
Identifiers: LCCN 2019040952 (print) | LCCN 2019040953 (ebook) | ISBN
    9781682474938 (hardcover) | ISBN 9781682475133 (pdf) | ISBN
    9781682475133 (epub)
Subjects: LCSH: Intercontinental ballistic missiles—United
    States—History. | Intercontinental ballistic missiles—United
    States—Historiography. | United States. Air Force—Weapons
    systems—History. | Strategic forces—United States—History. | Nuclear
    weapons—United States—History.
Classification: LCC UG1312.I2 B38 2020 (print) | LCC UG1312.I2 (ebook) |
    DDC 358.1/754820973—dc23
LC record available at https://lccn.loc.gov/2019040952
LC ebook record available at https://lccn.loc.gov/2019040953

♾Print editions meet the requirements of ANSI/NISO z39.48-1992 (Permanence of Paper).
Printed in the United States of America.

28 27 26 25 24 23 22 21 20   9 8 7 6 5 4 3 2 1
First printing

CONTENTS

ILLUSTRATIONS

ACKNOWLEDGMENTS

I owe immense gratitude to many who helped make this book a reality. First, I thank God for placing me in my current position. Thanks to Ken Hanushek for seeing potential and encouraging me down this path years ago. I also thank my dissertation committee, Joseph "Chip" Dawson III, Terry Anderson, Olga Dror, Angela Hudson, and Jim Burk, for guiding the initial study. The Smith Richardson Foundation and Texas A&M University provided generous grants supporting my research. Former missilemen, including Charlie Simpson and the Association of Air Force Missileers, provided their stories and encouragement. Librarians, staff, and archivists at the Air Force Historical Research Agency, the National Archives, the Library of Congress, the Eisenhower Presidential Library, the LBJ Presidential Library, the National Defense University Library, the Fairchild Research Information Center, and the Mudd Manuscript Library guided me to critical documents that revealed key insights into early missile development and operations. Neil Sheehan and Jeffrey Flannery provided access to interviews gathered for *A Fiery Peace in a Cold War*. The library staffs of Texas A&M, the University of Mississippi, and Rogers State University cheerfully responded to my many requests for assistance. Historians from Los Alamos Laboratories, the Department of Energy, Global Strike Command, Los Angeles AFB, and the Smithsonian provided incredible illustrations while Cyril Wilson created maps of the missile bases and colleagues from Rogers State University helped me enhance the images. Former students Elizabeth Walters, Sara Stefancik, and Jacob Fine reviewed chapters for me while numerous other friends helped in countless ways. Thanks to P. J. Springer and the Naval Institute Press for working with me to publish the book. Finally, I would like to thank my parents; my wife, Beth; and my children—Kristen and Sean—for encouraging me through this journey.

ASSURED
DESTRUCTION

INTRODUCTION AND HISTORIOGRAPHY

In December 1957 many people in the United States perceived the nuclear intercontinental ballistic missile (ICBM) as the ultimate weapon. By tying the newly developed atomic and hydrogen bombs to the ballistic missile and giving it intercontinental range, scientists created a revolution in military affairs as great as that of gunpowder or the rifled barrel. The new capability could devastate portions of an enemy country in minutes, and there was no defense against it. Although the United States had not yet successfully launched an ICBM to the required 5,000 mile range—achieving only 530 miles on its single successful long-range flight to this point—the hopes of America's future peace and security lay in this rocket and its successors, already under development. The nation prayed that its rival, the Soviet Union, would not develop a working ballistic nuclear missile first.

The Air Force planned to recruit capable and highly educated men to operate and maintain these awesome weapons for the defense of the nation and, American leaders proclaimed, for the protection of Europe, Asia, and other areas. Initially, these men—deemed missilemen at first and then later missileers—were expected to be geniuses, each with a degree in engineering as well as combat experience from World War II or Korea. They were expected to guide the Air Force and the United States into a future of stability and international harmony through strength as aircraft and other weapons became obsolete. Their own futures seemed boundless. Less than seven years later, in July 1964, the Atlas missile was decommissioned, along with the Titan I, the Thor, and the Jupiter, all ballistic nuclear missiles that were developed about the same time as the Atlas. The follow-on Minuteman and Titan II missiles were retained but held only as a necessary deterrent to the use of enemy nuclear weapons while military planners focused on a "limited war" in Vietnam. President Lyndon Johnson had no interest in using even one nuclear weapon, except in the most dire situation: a direct nuclear confrontation with the Soviet Union.

In fact, on September 18, 1967, the official who oversaw the largest buildup of U.S. ballistic missiles, Secretary of Defense Robert McNamara, stated, "I want, however, to make one point patently clear: our current numerical superiority over the Soviet Union in reliable, accurate and effective warheads is both greater than we had originally planned and in fact more than we require." He continued, "Moreover, in the larger equation of security, our 'superiority' is of limited significance, since even with our current superiority, or indeed with any numerical superiority realistically attainable, the blunt inescapable fact remains that the Soviet Union could still—with its present forces—effectively destroy the United States, even after absorbing the full weight of an American first strike."[1]

As McNamara shifted his focus to nonnuclear combat, the Air Force relegated missiles to a minor position, one significantly less important than flying operations and support to flying operations, and ignored the concerns of the missileers who controlled them. The service began to treat the men—for they were all men at the time—who controlled these missiles as second-class citizens, regarding them as support personnel rather than warriors.

But what led to such a development? How did such a promising field of military weaponry and its adherents drop so quickly in value? To be sure, this result was not predetermined. This study reveals how and why the U.S. Air Force missile community evolved as it did rather than how it was expected to progress. Three key factors powerfully shaped the perception and treatment of ballistic missiles in the United States and those who operated them, ensuring that neither the missiles nor the missileers attained their advertised prominence. The decisions made about the trajectory of missiles cost the nation millions while preventing it from fully realizing the potential of the new capability, impaired the careers of the military personnel who worked with the missiles, and—because of the lesson taken from these decisions—prevented the Air Force from properly engaging with emerging technology for decades.

First, during a time of national political turmoil and global discord, missiles were sold as the ultimate weapon without regard to the political and social implications of nuclear warfare. Between 1947 and 1957, as a cold war escalated between two former allies, rapid scientific advances allowed the United States to develop and build intercontinental ballistic nuclear missiles as quickly as possible. Political and military leaders who had just witnessed the most terrible and costly war the world had ever seen were determined to stay militarily ahead of their greatest international adversary as the two superpowers began to compete for global influence and prepare for conflict. The credible fear of a near-term World War III also influenced the public's perception of nuclear warfare. Consequently, both nations quickly developed and immediately incorporated the powerful new technology into their war plans.

In the United States, especially after the Soviet Union launched Sputnik, both Democrats and Republicans endeavored to prove their support for the new weapons, and the military services threw themselves into the effort in an attempt to not be left behind. Numerous careers were made and broken on the premise of whether the United States was behind the Soviet Union in its ability to launch nuclear ballistic missiles. This purported "missile gap" even influenced the election of the nation's thirty-fifth president: John F. Kennedy. Although President Dwight Eisenhower knew there was no "missile gap" and actively argued throughout his term of office that it did not exist, he too was forced to participate in this dangerous race. On September 13, 1955, he directed that the Department of Defense classify the ICBM research and development program the "highest priority above all others."[2] This ensured that missiles were accorded with status and significance in the short term but tied their value to political vagaries, potentially setting them up for a future demise when political support waned.

The second contributing factor was the creation of a separate air force and the intensified interservice rivalry that resulted from this act. The struggle to create a new service convinced many Air Force advocates of the need to protect and prize their cherished flying mission against any and all competitors. President Eisenhower, and others in his administration, perceived the new ballistic missile as the natural replacement for the manned strategic bomber. U.S. Air Force leaders, in response, believed they could best protect the manned bomber and their domination of the strategic air mission by controlling the new weapon so they could determine its future.

Conversely, the U.S. Army—stung from the loss of the Air Corps, especially as the Air Force became the nation's dominant military capability under President Eisenhower—believed the ballistic missile should belong with the ground forces. The U.S. Navy, too, recognized that this awesome new weapon had caught the attention of the nation and held the promise of extravagant funding and historical prominence. Therefore, each of the three major services struggled mightily to obtain control of the new mission in order to expand their credibility and funding, if not to ensure their survival. Thus, although the first successful ICBM was not built until 1957, this study examines how the creation of a separate air force in 1947 influenced the incorporation of the weapon into the new service and prejudiced the Air Force's treatment of the new capability after it was assimilated and political leaders returned their focus to nonnuclear conflict.

The third contributing factor, the Cuban Missile Crisis—arguably the pinnacle of success for U.S. Air Force missileers—rather than validating the nation's perception that missiles were the trend of future military operations, convinced the nation's leaders that nuclear missiles should never be used except to deter nuclear war. Therefore, as the nation became enmeshed in the Vietnam conflict, neither the Kennedy administration nor the Johnson administration seriously considered the first use of nuclear weapons. The political leaders became focused on fighting the war with conventional weapons, allowing the Air Force leaders to transfer money, personnel, and prestige away from the missiles and back to the flying mission.

Thus, as missileers moved into their second decade of existence, the meteoric rise that was promised to them disappeared as quickly as it had developed. They were no longer the exalted combatants of the future but were a proud, mostly unnoticed, and unappreciated cohort of warriors tied to the monotonous grind of underground, "push-button" warfare. Many of the concerns they had expressed, including the loneliness and tedium of missile duties, an inability to excel at daily operations, and poor promotion opportunities, were left to fester for decades.

This study began as an investigation into the actions of the missileers during the Cuban Missile Crisis, the only time in history that individual warriors have been tasked with the responsibility of destroying millions of people within minutes of notification, wreaking untold havoc on a significant portion of the Earth, without recourse to stop the devastation once they launched the missiles.[3] However, a significant amount of the material dealing with this topic is still classified after fifty years. The search was not futile, though, as it revealed the significant change in perspective toward missileers and their powerful weapons between 1957 and 1967. This book examines the human dimension of a new way of life—the era of the nuclear missile.

One of the difficulties of analyzing the social implications of the first decade of ballistic missiles in the Air Force is that most contemporary documents focus upon the scientific advancements of missiles and bureaucratic infighting involved in building them rather than on how the military incorporated the new weapons. Former Air Force historian Jacob Neufeld, in an interview with the author, revealed that no one at the time considered the human aspect of the missiles to be important.[4] The few documents from the time that do focus on the lives of the missileers remain difficult to obtain as most are still classified.[5] For this reason—and to gain a more personal understanding—this study uses the personal recollections of missileers who served during this time as well as contemporary papers produced in professional military education courses to unearth new insights.

There are several major historiographical arguments dealing with the study of Air Force ICBMs. One revolves around whether Air Force leaders began working to design and build the ICBM at the end of World War II or whether the service only started to seriously undertake developing the missiles as a response to the political firestorm created by the launch of Sputnik. This study acknowledges that work began well before Sputnik but also contends that the pace and funding wavered greatly until the Soviet threat appeared real. A closely related argument is whether the Air Force developed and built the ICBM to become a significant part of its inventory or whether its leadership fought the other services for control of the new mission so the service could retain the manned bomber as the premier weapon. This book proposes that Air Force leaders were divided on their advocacy of missiles and outside forces greatly influenced their willingness and ability to actively incorporate the new weapons into their plans but that when Gen. Curtis LeMay became chief of staff of the Air Force in 1961, the forces against missiles prevailed. This project also argues that the extensive manipulation of the career field by outside forces, including the Cuban Missile Crisis and the war in Vietnam, greatly influenced the nascent culture of missileers, preventing the group from adequately addressing significant concerns that haunted missileers into the twenty-first century.

There have been several outstanding books on missile-related topics. Several books written in the late 1950s and early 1960s reveal early thoughts about ballistic nuclear missiles and how they would be used. In 1958 Lt. Col. Kenneth Gantz, the editor of the *Air Force Quarterly Review*, assembled several key articles dealing Air Force ballistic missiles from the review, along with comments from senior Air Force leaders, to create *The United States Air Force Report on the Ballistic Missile: Its Technology, Logistics, and Strategy*.[6] This was almost certainly the first nonfiction book published on ballistic missiles, and it accurately reveals the Air Force understanding of missiles at the time. However, when the articles were written, there were not operational ICBMs in the United States, so the book is full of predictions rather than descriptions of actual missile units or personnel.

In 1959 Bernard Brodie approached the new weapons from a different perspective. The well-known military strategist published his concepts of nuclear strategy in *Strategy in the Missile Age*. He addressed critical changes that needed to be made to military strategy with the advent of nuclear weapons and strongly influenced the nation's perspective on deterring the use of nuclear weapons by maintaining an equal nuclear capability.[7]

At almost the same time Herman Kahn added a different perspective to nuclear strategy, using quantitative analysis techniques in lectures at Princeton University to contend that nuclear war did not necessarily mean mutual annihilation. He argued that nations should not only prepare plans to prevent nuclear war but plan to win or at least survive a nuclear war if one could not be prevented. His innovative ideas were then translated into book form and published in 1960 as *On Thermonuclear War*.[8]

James Baar and William E. Howard followed up with another authoritative book, *Combat Missileman*, that relied on interviews and personal experiences to reveal the lives and struggles of the early missileers. This book is another outstanding reflection of the early perspective of missiles, but since the book was published in 1961, it was still too early for the authors to analyze how the missile culture would develop or to comprehend what would happen by the end of the 1960s.[9]

Most other early works detail the creation of the ICBM. Roy Neal interviewed the scientists and engineers who developed the second-generation missile, Minuteman, to write *Ace in the Hole* in 1962.[10] Three years later Ernest Schwiebert published *A History of the U.S. Air Force Ballistic Missiles*, working with many of the same people to detail the scientific and logistical development of the Atlas, Titan, and Minuteman missiles.[11] Jacob Neufeld authored an update to Schwiebert's work in 1990 with *The Development of Ballistic Missiles in the United States Air Force, 1945–1960*.[12] Each of these authors focused their studies on the scientific and engineering aspects of the ICBM rather than the operations and management of missiles.

Edmund Beard, in *Developing the ICBM: A Study in Bureaucratic Politics*, expanded the study of missiles to reveal the bureaucratic and political machinations involved in building the ballistic missile and instigated the most prolific argument on the subject by stating that Air Force leaders did not want the missile to succeed as they were concerned it would replace the manned bomber.[13] Christopher Gainor argued against Beard's thesis in "The United States Air Force and the Emergence of the Intercontinental Ballistic Missile, 1945–1954."[14] Once again, though, both remain concentrated on the creation of missiles rather than addressing what happened to them after their construction.

Desmond Ball, in *Politics and Force Levels: The Strategic Missile Program of the Kennedy Administration*, broadened the focus again to include the influence of the political arena on missiles and vice versa.[15] Later, Neil Sheehan entered the fray, authoring *A Fiery Peace in a Cold War: Bernard Schriever and the Ultimate Weapon* in 2009.[16] All of these authors center on missiles as a piece of technology or on the political machinations involved in gaining control of and building such weapons rather than on how they were incorporated into the Air Force inventory as a key weapon in national defense or on the struggles of the personnel assigned to control them.

Finally, in 2012 David Spires wrote *On Alert: An Operational History of the United States Air Force Intercontinental Ballistic Missile Program, 1945–2011.*[17] This tome is one of the few that deal with the operations of missiles and the day-to-day activities of missileers, but Spires focuses primarily on the time after 1965, with minimal concentration on the critical time period between 1957 and 1967. This study intends to fill this historiographical chasm while placing the era into historical and political context by documenting the impact that the Cold War and establishment of the Air Force as a separate service had on the new ballistic missiles and those who worked with them.

Since the study relates the growth of missiles in the Air Force to the growth of airpower in the Army just a few years prior, readers can find a valuable resource to understanding this earlier revolution and its sociological impact in James P. Tate's *The Army and Its Air Corps: Army Policy toward Aviation, 1919–1941.*[18]

Those who are searching for valuable insights on the Cold War are well served by John Lewis Gaddis' *The Cold War: A New History*, which presents a balanced perspective of the Cold War from its rise at the end of World War II through its demise in December 1991 when the leader of the former Soviet Union declared the conflict over.[19] Carole Fink has also written a valuable resource in *Cold War: An International History*, which includes what she labels the prelude to the Cold War, the time between the creation of the Soviet Union in 1917 and the emergence of the full-fledged rivalry in 1949.[20] Although there are numerous other valuable books that reveal aspects of the Cold War, Norman Friedman's *The Fifty Year War: Conflict and Strategy in the Cold War* is another that I would highly recommend.[21]

Readers hoping to find more on what I consider the most influential event of the Cold War, and probably of the twentieth century, which is centered in this study—the Cuban Missile Crisis—should read Michael Dobbs' *One Minute to Midnight*, which reveals the multitude of events that made up this decisive episode, and David G. Coleman's *The Fourteenth*

Day, which does an outstanding job of revealing the less-known political actions and implications following the legendary thirteen days made famous by Bobby Kennedy's memoir.[22]

Information on the Soviet side is still difficult to obtain. For more information on the Soviet development of a nuclear bomb, the best book that I have found is David Holloway's *Stalin and the Bomb*.[23] This tome provides a very clear perspective of the Soviet effort to build their first atomic weapon. Asif Siddiqi has conducted outstanding research on the development of early Soviet rockets, translating and editing the four-volume *Rockets and People*, a first-hand account of Boris Chertok, a Soviet rocket engineer, as well as writing *Challenge to Apollo: The Soviet Union and the Space Race, 1945–1974* and *The Red Rockets' Glare: Spaceflight and the Soviet Imagination, 1857–1957*.[24] Finally, for a solid understanding of Russia's Strategic Rocket Forces, see *Russian Strategic Nuclear Forces*, edited by Pavel Podvig, the most thorough book on the topic that I have found.[25]

This book conveys its historical argument in a chronological narrative. The introduction presents the thesis and provides the historical context, addressing the historiographical gap that this study intends to fill. Chapters 1 through 3 review the initial development of nuclear missiles while chapters 4 through the conclusion reveal the impact of incorporating missiles into the Air Force in the manner that they were. Chapter 1 addresses the creation of the nuclear bomb, its use in World War II, and the Soviet response. Chapter 2 reveals the intermittent and convoluted development of the ballistic missile during the Roosevelt and Truman presidencies, addressing the internal and interservice struggles to wrest control of the new capability into a single branch of the military services. Chapter 3 explores how Trevor Gardner influenced the Air Force's control and development of missiles under the Eisenhower administration and how the intensifying Cold War increased the pressure for both countries to quickly field the new capability. Chapter 4 deals with the problems caused by the rush to build and incorporate missiles into the Air Force, including damage to the missiles' credibility within the service and hostility engendered by the political maneuvers to support them. Chapter 5 addresses the changes brought about by the Cuban Missile Crisis, including Strategic

Air Command's herculean efforts to mobilize the new weapons during the crisis and the Kennedy administration's dramatic reversal in perspective, from aggressively advocating for missiles before the Cuban Missile Crisis to retreating from almost any use afterward. Chapter 6 analyzes the impact within the Air Force of the political decision to move toward limited warfare, detailing the impact on the missile career fields. The conclusion reviews the political and military decisions affecting ICBMs during their first decade and explores the long-lasting impact of those decisions on the Air Force, including decisions impacting other military capabilities that reduced the need for piloted aircraft like operations in space, computer network operations, and unmanned aerial vehicles.

CHAPTER 1

The Atomic Bomb

World War II ushered in a time of significant scientific and technological advancement. Scientists became aware of the double helix structure that makes up DNA, opening the door for major advances in understanding hereditary diseases. Penicillin proved to be an extremely effective antibacterial agent, approved for medical use, and drug companies began to produce it in vast quantities. Bell Laboratories revealed the capabilities of the transistor, beginning a revolution in solid-state electronics. Jonas Salk identified a vaccine that would all but eradicate the deadly disease that crippled President Franklin Delano Roosevelt—polio. Significant political upheaval throughout much of the world led to continued scientific progress in weapons of war as well as agents of peace. Hans von Ohain and Frank Whittle separately designed and constructed jet engines. Other scientists used Enrico Fermi's studies about triggering an atomic chain reaction to produce the most powerful weapon ever known—the nuclear bomb.

As the fight against the Nazis wore down, the ties between the Allies began to wear thin. Soviet, British, and American leaders found that, without the chilling threat of Nazi expansion, diverging national interests prevailed over the concerns of their partners in the conflict. Soon the former Allies became enmeshed in a struggle of their own—the Cold War. This chapter reveals how the end of World War II and the emerging Cold War motivated United States leaders to accelerate their weapons programs to create an almost unstoppable and destructive weapon—the nuclear ballistic missile—and amplified the criticality of the nuclear ballistic missile to both Cold War adversaries.

The manufacture of the nuclear ballistic missile was made possible by remarkable scientific advances in two separate fields that took place roughly twenty years apart. The first was the creation of the ballistic rocket in 1926, although more than a decade passed before it was used to transport weaponry. The second was the creation of the atomic bomb in 1945. Sadly, although the initial studies done on ballistic missiles were conducted in the United States, the Nazis dominated the early development of both as weapons.

Germany led the initial development efforts to produce a bomb using the fission of atoms to create energy. In 1938 Otto Hahn and Fritz Strassmann discovered that they could make a uranium atom become unstable by bombarding it with neutrons. With the help of Lise Meitner and Otto Frisch, they discovered that—under the right conditions—the unstable atom split, creating smaller atomic particles in a process called nuclear fission. During this process, the splitting atom discharged several neutrons itself. Hahn and Strassmann published their findings in January 1939. Soon after, scientists around the world speculated that the process of nuclear fission could create further fissions, establishing a chain reaction that would generate an explosion with power far greater than any seen up to that time. By December of that year scientific journals had published almost one hundred articles on the topic. The Germans almost immediately began studying the military applications of this atomic capability.

This threat did not escape Allied notice. In August 1939 a Jewish immigrant who left Germany when the Nazis came to power, physicist Leo Szilard, became greatly concerned about the German work on nuclear explosions. He convinced Albert Einstein of the threat and persuaded him to sign a letter to President Roosevelt warning that scientists were close to creating a nuclear chain reaction using uranium. This reaction, the letter cautioned, would allow the construction of "extremely powerful bombs of a new type." He further revealed that Germany had "stopped the sale of uranium," leading him to believe the Germans might be conducting the same research. The decision to have Einstein send the letter was not arbitrary. Einstein had been awarded the Nobel Prize nearly two decades earlier and was widely recognized for his genius. Alexander Sachs, a friend of Roosevelt, personally delivered Einstein's letter to the president. Einstein's warning convinced Roosevelt to establish a board that would investigate the concerns. However, other than continued research, little more was accomplished until 1941, when U.S. and British researchers shared their research on inducing chain reactions.[1]

Two German refugees living in England had better success in convincing their government of the threat in 1941. After more accurately determining the critical mass required for an atomic bomb, Rudolf Peierls and Otto Frisch prepared a paper for the British government on the prospect of an atomic bomb. They argued that a bomb could be made from a much smaller amount of U-235 than previously believed, which meant that it could be delivered by aircraft rather than by ship. They also contended that no shelters would effectively protect citizens from the explosion. Therefore, they strongly urged the British government to begin preparing their own bomb as a counter threat. The paper must have been persuasive, as the British government organized a secret committee, christened the MAUD Committee, to study the bomb further. The MAUD Committee agreed with Peierls' and Frisch's assessment and reported that the bomb could be built in time to sway the outcome of the war.

After substantiating the research and informing their own government, the MAUD Committee shared its research with the United States, requesting that the Americans cooperate with them to develop and build an atomic bomb. When they failed to receive a reply, Marcus Oliphant, an Australian heavily involved with the MAUD Committee, approached Vannevar Bush, Roosevelt's science advisor, and Bush's National Defense Research Council to ensure they were aware of the British research. They had not been. Once Bush became aware of the new information, he summarized the MAUD research, along with American reports on nuclear fission, and provided the information to Roosevelt on October 9, 1941. Roosevelt authorized extensive research but did not authorize creation of a bomb itself.

A month and a half later, after American scientists again confirmed the original research, Bush once more broached the topic with Roosevelt. Soon after, with Roosevelt's blessing, Bush expedited research on the atomic bomb. On June 17, 1942, Bush informed the president that U.S. scientists could produce a nuclear weapon that could decisively impact combat. He further declared that, under the right conditions, it could be prepared quickly enough to affect the outcome of the war. The next day, the military was tasked to join the work. Then, on December 28, 1942, Roosevelt authorized the group, known now as the Manhattan Project, to build the required plants and facilities to construct an atomic bomb.

Henry Stimson, the U.S. secretary of war, later explained Roosevelt's policy on atomic weapons, a policy similar to the one that would be followed in the development of ICBMs: "It was to spare no effort in securing the earliest possible successful development of an atomic weapon. . . . In 1941 and 1942 they [the Germans] were believed to be ahead of us, and it was vital that they should not be the first to bring atomic weapons into the field of battle."[2]

The British and Americans were not alone in their concerns. On June 23, 1941, the day after the German attack on the Soviet Union, Soviet scientists met to volunteer their efforts toward the defense of their nation. Soon most Soviet research was focused completely on supporting the war effort. Those who had been focused in other areas dropped their research to reengage on critical wartime tasks like improving radar and armor. This included the nuclear scientists, who felt their study would be more beneficial in less esoteric areas.

One physicist, however, remained concerned about nuclear research. In 1939 Georgii Flerov and Konstantin Petrzhak discovered that a fission reaction could occur spontaneously with uranium. Later, while in the Soviet Air Forces, Flerov looked in Western journals to see if his discovery had been noticed by Western academics. Instead he noticed that Western scientists had stopped publishing on nuclear fission. But what he found even more intriguing was that the scholars who had been working in this area were not writing about other topics. This situation led him to the conclusion that the West, specifically the United States and Great Britain, had begun working on a nuclear bomb and did not want others to know. He became even more concerned when he recognized that the Germans were not publishing on the topic either, although they had very capable researchers in the field.

After addressing his concerns with everyone that he could think of, Flerov finally wrote a letter to Soviet leader Joseph Stalin in April 1942, imploring him to open a scientific discussion of nuclear research. Flerov's efforts appear to have met with no success, possibly because the Soviet leaders were suspicious of scientists, believing that they were not politically reliable. However, a similar concern emerging from a different arena had a much greater impact.

Beginning in September 1941 Soviet spies began to warn that England was preparing to produce uranium bombs. Lavrentiy Beria, the deputy commissar of the People's Commissariat for Internal Affairs (NKVD), informed Stalin, but Stalin reportedly dismissed the concerns, proclaiming the information as foreign propaganda. Thus, the Soviet leadership took no action until 1942. Only then did Beria, now head of the NKVD and a deputy prime minister as well, find proof that the Germans had been working on an atomic bomb and discover that the military intelligence organization, the GRU, corroborated his information on U.S. and British efforts to develop an atomic weapon.[3]

Intriguingly, and unknown to the Americans or their allies, the Germans had moved in the opposite direction. In early 1942 German army ordnance officers ranked the different weapon systems development programs that their service was supporting. Since they believed it unlikely that a working nuclear weapon could be developed in the next two years, by which time they believed the war would be over, they ranked the nuclear bomb very low, ensuring the failure of the Nazi's nascent nuclear project.[4]

Nevertheless, the U.S. response to the atomic threat remained focused, and even though the German threat had dissipated, a race to develop nuclear weapons began between the United States and the Soviet Union. U.S. scientists conducted studies to determine the most effective method of creating the fuel needed to produce an atomic bomb while others collaborated in a search for the best method of creating and detonating the bomb.

Robert Oppenheimer led a team to conduct the theoretical calculations that would determine the critical mass required to detonate a weapon, along with the most feasible method to do so. In July 1942 they determined that a bomb using nuclear fission was theoretically possible. Seth Neddermeyer then led a study that determined that the critical mass required to sustain a bomb could be produced in much less time by imploding, or causing the nuclear material to collapse inwardly in a violent manner, than using previous methods.

Several teams of scientists searched for the best method to enrich the required uranium and, later, to isolate plutonium, which would be used to create larger nuclear explosions. After months of study, key leaders of each group met in Washington on May 23, 1942, to determine which method could best enrich uranium. After concluding that the Germans probably had a two-year head start on the Americans, the group decided to rec-ommend development of all five possible methods in hope that one could be completed quickly enough to prevent the Germans from completing their bomb first. Difficulties in two of the processes quickly convinced the United States to narrow the field to three primary methods.

Near the same time, in August 1942, Glenn Seaborg led a team to sepa-rate microscopic samples of pure plutonium, which they believed would be able to create an even more powerful explosion than uranium. In the meantime, Gen. Leslie Groves, the director of the Manhattan Project, enlisted several contractors to build the facilities to separate uranium, including the DuPont Corporation, which designed and built the chemical separation plant required for plutonium.

Meanwhile, Enrico Fermi led a group of scientists at the University of Chicago to build a large lattice pile on a squash court under the western stands of old Stagg Field. The lattice was created from six tons of uranium metal, fifty tons of uranium oxide, and four hundred tons of graphite bricks, the latter to moderate the expected nuclear reaction. On December 2, 1942, at 3:25 p.m., they generated the first controlled, self-sustaining nuclear chain reaction. Less than a year later, on November 4, 1943, Oak Ridge National Laboratory's first experimental pile began producing plutonium.

In just two years, Oppenheimer's teams had developed not just one but two different kinds of weapons using atomic fission. The initial design, termed a "gun design," fired a uranium projectile into a cavity created in a second mass of uranium. Early studies showed that this method should be effective when using uranium, but by July 1944 it was clear that a plu-tonium bomb could not use the gun design. Thus, Oppenheimer's team returned to Neddermeyer's concept of using implosion for the plutonium bomb. This was a much more complex process since outside pressures would be required to compress a sphere of plutonium in equal force from all sides at one time. The physicists involved determined that there was

Man standing next to an experimental pile. These stacks of uranium rods, twenty-nine of which were built, proved the concept of nuclear fission. *Argonne National Laboratory, picture 1-828*

an extremely narrow margin between success and failure, but this was the most reasonable chance for creating a successful plutonium bomb. With help from visiting British scientists, the theory became reality.

By early 1944 Oppenheimer believed that his team was ready to conduct a full-scale nuclear test. Since there was so little of the required atomic material available, the decision was made to just test one of the models of the bomb. The uranium "gun design" bomb was designed around fairly simple and uncomplicated principles while the plutonium bomb's concepts were more novel, so Oppenheimer decided to test the plutonium bomb, theorizing that if the more complicated bomb would work, the simpler design would work as well. General Groves approved the test, so in March of that year Oppenheimer's organization began planning for the test and selected the location—the Alamogordo Bombing Range in New Mexico. Oppenheimer proposed that the test be called "Trinity."

On July 16, 1945, at 5:30 in the morning, the scientists at Alamogordo created the first nuclear explosion. Two days after the test, Groves declared it "successful beyond the most optimistic expectations of anyone." He described the energy from the blast conservatively, as more than equivalent to 15,000 to 20,000 tons of dynamite. The blast created a 1,200-foot-wide crater that was up to 25 feet deep in the center, and the tower that had held the bomb evaporated in the explosion. Light from the explosion was seen up to 180 miles away.[5]

To test the power of the bomb, workers for the Manhattan Project had built a second tower a half mile from the explosion site. This 40-ton steel tower was 70 feet high, anchored in concrete, surrounding a massive steel cylinder weighing another 220 tons, which was also held in a concrete base. Groves reported that the "blast tore the [second] tower from its foundations, twisted it, ripped it apart and left it flat on the ground. The effects on the tower indicate that, at that distance, unshielded permanent steel and masonry buildings would have been destroyed."[6]

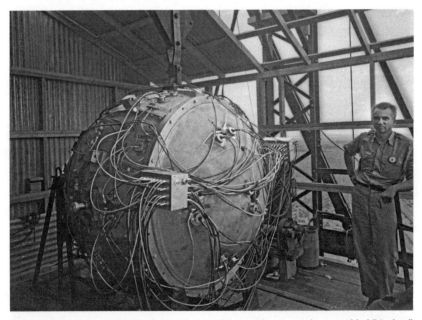

Norris Bradbury, group leader for bomb assembly, stands next to the assembled "Gadget" nuclear bomb at the top of the test tower at the Alamogordo Bombing and Gunnery Range, where it was later detonated. *U.S. Department of Energy, photo HD.4G.053*

Two days later President Harry Truman and British prime minister Winston Churchill, discussing the successful test, agreed to deploy the new weapons into combat as soon as possible. Roosevelt had planned to use the atomic bombs against Germany, but the war in Europe was won more than two months before the Trinity test proved the bombs would work. Although there had been some previous discussion of whether a demonstration of the bomb might be enough to convince the Japanese to surrender, this plan was rejected because of concerns that the demonstration would not work effectively or that the Japanese might be able to determine a way to defend against the attack. Thus, the decision to use the new bombs in actual combat was made.

While the scientists at Los Alamos, New Mexico, and other Manhattan Project research facilities designed the new weapons, General Groves guided the planning for the bomb's employment in combat. After determining that there were no U.S. aircraft at the time that could carry the bombs, Groves approached the commanding general of the Army Air Forces, Gen. Henry "Hap" Arnold, notifying him of the concern. Groves later recalled that Arnold responded that "the Air Force would make every effort to ensure we had a B-29 capable of doing the job."[7] By reducing the size of the bombs themselves and specially modifying the B-29, the two generals were able to accomplish that task. With the support of Col. Roscoe Wilson, one of two Army Air Forces liaisons to the Manhattan Project, the organization built a composite group around a special heavy bomber squadron to train for the critical mission. By October 1944 the unit, the 509th Composite Group, was together and practicing for its ominous assignment.

In April Col. Paul W. Tibbets began moving his crews to Tinian, a small island in the Pacific that had been selected as the launch point for the 509th Composite Group's attack. On July 14, 1945, the main nonnuclear parts of the first atomic bomb to be used in combat, a uranium bomb christened Little Boy, were transported by rail to San Francisco, where they were loaded on the USS *Indianapolis* and carried to Tinian. Three C-54 Skymasters then flew the bomb's nuclear components there. Soon after, on August 2, a specially designed C-54 along with B-29s from the 509th Composite Group carried the pieces of the plutonium bomb, designated Fat Man, to the same island.

On July 25, 1945, Gen. Thomas Handy, the acting chief of staff of the Army, ordered the commander of U.S. Strategic Air Forces in the Pacific, Gen. Carl "Tooey" Spaatz, to attack Japan with a nuclear bomb after about August 3 if they had not yet surrendered. The 509th Composite Group was directed to launch the first bomb on Hiroshima, Kokura, Niigata, or Nagasaki on the first day that weather permitted visual bombing following August 3. The cities were chosen because they were deemed the most likely to negatively affect the will of the Japanese people to continue the war. Each contained a military headquarters, a large concentration of troops, or military production facilities that had not been previously targeted.

The next day, on July 26, Allied leaders in Potsdam, Germany, made a final call for the Japanese to surrender, warning that the alternative was "prompt and utter destruction." Since the Japanese continued to fight on, the 509th prepared their destructive device. Poor weather prevented the Army Air Force from acting for several days, but at 8:15 a.m. local time on August 6, a U.S. Army Air Force aircrew dropped—to devastating effect— the first atomic bomb used in combat on Hiroshima.

The bomb fell 57 seconds before detonating at 1,900 feet in altitude. The resulting blast was equivalent to 13,000 to 15,000 tons of trinitrotoluene, or TNT. The bomb effectively destroyed 4.7 square miles—approximately 60 percent of the city, killing between 70,000 and 80,000 people and injuring another 70,000. The area nearest the explosion, approximately 2 miles in diameter, was completely devastated. This was not the most devastating attack of the war. On March 8, the Army Air Force had fire-bombed Tokyo with 334 bombers, incinerating nearly 16 square miles of the city and killing over 80,000. However, at Hiroshima, the destruction was accomplished with one bomb.

After the attack on Hiroshima, Truman released a press report warning of further attacks: "It was to spare the Japanese people from utter destruction that the ultimatum of July 26 was issued at Potsdam. Their leaders promptly rejected that ultimatum. If they do not now accept our terms, they may expect a rain of ruin from the air, the like of which has never been seen on this earth."[8] Although several senior Japanese leaders were convinced to surrender, including the emperor, the senior military leaders refused to even discuss it, so nothing was done.

The United States, continuing its research on plutonium bombs, decided to drop the second bomb as soon as there was enough fissionable plutonium. The target date was initially August 20, but by August 7 the date had moved forward to August 10. Weather again proved a factor, with bad conditions predicted for five days following August 9. Thus, even though the scientists were concerned that the bomb might not work properly if used on that date, General Groves scheduled a second attack for August 9.

The city originally targeted was Kokura, the location of one of the largest war plants in Japan, but weather prevented the crew from bombing the city visually, which was required by orders. After unsuccessfully attempting three bombing runs over the city, Navy commander Frederick "Dick" Ashworth, the weaponeer, decided to move to the secondary target— Nagasaki. Since clouds also covered Nagasaki, Ashworth grew concerned. After Ashworth decided to violate orders and drop the bomb by radar, if necessary, the cloud cover opened briefly and Capt. Kermit Beahan, the bombardier, dropped Fat Man on the city. Therefore, three days after Hiroshima, just before 11 a.m. local time on August 9, the first plutonium bomb to be used in combat was dropped on the city of Nagasaki, again to ruinous effect. The bomb, equivalent to twenty-one kilotons of TNT, exploded at 1,840 feet. Because the city was extremely hilly, the casualties were much less than at Hiroshima, but still tremendous—between 25,000 and 35,000 killed and up to 60,000 more wounded. More than 40 percent of the city was flattened.

That same day the Soviets entered the fray. On August 8, they had informed the Japanese that they would consider themselves at war with Japan the next day. Then, the morning of August 9, Soviet troops swept into Japanese-occupied China and Korea.

When two nuclear bombs and the Soviet invasion of Japanese-held territory did not convince Japan's Supreme War Direction Council to surrender, the prime minister asked the emperor to decide. Hirohito, shockingly, stepped out of his usual role and addressed the group, agreeing to surrender as long as he continued as sovereign. On August 10, the Japanese notified the Allies that they accepted the Potsdam Declaration and would surrender if Allies allowed the emperor to retain his rights and privileges as sovereign. On August 15, 1945, after a military coup attempting to prolong

Nuclear cloud as seen from an American aircraft, likely the B-29 bomber *Big Stink*, which was at the site to photograph the explosion. *U.S. Department of Energy, Los Alamos Laboratory, IM-4: di05-210*

the war was put down, Hirohito announced on a national radio broadcast that the Japanese had officially surrendered.

The Trinity test and nuclear attacks on Japan had a tremendous impact in other areas as well. At the end of 1942 Stalin had approved a nuclear scientist named Igor Kurchatov to run the Soviet program on atomic research. However, even Kurchatov was not completely convinced of the viability of nuclear weapons until Premier Vyacheslav Molotov provided him with the intelligence materials gathered from the United States and England. After a careful review of the intelligence, Kurchatov concluded that the Soviets could build a plutonium bomb but that it would take a while because the Soviets did not at that time have the necessary equipment or supplies to do the required work. Because Kurchatov was not allowed to provide the atomic intelligence to the others he worked with, unless specifically approved, he guided his colleagues to follow Western research by suggesting areas of research and guiding their actions in other ways. However, the Soviet leaders still perceived atomic research as a long-term concern rather than a pressing problem that needed to be addressed immediately, so these studies were not prioritized or well-funded.

Even when Klaus Fuchs, a key British scientist working at Los Alamos, informed the Soviets that the United States would be testing an atomic bomb on July 10, 1945, and planned to use it against Japan if it proved to be successful, the Soviets did not change their minds. This change in perspective did not come about until after the Trinity test. Presumably, the Soviet leaders, including Stalin, believed that the intelligence received from the West was overexaggerating the American capabilities.

Thus, when Stalin received word that the Trinity test had proven the viability of nuclear weapons and Truman validated its importance, he finally comprehended the importance of the atomic program and quickly established a crash program to catch up with the United States. The point was made even more clear on August 6, when the Americans dropped the atomic bomb on Hiroshima. Soon after, Stalin told Kurchatov's team, "A single demand of you, comrades, . . . provide us with atomic weapons in the shortest time. You know that Hiroshima has shaken the whole world. The equilibrium has been destroyed. Provide the bomb—it will remove a great danger from us."[9] Those engaged in the development of the Soviet bomb realized "the creation of our own atomic weapons, the restoration of equilibrium [had become] a categorical imperative."[10] The nuclear race was on.

On August 20, 1945, Lavrentiy Beria, the head of the NKVD, was given two years to deliver an atomic bomb. Soviet intelligence organizations were ordered to find out everything that they could on the atomic bomb, including how it was built and how much destruction it caused in Japan. Former German scientists, detained after the Nazi surrender, were engaged to separate the isotopes required for nuclear fission. Stalin informed Kurchatov that he should "ask for whatever you like. You won't be refused."[11]

Based on the difficulties of obtaining the highly enriched uranium required for a bomb like that used on Hiroshima, Kurchatov decided to follow the second plan of the U.S. nuclear scientists, building a plutonium bomb. The plutonium bomb still required uranium, but not the exceedingly rare enriched uranium. The Soviets, despite the efforts of the Americans to purchase or control all uranium mines that they could, used captives in forced labor camps to mine for uranium in central Asia. They also found significant deposits in Soviet-occupied Czechoslovakia and Germany. Once the required materials were obtained, Kurchatov's team began assembling a nuclear reactor. They began to insert the uranium fuel rods on November 15, 1946, and the reactor went critical, with a controlled chain reaction, on December 25 of that same year. An operational reactor to produce the required plutonium became operational a little over a year and a half later, on June 10, 1948.

Using American plans obtained through espionage, the Soviets determined the exact specifications of a bomb that could properly implode the plutonium in order to create a nuclear explosion. Stalin approved the design of a bomb that could be delivered by the Tupolev TU-4, a Soviet copy of the American B-29 Superfortress long-range bomber, which was built starting in 1947. Even with the intelligence obtained from the West, however, Soviet scientists, engineers, and physicists had to work hard to devise the perfectly fabricated parts to ensure a nuclear explosion, as Soviet technology was not as advanced as that in the West.

As the new weapon was being designed and built, the Soviets began preparing to test the bomb. They selected a site on the steppes of Kazakhstan, about 87 miles northwest of Semipalatinsk. The original plan was to drop the bomb from an aircraft. However, the Soviets suffered from the same problem that the Americans originally struggled with: there was no Soviet aircraft that could carry the bomb in order to test it. Therefore, the Soviets decided to conduct the test similarly to the Trinity test. Workers erected a thirty-meter tower and built a workshop to assemble the key parts of the bomb. To test the destructive capability of the bomb, they also constructed several buildings nearby made of wood or brick and at various heights. They also built other structures like bridges and tunnels to determine the effect of the bomb on these architectural designs. They placed animals in buildings and pens so they could determine the effects of the bomb on living creatures. They also positioned numerous test instruments throughout the area in order to capture scientific data about the explosion as the bomb detonated.

By the spring of 1949 the Soviets had finished preparing for their first bomb, and Kurchatov asked Stalin for permission to test the bomb in June. Reportedly, Stalin was shocked that they had only created one bomb. He approved the test but ordered the creation of a second bomb as soon as possible. Kurchatov traveled to Semipalatinsk to finalize the work required to test the bomb. Then, after Beria conducted a final inspection of the test site and reported to Stalin that the test site was ready, Kurchatov declared that the bomb would be tested at 6 a.m. on August 29.

Around two in the morning, the bomb was raised to the top of the tower and the detonators placed around the nuclear material. Several hours later, with the key leaders gathered safely in a protected command post, Kurchatov directed the test to start, and the Soviets exploded their first nuclear device.[12]

CHAPTER 2

Creating a Working Missile

With the force of the U.S. atomic bomb proven, military leaders now had to determine the best method for deploying the bomb. The U.S. Air Force had modified aircraft specifically for the purpose, but both the United States and the Soviet Union recognized the value of Germany's embryonic missile technology as a potential vehicle for the newly developed nuclear weapons. Many believed the two technologies, atomic weapons and ballistic missiles, could be combined to create a revolution in military affairs that would make other military weapons and strategies obsolete.[1] Yet Maj. Gen. Curtis LeMay, the Army's first and only deputy chief of Air Staff for research and development, noted after Japan's surrender that the United States was "at least ten years behind the Germans at the end of the war in aerodynamics and jet propulsion and missiles and things of that sort."[2]

This was surprising since much of the initial work on missiles was conducted in the United States. A quarter century before the end of World War II, in December 1919, Robert H. Goddard published "A Method of Reaching Extreme Altitudes" in the *Smithsonian Miscellaneous Collections*, the first public proof that rockets could work in a vacuum.[3] Then, on March 16, 1926, Goddard became the first person to successfully launch a rocket using liquid fuel. Years later, as World War II loomed, Goddard met with representatives from Army Ordnance, the Army Air Corps, and the Navy Bureau of Aeronautics on May 28, 1940, and offered to provide them with his research data, his patents, and the facilities that he used to test his theories of rocketry, but none of the services were interested in his work at that time.

The Germans, on the other hand, expressed great interest in Goddard's work. They initiated work on rocket technology in the 1930s, and as the Nazis rose to power, German military leaders substantially expanded the program. They hoped to use missiles to replace the long-range artillery that was banned to them by the Versailles Treaty following World War I. In the 1930s scientists working with the German Army began to develop the A-4 rocket (Aggregat 4), later designated as the V-2 or Vergeitungswaffen-2. The missile was capable of propelling an explosive warhead that weighed over a ton a little over two hundred miles.[4] It used alcohol and liquid oxygen to fly faster than the speed of sound in order to drop its explosive payload onto an enemy target without warning. Despite its unprecedented range, speed, and explosive power, the V-2 was not accurate, with only a 50 percent chance of falling within ten miles of its designated target, so it could not be used against small or hardened targets. Nevertheless, the Nazis were able to use it with great effect against Allied cities.[5]

The Nazis successfully tested the V-2 on October 3, 1942, but they did not use the new technology in combat for almost two years. Then, on Wednesday, September 6, 1944, Gruppe Süd Battery 444 attempted to launch two V-2s against Paris from occupied Belgium. Both rockets misfired, rising only a few feet from the launchers before the engines cut off and the missiles fell back to the launch platform. Two days later, on September 8, 1944, Battery 444 again tried to launch two V-2 rockets against Paris while its sister unit, Gruppe Nord Battery 485, launched a second pair against London. Although the first missile fired against Paris appears to have exploded at high altitude, causing little or no damage, the second missile struck Charentonneau, southeast of Paris, a little before noon, killing six and injuring thirty-six others.[6]

The attack on London was also successful. About 7:00 p.m., one rocket struck a residential area on Staveley Road in West London, killing three and injuring seventeen. It demolished 11 homes, seriously damaged 12 others, and caused some level of wreckage to 556 others. It also wreaked havoc on gas and water mains in the area. A second missile impacted in Epping, Essex, causing minor loss to two cottages. Undaunted by their moderate success, the Germans continued to launch the missiles against allied towns and cities on an almost daily basis for months. These attacks created quite a stir within the American and British military because the missiles struck so quickly and without warning, and the Allies had no countermeasures to shoot down the missiles or stop them.[7]

Before these attacks, U.S. Army Air Forces leaders gave little attention to guided missiles, but the V-2 attacks, along with similar attacks by V-1 "buzz bombs," quickly garnered their attention. Historian John Chapman noted in 1960 that for many officers in what would become the U.S. Air Force, Germany's V-2 missile "changed the complexion of modern war. It wiped out much of our antiquated thinking about rockets. It took the guided missile out of the artillery class and established it as a strategic weapon of devastating potential."[8]

By 1945 the Germans were working on newer versions of the V-2, including a two-stage rocket that was expected to travel about three thousand miles, a distance that threatened the United States. Americans became extremely concerned that the German atomic program would develop a successful atomic bomb and that the Nazis would use the V-2s to carry this terrible weapon to Allied cities, including ones in the United States.

Gen. Henry "Hap" Arnold, the commanding general of Army Air Forces from 1942 to 1946, responded to reports of German advances in rocketry by prophetically exclaiming, "Someday, not too far distant, there can come streaking out of somewhere (we won't be able to hear it, it will come so fast) some kind of a gadget with an explosive so powerful that one projectile will be able to wipe out completely this city of Washington."[9]

General Arnold expounded further on these ideas in a letter to Gen. George C. Kenney, noting that "at present it appears that there will be probably two and possibly five great powers in the next 20 years. Certainly, presently conceived weapons will not be successfully used against any of these powers because of distance and weather limitations and I for one propose to be the leader and not the follower in the experimental development." Arnold continued, "Whether we have rockets, menless [unmanned] aircraft, or something that replaces the aircraft in its entirety, I want to be very sure that the Air Forces are not again slightly behind our enemies in pre-war development and potential offensive capabilities and countermeasures."[10]

Others agreed. Thus, while the U.S. military responded quickly to the threat of the German ballistic missiles, the three major Army elements

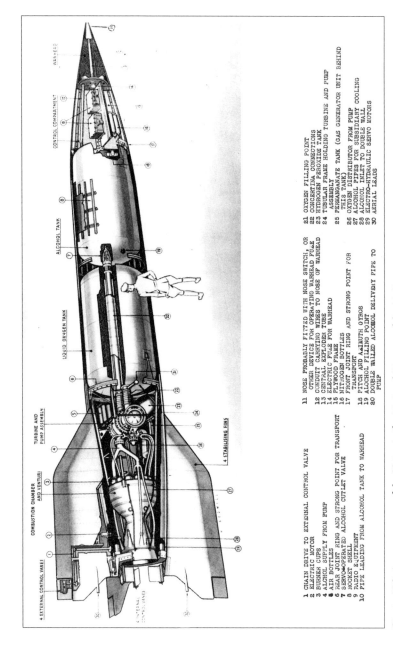

4 EXTERNAL CONTROL VANES

COMBUSTION CHAMBER
AND VENTURI

TURBINE AND
PUMP ASSEMBLY

LIQUID OXYGEN TANK

ALCOHOL TANK

CONTROL COMPARTMENT

WARHEAD

4 STABILISING FINS

4 INTERNAL CONTROL VANES

1 CHAIN DRIVE TO EXTERNAL CONTROL VALVE
2 ELECTRIC MOTOR
3 BURNER CUPS
4 ALCOHOL SUPPLY FROM PUMP
5 AIR BOTTLES
6 REAR JOINT RING AND STRONG POINT FOR TRANSPORT
7 SERVO-OPERATED ALCOHOL OUTLET VALVE
8 ROCKET SHELL
9 RADIO EQUIPMENT
10 PIPE LEADING FROM ALCOHOL TANK TO WARHEAD

11 NOSE PROBABLY FITTED WITH NOSE SWITCH, OR
    OTHER DEVICE FOR OPERATING WARHEAD FUZE
12 CONDUIT CARRYING WIRES TO NOSE OF WARHEAD
13 CENTRAL EXPLODER TUBE
14 ELECTRIC FUZE FOR WARHEAD
15 PLYWOOD FRAME
16 NITROGEN BOTTLES
17 FRONT JOINT RING AND STRONG POINT FOR
    TRANSPORT
18 PITCH AND AZIMUTH GYROS
19 ALCOHOL FILLING POINT
20 DOUBLE WALLED ALCOHOL DELIVERY PIPE TO
    PUMP

21 OXYGEN FILLING POINT
22 CONCERTINA CONNECTIONS
23 HYDROGEN PEROXIDE TANK
24 TUBULAR FRAME HOLDING TURBINE AND PUMP
    ASSEMBLY
25 PERMANGANATE TANK (GAS GENERATOR UNIT BEHIND
    THIS TANK)
26 OXYGEN DISTRIBUTOR FROM PUMP
27 ALCOHOL PIPES FOR SUBSIDIARY COOLING
28 ALCOHOL INLET TO DOUBLE WALL
29 ELECTRO-HYDRAULIC SERVO MOTORS
30 AERIAL LEADS

Fig. 1. U.S. Army cutaway of the V-2 missile. *National Museum of the Air Force*

that reacted—the Army Ground Forces, the Army Service Forces, and the Army Air Forces—began competing with each other and with the Navy to build and operate the new weapon. This intra- and interservice competition would plague missile development for years, with each side using a variety of bureaucratic and political maneuvers to gain control of the new capability. This discord also influenced the reception and incorporation of ballistic missiles into the services and, as the Air Force became a separate service, prejudiced the service's perception of those selected to manage these powerful weapons.

The leaders of the Army Service Forces, who controlled the procurement of the army's artillery were the first to respond effectively to the new weapon. In September 1943 Army Ordnance, under the Service Forces, created a rocket development branch. Two months later, in November, Dr. Theodore von Karman, the director of the Guggenheim Aeronautical Laboratory of the California Institute of Technology (often known as Caltech), submitted a proposal to Army Ordnance to develop long-range, surface-to-surface missiles. In that same month, General Arnold directed that Army Air Forces emphasize research, development, and procurement of guided missiles—termed aircraft rockets.[11]

With their head start, in January 1944, Caltech scientists working for Army Ordnance began developing tactical ballistic missiles capable of carrying warheads less than one hundred miles, the Private A and Corporal missiles. The Army launched the first twenty-four Private A rockets in December of that year and launched the Corporal the next September.

The Army Air Forces began their work on missiles six months after the Ordnance Department, focusing on aeronautical missiles—missiles that remained within the atmosphere and had wings—rather than ballistic ones. In July 1944 the Army Air Forces offered Northrop Aircraft a contract to develop the JB-1, a jet-propelled pilotless aircraft more similar to the German V-1 than its ballistic counterpart, the V-2. The first prototype of the JB-1 was delivered to the Army Air Forces on September 8, 1944, but these missiles were plagued with problems. Therefore, General Arnold requested the production of JB-2s, a copy of the German V-1 designed by piecing together parts from exploded V-1 missiles. He wanted to produce enough JB-2s to launch one thousand per month, but the War Department countermanded this requirement, saying it would disrupt the production of essential war material.

Arnold continued to press for missiles. Even when Lt. Gen. Carl Spaatz, the commander of the U.S. Strategic Air Forces in Europe, contended that the missiles would not be needed by the time they could be available, Arnold thought that the JB-2 "would not only be effective, but might well be essential to continue the air offensive."[12] His thoughts would not prevail. General Eisenhower, concerned the missiles might interfere with the shipment of matériel needed in theater, opposed the program. The contracts for the JB-2 missiles were terminated by early 1946, and none of the missiles were ever used in combat.

As the war came to a close, both the Soviet Union and the United States raced to seize from the defeated country the scientists who had designed and built the German missiles along with their associated equipment. In the United States, Army Ordnance again won the quest, "liberating" Wernher von Braun, providing him with resources, and watching him advance the development of missile technology. Von Braun said he was going to build a rocket that would take man to the moon, and he didn't appear to care who helped him do so. At the same time, however, the Soviet Union captured several German scientists and began their own missile program as well.[13]

Soon, within the United States, three Army organizations—the Ground Forces, the Service Forces, and the Air Forces—were competing heavily to control the development and operation of missiles for the Army. Not to be outdone, the Navy struggled to assert its own control over the new weapon. Between 1945 and 1950, even though Congress drastically cut service budgets, naval planners prioritized the development and acquisition of an air-atomic capability and spent more money on missiles than either the Army or the Air Force. As in the Army, the Navy programs were divided, this time between the Bureau of Aeronautics and the Bureau of Ordnance.

To reduce the tension and discord between the Army's contending military organizations, Lt. Gen. Joseph McNarney, the Army deputy chief of staff, decided to provide each of his service's competing organizations with specific responsibilities in creating the new ballistic missile. In a policy statement signed on October 2, 1944, he divided the responsibilities for missile development between the three groups. He focused on each element's specified mission and proven capabilities, granting the Army Air Forces control over all "guided or homing missiles dropped or launched from aircraft," including the responsibility for determining the military characteristics of these weapons. He also assigned the Army Air Forces authority over "all guided or homing missiles launched from the ground which depend for sustenance primarily on the lift of aerodynamic forces." McNarney assigned the Army Service Forces, who controlled the Ordnance Command and the procurement of its artillery, authority for designing and building ballistic missiles like the V-2, specifically designating them "research and development responsibilities for guided or homing missiles launched from the ground which depend for sustenance primarily on momentum of the missile."[14] The Army Ground Forces, which focused on operations rather than the procurement of artillery or airpower assets, were not allocated authority to develop their own ballistic missiles but were told to establish any unique requirements that they had for missiles and to provide these requirements to one of the other organizations for development.

General McNarney refused to give operational control of ballistic missiles to any of the three Army organizations. Since there were no missiles ready for operational use at the time, he concluded that assigning operational control "would jeopardize the future development of the potential weapon."[15] He was correct in this assessment because even his clear direction did not prevent the organizations from conducting research into the areas assigned their competitors.

In 1945, six months after Harry Truman replaced Franklin Roosevelt as president and about a month after World War II was over, the Army Air Forces expanded its work on missiles, sending letters to many of the companies in the retrenching aviation industry and inviting them to send proposals to conduct essential research and development on missiles for the military over the next ten years. Contracting officers requested input on four types of missiles: air-to-air, air-to-surface, surface-to-air, and surface-to-surface.

The Army Air Forces do not appear to have been concerned about abiding by General McNarney's guidance on missiles; by the next spring they were working with several contractors on twenty-eight different missile projects, including one with Consolidated Vultee Aircraft Corporation (also known as Convair) to develop a ballistic missile, even though these had been assigned to Army Service Forces.

The $1.4 million contract with Convair requested that the company research two separate missiles, both meeting a requirement for a long-range missile capable of launching a 5,000-pound warhead over 5,000 miles to within one mile of its planned target. The company was not expected to produce the missiles but to review possible options that could be built in five to ten years. The first possible option was a subsonic, jet-powered winged missile while the second, called Project MX-774B, would be supersonic and rocket powered. Soon after, the Army Air Forces offered a second contract to Northrop Aircraft, the only other company to be contracted to develop a missile for the long-range requirement. Northrop's contract required the company to design a supersonic turbojet aeronautical missile.[16]

The disregard of McNarney's directive seems to have been a common problem as each of the military organizations complained about the others conducting work in the areas not assigned to them.[17] To resolve these concerns, in March 1946 Brig. Gen. R. C. Coupland, the Army Air Forces air ordnance officer who had experience in two of the opposing camps, recommended creating "a single government agency similar in scope to the Manhattan Project with exclusive control over research, development, production, and operational application" to resolve the problem.[18] In a foreshadowing, the recommendation was not accepted even within the Army Air Forces, and it never went further. The one thing that the service leaders could agree upon was that they wanted control of missiles and missile development to remain in the military services.

Shortly thereafter funding began to quickly dry up. The Cold War had not started in earnest, and the nation cared much more about demobilizing from World War II than about preparing for another potential war. Thus began a second American struggle over the fate of missiles. While some politicians, scientists, and military officers, including General Arnold and Dr. von Karman, by then chairman of the Air Forces' Scientific Advisory Group, believed the nation should obtain the new "ultimate weapon"—an intercontinental ballistic missile carrying a nuclear warhead—as soon as possible, others felt that it was too soon.[19] Many, like Vannevar Bush, the highly influential head of the U.S. Office of Scientific Research and Development during World War II, thought ballistic missiles were not yet ready to power the proposed nuclear revolution. Bush ridiculed the idea of an intercontinental ballistic missile, saying that such an idea was not feasible and arguing that even if a long-range ballistic missile could be built that would reach a predicted target, its cost would be astronomical and would economically exhaust the nation before its use affected the enemy.[20]

Bush's perspective seemed reasonable at the time. The V-2 missile, the most powerful ballistic missile operational at the end of World War II, had a range of only about 180 miles, not the thousands of miles required to accomplish the long-range nuclear mission. Moreover, the V-2 missile was notoriously inaccurate. Bush believed that the scientific knowledge and technology of the time could not adequately extend the range and accuracy of the missiles to make them practical, so he argued that the time and money should be put toward improving the ability of bombers to deliver the nuclear weapons rather than being wasted on dubious missile technology.

The President's Air Policy Commission, headed by Thomas K. Finletter, agreed. The commission, charged with formulating an integrated aviation policy for the nation, argued that "push-button warfare" protagonists were pushing too hard to make the transition to missiles. Thus, they recommended that the United States be patient, first ensuring that missiles were the best decision for the nation and not a "blind alley." Missiles, they declared, were "a case where making haste slowly will certainly pay" by ensuring that the nation would not overrun "our basic knowledge in an effort to develop production articles too soon."[21] In addition, because many believed the nuclear bomb had established the United States as the dominant world power and that America would retain exclusive control of it for several years, if not decades, there was no need to rush to develop a new weapon.

General Arnold remained one of the most powerful voices in support of missile research. Even when the United States was focused on ending the war in Japan, Arnold directed more funding toward guided-missile programs, eventually budgeting $34 million for the new weapon systems. However, on June 30, 1946, when he retired from active duty, the Army Air Forces' support for missiles began to diminish. Thus, when Congress cut the services' research and development budget by 40 percent for fiscal year 1947, the Army Air Forces cut the guided-missile budget drastically.

Instead, the organization focused on jet-powered bombers and aerodynamic missiles, weapons that service leaders said would be operational sooner, were cheaper, and could travel further with a larger payload. Gen. Donald Putt, director of research and development for the Air Force deputy chief of staff for matériel, had an alternate explanation. He believed that the Air Force put wings on its missiles and kept them in the atmosphere to distance itself from the Army's interpretation of missiles. "We were afraid that if we developed them to look like rockets or a big artillery shell, that eventually the Department of Defense would give the mission to the Army." He also conjectured that, psychologically, air-breathing missiles closely resembling aircraft were easier for the service to accept than ballistic missiles.[22] Regardless of the reason, in December 1946, the Army Air Forces cut its budget for missile development to $22 million. This forced research and development leaders to cancel over a third of its twenty-eight missile projects, including Convair's subsonic missile, and to reduce funding for the company's long-range rocket-powered missile.

Seven months later, in July 1947, when the budget was cut again, the Army Air Forces terminated Convair's contract, stating that the MX-774 missile did "not promise any tangible results in the next eight to ten years."[23] In fact, an Army Air Forces staff evaluation of the guided-missile program proclaimed that "for the next ten years, at least, the subsonic bomber will be the only means available for the delivery of long-range (1,000 miles and over) air bombardment."[24] Fortunately for both the nation and for Convair, the officers controlling the contract allowed the company to retain the funding it had already received and to continue work on the project with the remaining resources. This decision was probably one of the most critical affecting the future Air Force's development of ballistic missiles as work only continued based on the money that Convair was willing to put into the program.

Soon after, another event—possibly just as critical to the future of missiles—occurred. Since World War I, there had been a growing rift between what historian James Tate deems the "visionary" flyers who demanded "several hundred millions of dollars to acquire the newest airplanes and to train men to fly them" and the "realists" in the Army who wanted to spend the money on what they believed were current needs. Brig. Gen. William "Billy" Mitchell became the primary voice for the flyers. Tate contends that, as the disagreement intensified, Mitchell began to perceive his nonflying antagonists as stupid or immoral, arguing that "the Army feared innovation . . . because it might curtail 'their ancient prerogatives, privileges, and authority'"—earning himself a court-martial. Because of Mitchell's haughty antagonism, Tate asserts that Mitchell's "chief legacy to the Air Corps" was a "self-confident, self-righteous attitude . . . conditioning his followers and those they would later indoctrinate never to be satisfied with anything short of independence from the Army."[25]

However, based on many of the service members' future attitudes toward missiles and any other technology that threatened manned flight, the primary lesson appears to have been what historian John Darrell Sherwood terms a "flight suit attitude." This attitude, explained Korean-era pilot George Berke, one of Sherwood's biographical subjects, meant, "If you could fly, we accepted you, and if you couldn't, out!!! We didn't want you around."[26] Thus, nonflying missileers were not acceptable to many Air Force pilots.

On July 26, 1947, when Truman signed the National Security Act of 1947, the "visionaries" saw their dream of a separate Air Force coming true. Less than two months later, on September 18, Stuart Symington became the first secretary of the independent U.S. Air Force. The act did not resolve the conflict between the flyers and the soldiers, however, as many roles and missions had to be allocated between the two services, including the acquisition of new missiles. Planners and commanders from both the Army and Air Force met to determine how to best separate responsibilities and resources. One month later, Secretary of Defense James V. Forrestal approved the document they hammered out, the "Army-Air Force Agreements: As to the Initial Implementation of the National Security Act of 1947."

Among other things, this document redefined the relationship between the services and the missile, declaring that "strategic missiles will be assigned to the U.S. Air Force. Missiles within this category are those designed for employment against targets, the destruction or neutralization of which are normally the targets of bombers." Tactical missiles, those "which will have a direct effect on current Army tactical operations," were assigned to the Army. However, the agreement asserted that this was "no change" to present agreements, and it did little to prevent continued contention over roles and missions and duplication of efforts.

Vannevar Bush, director of the Office of Scientific Research and Development, who believed that research should be performed by civilian agencies rather than the military, then tried to resolve the issue by creating a guided missiles committee composed of three civilians and two officers from each of the three competing services, but all three of the military services ignored the group.[27]

Consequently, when Louis Johnson became President Truman's Secretary of Defense on March 28, 1949, and reduced service budgets again, interservice struggles over who would control missiles erupted once more. The Army tried to regain control of surface-to-surface ballistic missiles by recommending that the Air Force focus on air-launched missiles and the Navy control sea-launched missiles, leaving the ground-launched missiles to the Army. Because the services could not come to agreement, Johnson ordered a complete review of all Defense Department missile programs. The review accomplished little as the Joint Chiefs of Staff recommended that the services hold joint control rather than defining clear roles and responsibilities as Johnson had desired. Therefore, Johnson ordered Secretary of the Air Force Symington to come up with a better plan. Symington established the Special Interdepartmental Guided Missiles Board, known better as the Stuart Board after its head, Harold Stuart. Another round of bickering and finger-pointing followed but still accomplished little.

Secretary Johnson was frustrated at the lack of cooperation. He considered bringing in someone from outside of the Defense Department to help resolve the issue, but the services did not want to lose control of this potentially valuable weapon as they had with the nuclear bomb. Symington convinced Johnson to allow the Joint Chiefs of Staff one last opportunity to prioritize defense missile projects and establish order. This time, the Joint Chiefs recommended "that the Air Force be given operational responsibility for surface-to-surface missiles that replaced aircraft other than close air support aircraft" while the Navy was assigned "responsibility for surface-to-surface missiles that replaced naval aircraft" and the Army was assigned joint responsibility with the Air Force over control of "surface-to-surface missiles that replaced close support aircraft." The agreement should have reduced the antagonism, but the services continued to "study" missiles that were not within their purview, wanting to be ready if—when—the guidance changed again.[28]

In the midst of all of the maneuvering, the Joint Chiefs prioritized the existing missile programs and relegated long-range strategic missiles to eighth on their priority list. Air Force missile advocates were angry over this low ranking, but their own service had not prioritized long-range strategic missiles, focusing instead on the air-launched missiles that enhanced the role of strategic bombers and air defense missiles.

All these disputes mattered less than it appeared as, in July 1949, the National Security Council recommended that the president set the production of the atomic bomb as the nation's highest priority and the production of the B-36 bomber to carry it as the second-highest priority. Nothing was said about the long-range missile. Significantly, when U.S. intelligence reported that the Soviet Union had successfully tested an atomic bomb on August 29, 1949, it only solidified the decision to ignore ballistic missiles. After careful study and deliberation, on January 31, 1950, Truman announced that he had "directed the Atomic Energy Commission to continue its work on all forms of atomic weapons, including the so-called hydrogen or superbomb."[29]

The military services had believed it would take a lot longer for the Soviet Union to create an atomic bomb (the Air Force, who was termed alarmist by the other services, estimated it could happen by 1952, while the Army predicted 1960 and the Navy 1965) but feared that the Soviet Union might gain the upper hand militarily, so they funded "current" technology—aircraft and aeronautic missiles—to combat this threat rather than "technology of the future" including ballistic missiles. Thus, work on missiles waned until mid-1950.

On June 25, 1950, a critical shift in the Cold War again altered the status quo, but this time in a positive direction for ballistic missiles. Communists from North Korea invaded a U.S. ally, South Korea. As war broke out on the Korean peninsula, President Truman replaced Louis Johnson, known for drastically reducing the defense budget, with a new secretary of defense, former general George C. Marshall, and initiated a partial mobilization of the Defense Department. General Marshall, preparing to combat the communist aggression, increased defense funding considerably. Some of this added funding was allocated to support further research and development for missiles.

Convair had prepared for this moment. Even though government support for its missile development program had run out, Convair had provided Karel "Charlie" Bossart, the primary engineer for the MX-774 contract, with about $3 million to conduct further research on the project between 1949 and 1950, believing that their advances would lead to future contracts. This foresight paid substantial dividends. With the money provided from the earlier contract, Convair had built a working ballistic missile, launching the first on July 13, 1948. Although it had never traveled further than about thirty miles, the Convair missile was the most promising ballistic missile America had to offer.

Launch of an MX-774 (RTV-A-2) rocket at White Sands, New Mexico, possibly 1948. *Smithsonian Air and Space Museum*

Like other manufacturers of the time, Convair based its MX-774B ballistic missile on the German V-2 but improved the German missile's weak guidance system to enhance its accuracy. Charlie Bossart also decided that the only way to extend the range was to reduce the weight of the airframe. Therefore, he made the entire area between the warhead and the rocket into a large fuel tank of thin aluminum rather than designing separate tanks inside a strong metal exterior. The only thing separating the fuel from the oxidizer was a single bulkhead, which was not strong enough to hold the weight of the warhead by itself. Thus, the fuel and oxidizer inside the missile held the warhead in place.[30]

This unique design was expected to increase the range of the missile significantly. In addition, the company redesigned the rocket's engines, increasing their thrust and designing a control system to move the engines in flight so the rocket could be steered. While the contract did not require the designers to produce a missile, they thought that building one would help them learn more quickly. Therefore, Convair had requested permission to build the MX-774B, and, since it had not cost the Army Air Forces any more money, the military allowed it.

Hearing that the newly created Air Force was again considering research on missiles, in October 1950 the company proposed several options to officers in the Air Materiel Command, including a ramjet missile that Convair thought the Air Force favored.[31] Two months later, when the service's engineering division wanted to determine the best approach to build a long-range surface-to-surface missile, the Air Force turned to Convair, the only company with any real experience and operational concepts in this arena.

Thus, on January 23, 1951—three and a half years after it cancelled its original agreement with Convair, the Air Force signed a new $500,000 contract with the company to study "an intercontinental missile with a minimum range of 5,000 miles, a minimum speed of Mach 6 over the target, a circular error probable (CEP) of 1,500 feet, and a nuclear warhead." Donald MacKenzie, in *Inventing Accuracy*, speculates that the CEP requirement was designed to mimic the target area believed to be achievable by 1950s-era bombers dropping bombs by radar from 25,000 feet. These requirements were deemed impossible at the time, leading some historians to contend that Air Force leaders established the requirement to prevent Convair from succeeding. Cruise missiles, the closest weapon to the missile, had still not achieved a CEP of 5,000 feet, over three times larger than the target established for Convair's ballistic missile.[32]

The new opportunity thus, ironically, created conflict in the new service. Richard Curtin, a lower-ranking officer on the Air Staff at the time, explained the controversy. "Many of the people who were real airplane types. . . . [were] not sure that we [in the Air Force] should have these new things [missiles]. The new things might take over some of the jobs of the airplanes and so forth."[33] However, others—like Curtin—remembered the contest between the various branches of the Army over missiles and desperately wanted to retain control over the new weapon and its role in national defense. These missile advocates advised Gen. Nathan Twining (who served as vice chief of staff, then as chief of staff of the Air Force, then as chairman of the Joint Chiefs) and Thomas White (who followed as vice chief of staff and chief of staff) that the Air Force must develop missiles or the strategic mission would be taken away from them. If the Army controlled missiles, Curtin explained, "Why should we [the Air Force] have the mission of bombing targets 500 miles away, as opposed to the Army who said they could do it."[34]

This was not an idle threat. Dwight D. Eisenhower, who would soon become president, along with many other influential people of the day, believed that missiles would carry the burden of warfare within a decade, replacing the manned airplane for most missions. Airpower advocate Gill Robb Wilson later acknowledged the concern most explicitly, stating, "The Air Force could make no sadder mistake than to believe that public concern about air power is ipso facto zeal for the Department of the Air Force. The fact is that Army and Navy could quietly absorb every major role of the Air Force without enough public outcry to disturb a nursery."[35] Senior Air Force leaders remembered General Arnold's concern that "whether we have rockets, menless [unmanned] aircraft, or something that replaces the aircraft in its entirety, I want to be very sure that the Air Forces are not again slightly behind our enemies." Therefore, Air Force pilots struggled fiercely to retain missiles even though many were terrified that the new weapons might replace the aircraft they loved.[36]

If the Air Force controlled missiles, presumably it could ensure the new weapons would not completely replace the manned airplane. To ensure the latter did not happen, Air Force leaders began to argue that "missiles and aircraft can be combined, capitalizing on the performance and characteristics of each, to create a formidable instrument of air power considerably greater than the use of missiles or aircraft alone. The creation of such an instrument is a primary objective of the Air Force."[37] As early as May 1951, the Air Force Council began assigning aircraft designations to missiles, and soon after airmen working in missile programs were ordered to refer to their creations as "pilotless aircraft" rather than missiles. The leaders also expressed a different vision for the future.[38]

Several Air Force leaders presumed that missiles were an early step to space flight. Therefore, even if manned flight was not immediately threatened, they believed the Air Force must control missiles to ensure the service's future in space flight. Col. Claude Putnam, the Air War College's deputy for evaluation, would later present this argument in the *Air University Quarterly Review*, contending that "man is headed for outer space, and the missile is just another step in the long process of evolutionary development which will allow him to get there. Just as the evolution of the airplane furnished the basic technology for the missile, so will the art of missilery make important contributions to the development of the space vehicle."[39] Gen. Clarence Irvine, the Air Force deputy chief of staff for matériel, concurred, saying in congressional testimony that "the ballistic missile is only a short step in the evolution of a weapon system; . . . out of it comes things like a ballistically boosted manned machine, whether this is made as an airplane to not quite go in orbit, or whether it is a true orbital type machine."[40]

Historian John Lonnquest contends that, paradoxically, even though the Air Force struggled desperately to control ballistic missiles, between 1946 and 1952 Air Force leaders never prepared adequate operational concepts for the ballistic missile, refused to allocate appropriate resources, and failed to monitor the development of the ballistic missile.[41] Ray Soper, an Air Force veteran of the time, agreed. "The Op[eration]'s attitude, at the Pentagon, was to let the 'longhairs' develop the system—they didn't take a very serious view of the ballistic missile, for it was thought to be more a psychological weapon than anything else," he remembered. "The main Air Staff support was from the Vice Chief—later Chief of Staff, General [Thomas] White—and from General Don Putt, the [Deputy Chief of Staff for Development]. I remember many times General White lectured the Air Staff on ballistic missiles—they were here to stay, he told them, and the Air Staff had better realize this fact and get on with it."[42]

Roy Ferguson, who was assigned to the Air Staff in 1951 as a major, reinforced Lonnquest's argument. Years later he recalled that he was "the only missile enthusiast in the Directorate of Operations." Although the Air Force had taken on several missiles, no one had any idea of how the service would use them. Therefore, when Ferguson mentioned his interest in missiles, his leadership "was tickled pink because . . . the Air Force didn't want missiles" and they needed someone in the organization who cared about them.[43] However, men like Ferguson and Curtin did help the service move forward on missiles. In April 1951, Strategic Air Command published "Preliminary Plans for Activation and Employment of USAF Guided Missile Units." A year later, General White, another supporter of missiles, created a new office, the Assistant Deputy Chief of Staff, Operations (Guided Missiles), to help incorporate missiles into the service and to develop operational concepts for them. This action still did not heal the widening rift between those who supported missiles and those who did not.[44]

Within the Air Force, most thought the optimum missile would be a "glide" missile, launched into orbit and remotely guided to its target by the use of attached wings after reentry into the atmosphere. However, Convair engineers chose the ballistic rocket. They believed that the glide rocket would be too easily intercepted and that building a winged system to reenter the atmosphere would be much more difficult than creating a solid warhead to do the same. Even though they were roundly excoriated by the Air Force Scientific Advisory Board for "promoting a comet that would burn up upon atmospheric reentry," the Air Research and Development Command supported the company's premise, predicting that a working ballistic missile could be operational in the early 1960s.[45]

Over the summer the Air Force perspective on glide missiles changed as it became apparent that these missiles combined the disadvantages of both cruise missiles and ballistic missiles without offering the advantages of either. Thus, in September 1951, Headquarters USAF directed that all work on Project Atlas, the Convair study, "be directed towards the development of a rocket-powered ballistic missile rather than a rocket-powered glide missile."[46]

On November 1, 1952, another technological development greatly improved the prospects of the Air Force ballistic missile program, although it was not immediately evident to all. American scientists successfully tested a thermonuclear or hydrogen bomb, producing a warhead with much greater explosive capability. Its makers believed that they could reduce the new bomb to fit into a missile and that the greater explosive capacity would significantly reduce the need for accuracy. This advancement made intercontinental ballistic nuclear missiles feasible in the near term. A preliminary Air Force Special Weapons Center study dated September 15, 1953, explained how the new development made ballistic missiles viable, but many in the Air Force did not yet appear to be ready to understand or accept this concept.

CHAPTER 3

Race to the Finish

In December 1952, after Dwight Eisenhower was elected president, Roswell Gilpatric, Truman's undersecretary of the Air Force, explained the official Air Force position on ICBMs to the incoming secretary and undersecretary of the Air Force, stating that "many years will elapse before major dependence can be placed on these new weapons and that meanwhile another generation of piloted aircraft . . . will be needed."[1] Many in the Air Force agreed. Roy Ferguson later elaborated, "The Air Force didn't want missiles because any money you spent on missiles took away from the manned fleet. That's the reason General [Curtis] LeMay hated us so." He continued, "[LeMay] wanted new airplanes and lots of them. And with these missile things we were spending money that they [Air Force pilots] thought was rightfully theirs. Not only that, they kept saying we were throwing pilots out of work." In fact, when the Air Force began awarding missile badges, Ferguson remembered taunts that "the missile badge, it was shooting down the wings, which are right above it."[2] Ray Soper, another missileer, recalled LeMay saying, "You guys are going to regret everything you're doing. You're going to regret every penny spent on this damned [Atlas] missile."[3]

Thus, in January 1953, the commander of Air Research and Development Command, Lt. Gen. Earl Partridge, complained that a lack of centralized Air Force guidance on missiles made it difficult for his command to coordinate their development. Bomber advocates, he argued, were able to push the ICBM program to the side over the objections of a "small but vigorous missile group." He then warned that if the Air Force failed to work aggressively to integrate missiles, the Air Force would split into two hostile camps: missile advocates and "old fogies," those who fought for the dominance of piloted aircraft.[4]

Partridge was not far off the mark. In February 1953 Eisenhower appointed Trevor Gardner to be the special assistant to the secretary of the Air Force for research and development. His selection greatly strengthened the lot of those who sought to incorporate missiles into the service, as Gardner believed "the era of the unmanned missile in warfare . . . [was] very much at hand" and contended that "the United States must have 'weapons of such superior ingenuity, performance and effect as override the enemy's ability to attack or defend himself.'"[5]

Thus, in his opinion, the current military requirements for missiles were "unnecessarily complex, and occasionally impossible . . . , especially those concerning CEP's [the expected ability to hit within a defined target area], payloads, and guidance." Gardner wanted Congress and the president to vigorously back the creation of an operational ICBM capability "to assure that the peacetime checks and balances which are necessary in our system of government will not be the cause of time delays in the accelerated progress of the program."[6]

Gardner's attitude and actions further exacerbated the antagonism between the divergent Air Force officers. He wanted a "crash" program, one unhindered by anything or anyone, to produce missiles as quickly as possible. Ray Soper remembered that there was a "feeling [on the Air Staff] that Gardner was out to create a personal empire, employing Air Force operational needs for ballistic missiles to further this aim." He used his position to lobby the nation's political leaders to accelerate Air Force research into and production of ballistic missiles but found himself struggling against the tide.[7]

After assuming the presidency, Eisenhower worked to extricate the United States from the conflict in Korea and to reduce government spending. Eisenhower planned to achieve these goals by relying more heavily on nuclear weapons through his "New Look" defense philosophy. However, this did not include nuclear missiles at the time as missiles were still unproven.

Thus, in the spring of 1953, as the combatants in Korea worked toward a peace agreement, Charles Wilson, Eisenhower's secretary of defense, reduced research and development funding for the services by 25 percent.

This cut again highlighted the duplication between the services' work on missiles. For this reason, a few weeks later Wilson ordered a review of the guided-missile programs to eliminate duplication and identify a standard missile to accomplish the services' operational requirements.

Gardner made the most of this new opportunity. When Wilson charged the secretary of the Air Force to guide the study, Gardner became the point man for a tri-service study group on missiles. At the same time, he established an Air Force committee on strategic missiles, officially titled the Strategic Missile Evaluation Committee (codenamed the Teapot Committee) but sometimes called the von Neumann Committee after its leader, John von Neumann. Gardner charged the committee to evaluate the various Air Force missile programs against available technologies, especially in comparison to the expected capabilities of potential enemies, and to recommend solutions to any problems identified. To ensure the committee would recommend advancements in missiles, Gardner stacked the group with nationally esteemed scientists from prestigious universities and industry who were strongly in favor of missiles, as he was.[8]

Then, as the Soviets detonated their own hydrogen bomb in August 1953, less than a year after the Americans' own demonstration, Gardner's position was further solidified. By the end of the year, the Eisenhower administration set the primary focus of national defense on "nuclear weapons with the most advanced aerial delivery systems" in order to reduce costs. Gardner, with the backing of key scientists and politicians, "urged Air Force policy-makers to give over-riding priority to ballistic missiles as the most advanced nuclear weapons delivery systems."[9]

On February 10, 1954, the von Neumann Committee presented its findings. The report asserted that the new thermonuclear bomb, or hydrogen bomb, would indeed allow the military to reduce the size of warheads within a few years and recommended accelerating the ICBM program, strengthening Gardner's position immeasurably. Those who had been working closely with the future missile systems had recognized this fact over a year earlier but had been dismissed without serious consideration because their views seemed so incredible. Now they had credible backing.

In its report, the von Neumann Committee contended that the ICBM program should be accelerated because the Soviets could rapidly strengthen their defenses against U.S. bombers or quickly develop their own strategic missiles. Although the committee admitted that they did not have enough information to determine Soviet progress in the field, they asserted that they could not rule out that "the Russians are ahead of us."[10]

The committee also recommended relaxing the military requirement for a 1,500-foot CEP to "at least two, and probably three, nautical miles." By using the new thermonuclear warhead to reduce weight and increase the target size, some members of the committee believed the United States could produce a "preliminary [missile] system . . . sometime between mid-1958 and mid-1960." Thus, instead of reducing costs as the secretary of defense intended for it to do, the committee called for a tremendous increase in missile expenditures.[11]

A RAND Corporation report, released two days prior to the von Neumann Committee's recommendation, corroborated the committee's findings. In *A Revised Program for Ballistic Missiles of Intercontinental Range*, RAND predicted that an Atlas ICBM could achieve initial operational capability by the early 1960s if performance criteria were relaxed and the program were prioritized and funded appropriately. The von Neumann Committee and the RAND reports were intentionally similar since the von Neumann Committee used the RAND report and several briefings they received from RAND employees to prepare their own report.[12]

Gardner convinced Air Force Secretary Harold E. Talbott. The next week, Talbott notified the Air Force chief of staff, Gen. Nathan Twining, that "Mr. Trevor Gardner has developed a plan for accelerating our efforts so as to achieve . . . an intercontinental ballistic missile operational system within approximately five years." The secretary then directed that "the Air Force immediately accelerate the intercontinental ballistic missile program . . . at maximum effort . . . on the assumption that total funding required will ultimately be provided by Congress."[13]

While Gardner was pressuring a reluctant Air Force to quickly accept and develop ballistic missiles, he was also creating havoc in the contracting world. From the beginning, Gardner had struggled with Convair. Even though the company's engineers had designed the Atlas while the Air Force neglected ballistic missiles, Gardner argued that they did not have the scientific and engineering aptitude to create an ICBM. Therefore, he contracted two technological entrepreneurs from the Air Force's Scientific Advisory Board, Simon Ramo and Dean Wooldridge, to study the progress of strategic missile development. Not unsurprisingly, in February 1954 Ramo-Wooldridge, the company formed for the task, found that Convair was not acceptable and recommended that a new group be formed to run the program.

Convair argued that Gardner could not legally have his friends' company, Ramo-Wooldridge, oversee the Convair contract, so once he had both reports—and even before he presented them to the Air Force—he recommended the Air Force abandon the current Convair missile program and replace it with a new, more aggressive program run by a group focused only on ballistic missiles. By doing this, he insisted, the Air Force could attain an emergency capability between 1958 and 1960.

However, this time he was not as convincing. While Secretary Talbott approved acceleration of the ICBM program, he did not abandon Convair's Atlas program as Gardner had requested. Instead, when the Air Force Council convened and revised the payload and CEP standards of Air Force missiles, they also worked to protect the Atlas, specifically against poaching from the other services, advising that "the development and operation of [the Atlas] is a mission of the Air Force and must be under the control of the Air Force." Two months later, on May 14, 1954, the Air Force boosted Convair's missile to the top of the Air Force's research and development priority list and directed the Air Research and Development Command to "accelerate the revised ATLAS program to the maximum extent permitted by technology." The timing was impeccable because, although it is doubtful that Secretary Talbott was aware of it at the time, less than a week later, the Soviet Council of Ministers and Soviet Central Committee issued a resolution to develop the R-7 intercontinental missile.[14] While the United States had been conducting their "on again / off again" development of missiles, the Soviets had been making similar progress. They too initially planned to deliver nuclear weapons with aircraft but had no airplanes capable of conducting the mission. Stalin first created an exact replica of the U.S. B-29 Superfortress, the most capable bomber of the time. However, the U-4, as the plane was designated, was not able to deliver a nuclear warhead against significant portions of the

United States. Thus, the Soviets began to study the German V-2 program, just as the Americans had done.

Stalin selected Sergei Korolev, an engineer who had studied rocket propulsion, to guide the creation of ballistic missiles for the nation. With German assistance, the Soviets built thirty V-2 missiles in 1946, and German veterans trained Soviet military personnel to operate them. Korolev then built a Soviet equivalent, the R-1. The military did not fully appreciate the weapon but accepted it for use on November 28, 1950. Korolev also created the R-2, a much-improved version of the R-1. However, when the Soviet Union tested its first atom bomb on August 29, 1949, it became very clear that the R-1 and R-2 would not satisfy Soviet requirements for nuclear missiles. These rockets were not designed to carry nuclear weapons and had a range of less than four hundred miles, so Korolev began thinking about much more advanced capabilities. These concepts included a missile with intercontinental range and one that could use propellants that could be stored in the missile—the latter requested by the military because of the difficulty of controlling and operating missiles that used the volatile liquid oxygen. By December 1949 Korolev's team had plans for the R-3, a single-stage rocket that could "lob a three-ton separable warhead a distance of 3,000 kilometers."[15]

Because the Soviet rocket engineers had established a large number of advanced concepts for the R-3, this missile was never built. Instead, the ideas behind the missile were incorporated into other missiles, including the R-11, a smaller missile that used storable fuels; the R-11FM, a submarine-launched ballistic missile using those same fuels; the R-5, which increased the range of the R-1 to 1,500 kilometers and became the first Soviet nuclear ballistic missile; and, most importantly, the R-6, a two-stage missile designed to far exceed the proposed R-3 range, promising to launch a warhead of not less than 3,000 kilograms almost 8,000 kilometers. This would allow it to reach the United States.

On March 5, 1953, less than a month after Stalin approved the concept for the new ICBM, he died. Influential Soviet leaders struggled to assume Stalin's position of power, but the tumultuous change did not harm the advancement of the new ICBM concept. Nikita Khrushchev, who eventually took control of the Soviet Union, recalled in his memoirs that "while Stalin was alive he completely monopolized all decisions about our defenses, including—I'd say *especially* those involving nuclear weapons and their delivery systems. We were sometimes present when such matters were discussed, but weren't allowed to ask questions. Therefore, when Stalin died, we weren't really prepared to carry the burden which fell on our shoulders."[16]

Thus, Khrushchev remembered that when Korolev first presented his work to the new party leaders in the Politburo, "we gawked at what he showed us as if we were a bunch of sheep seeing a new gate for the first time." He further noted that "when [Korolev] showed us one of his rockets, we thought it looked like nothing but a huge cigar shaped tube, and we didn't believe it could fly." Upon seeing a missile launch pad, Khrushchev declared that "we were like peasants in a marketplace. We walked around and around the rocket, touching it, tapping it to see if it was sturdy enough—we did everything but lick it to see how it tasted." However, he claimed, "we had absolute confidence in Comrade Korolyov. We believed in him when he told us that his rocket would not fly, but that it would travel 7,000 miles."[17] Therefore, when the rocket engineers revealed plans for a missile even more capable than the R-6, including new engines, a new guidance system, and a newly designed launch platform, the Central Committee concurred, calling for an intercontinental ballistic nuclear missile designated the R-7 on May 20, 1954.[18]

Back in the United States, Gardner immediately hired Ramo-Wooldridge to guide his missile venture, giving them "the highest priority obtainable in all matters of development, production, and support" and relieving them "of all hindrances created by military regulations." David M. Fleming, who wrote the initial contract for Ramo-Wooldridge, mentioned that Ramo and Wooldridge became angry that he wrote their contract in a way that ensured that they could not select their own company to both guide and complete the work. Fleming also noted that "anyone who didn't hop to it when they wanted to get something done was [deemed] an obstructionist."[19]

Once in business, Ramo and Wooldridge cherry-picked the most capable employees from other organizations working in the field. This helped their company but quickly engendered the hostility of other aerospace

companies and Air Force commands when these organizations lost outstanding personnel to the missile effort but were shut out of the program
through classification and contracts.[20]

On June 21, still concerned that Gardner was attempting to create another Manhattan Project for missiles, the Air Staff tasked the Air
Research and Development Command to develop the missile systems
and to recommend the logistics, operational, and personnel concepts to
support the new weapon. Air Force leaders also directed the command to
establish a new division to work on missiles. The U.S. Air Force established
the Western Development Division (WDD) on July 1, 1954, to "exercise complete authority and control over all aspects of the development
program for WS-107A (ATLAS), including ground support, operational
logistic and personnel concepts, and all engineering decisions."[21] Gardner
accepted the decision but ensured that Brig. Gen. Bernard Schriever, a recognized expert on missiles who had developed a close relationship with
Gardner and a zealot in his own right, became the division's commander.[22]

The Air Force located the WDD near the offices of Ramo-Wooldridge
in California and included many of the company's workers as part of
the organization but placed the new division under the authority of the
Air Research and Development Command. In addition, Air Materiel
Command established a separate procurement office to support the new
group. Schriever quickly began to handpick his own personnel and established a symbiotic relationship between Ramo-Wooldridge and the WDD.

Jamie Wallace, who worked for Schriever, remembered that "the
bomber men like LeMay were in full control of the Air Force and so interest in guided missiles was low indeed." Nevertheless, when Schriever began
to look for workers, a cadre of officers with missile experience existed
because airmen like Wallace had acquired experience in the various early
missile programs. Wallace recalled, "When Schriever got the job a lot of us
came out of the woodwork. They knew where everybody was. . . . We were
delighted to finally find someone who had the mission because we knew
exactly what to do."[23]

In April 1955, motivated by the new opportunities and political support, Schriever revealed his plan to have a working missile at an operational
base by July 1959. A month later Schriever managed to accomplish another

of Gardner's agenda items. He established a second ICBM development program called Titan to compete with the Atlas program. The new program was ostensibly to "provide alternate development routes and greater assurance of successful accomplishment of the ICBM development mission within target dates." However, because of Gardner's ongoing feud with the company, Convair viewed the action as an intentional slight, which it probably was. Even with this tremendous success, Gardner was not satisfied and kept pressing for greater effort on the ballistic missile.[24]

In the coming years, Schriever's division began a tug-of-war with the established Air Force commands and Air Staff over the control of missiles within the Air Force. A similar struggle was occurring in the contracting world.[25] At the beginning of 1954 Convair was the primary weapon-system engineering manager, guiding all of the contracted work on the Atlas, and was expected to remain the primary weapon-system contractor throughout the design and production phases. Instead, the WDD transferred the systems engineering management job to Ramo-Wooldridge during the fall of 1954. Then, in a second precedent-setting act, the WDD decided to only request and review subsystem designs from select companies rather than requesting designs from all qualified companies and evaluating each proposal.

To introduce continuous competition into the process, Schriever convinced the Air Force to allow him to select a second contractor for each subsystem, calling the dual-track program parallel development. Thus, not only did Convair not get to design and build the missile that the company had exclusively worked on to that point, but the contracts it did earn forced it to compete with other companies to earn the final sale. This new requirement was unprecedented and Convair, along with other companies infuriated by the process, complained to Congress and senior Air Force leaders. It appears that the criticality of getting a missile developed and built overrode concerns with legality or propriety. When the Air Force established the Robertson Committee to review and approve the ICBM development plan, the committee "doubted that the source-selection procedures were entirely fair . . . , but suspended judgment pending further observation."[26]

In addition, because the Air Force did not have enough personnel to oversee all contracts in a timely manner, Ramo-Wooldridge was given authorization to guide the contractors themselves. Over the next few years, several people expressed legal concerns with how the process was being carried out, but "a joint Ramo-Wooldridge/Western Development Division/Ballistic Missiles Office committee explored the problem and concluded in August [1956] that almost everyone concerned had been more interested in getting his work done fast than in observing regulations. . . . To WDD and Ramo-Wooldridge leaders, these were examples of the 'law's delay,'" and such delays were not justified in slowing down the missile program.[27]

Finally, contractors complained that they were forced to reveal proprietary information to a competitor, Ramo-Wooldridge, since Ramo-Wooldridge participated in the selection of other contractors and wrote the contracts for these other companies. Because of parallel development, each company's ideas were provided to their opponents so that the programs could remain interchangeable. The WDD argued that there was no issue since Ramo-Wooldridge was prohibited from building missiles itself, but this did not resolve the ill will from many companies who felt cheated by the process.[28]

All of these internal and contractual Air Force struggles did nothing to resolve the conflict with the Army, which had continued to work on ground-to-ground strategic missiles. In the early 1950s the Army's Redstone Arsenal in Alabama developed the Redstone missile, a liquid-fueled missile with a range of up to two hundred miles, clearly within the Army's designated mission area. Then, advancing outside of its allocated field, the Redstone Arsenal began to promote plans for a family of missiles, including one having a range of one thousand miles.[29]

On December 2, 1954, possibly reacting to these Army advances, the Air Force established an operational requirement for a tactical ballistic missile even though the Air Force had no mission for a shorter-range ballistic missile. Ironically, in response to the new Air Force requirement "for the development of a 1,000-mile missile using existing hardware," the Army permitted the Redstone Arsenal to upgrade its Redstone missile early the next year. The Air Force agreed to consider the Army proposal but recommended breaking up the Army team and assigning portions of the team to accomplish specific tasks. The secretary of the Army objected strenuously to this recommendation and won.[30]

This continued interservice competition was given greater emphasis by political events occurring behind the scenes. In March 1954, just one month after the von Neumann Committee released its report, Eisenhower met with members of his Science Advisory Committee to discuss his concerns about a surprise attack on the United States. Lee DuBridge, the chairman, recommended that an ad hoc committee be set up to study the problem. On July 26, 1954, Eisenhower established the Technological Capabilities Panel of the Scientific Advisory Committee—later deemed the Killian Committee because it was headed by James Killian, the president of the Massachusetts Institute of Technology—to "consider the vulnerability of the United States to surprise attack."[31]

Historians do not know why Eisenhower requested this study, but he faced many threats and was concerned about a Pearl Harbor–type nuclear attack. Communists were invading Guatemala and threatened Taiwan, and the French were struggling against communist nationalists in Vietnam. In addition, just a little over a month earlier, Sen. Joseph McCarthy (R-Wisc.) had attacked the Army for coddling communists, although this proved to be his undoing. Eisenhower was also struggling with political pressure to increase the defense budget, an action he was loath to do. Thus, he probably established the committee to show that he was taking all necessary actions to protect the nation without dramatically increasing spending on defense.

In February 1955 the forty-two-member Killian Committee released its report, stating that "the intercontinental ballistic missile [could] profoundly affect the military posture of either" the United States or the Soviet Union in the future and recommending that the "National Security Council formally recognize the present Air Force program for the development of an intercontinental ballistic missile as a nationally supported effort of highest priority."[32] The National Security Council asked the Department of Defense to comment on the Killian report. Gardner again took advantage of the incredible opportunity. Gardner discovered that Sen. Clinton Anderson (D–N.M.), the chairman of the Joint Congressional Committee on Atomic Energy, and Sen. Henry Jackson (D–Wash.), the chairman of the Subcommittee on Military Appropriations for Anderson's committee, both strongly concurred with Gardner's views on missiles. Thus, even before he presented his response to the secretary of the Air Force, Gardner provided a significant amount of information to Senator Jackson's subcommittee—in response to their queries. Then, when he provided the information to Secretary Talbott, Gardner suggested that Talbott forward a copy of his report to the two senators as well. Within days, Senators Anderson and Jackson sent Eisenhower a report titled *Findings and Recommendations Concerning the Intercontinental Ballistic Missile.*

In their document the congressmen warned that "the question of war or peace may depend upon who gets the ICBM first" and contended that "the ICBM . . . is the natural weapon of an aggressor bent upon carrying out a nuclear Pearl Harbor. If the Soviets win the race for the ICBM, and if they thereupon use it in a massive surprise attack against our cities and industries and the bases of the Strategic Air Command, effective retaliation may be impossible." To resolve these concerns, the Joint Committee strongly recommended that the president "immediately issue a directive singling out the ICBM as the most important project in our entire defense effort, assigning it unique and over-riding priority within the entire defense establishment."[33]

Other alarm bells were ringing as well. Thomas Phillips, a retired U.S. Army brigadier general, publicly expressed his concerns that the Soviets "started two years later than we to make a jet intercontinental bomber and now they have it in formations while we don't; . . . they have built more jet aircraft of a single type—the MiG-15—than we have of all jet aircraft combined and have built more light two-engined jet bombers than all the free world put together." He then criticized the fledgling U.S. missile program, proclaiming, "At the same time that the Soviets were involved in crash programs for medium and heavy bombers, they also had crash programs on long-range missiles. The United States, in contrast," Phillips contended, "completely dropped its intercontinental ballistic missile for two years and was progressing at a leisurely pace until Soviet progress forced a top priority on our missile programs."[34]

A week after receiving the congressional report, on July 6, 1955, Eisenhower met with Wilson and Talbott and requested a briefing on ballistic missiles. Gardner and his executive assistant, Lt. Col. Vincent Ford, had been working behind the scenes to convince like-minded presidential staffers to schedule them an opportunity to brief the president and the National Security Council on the nascent U.S. missile capability while the senators pushed from the front. Consequently, on July 28 Gardner, von Neumann, and Schriever briefed the president on their endeavor to build a ballistic weapon that could carry nuclear weapons across the world. While they explained their goals, they warned of the threat of a similar Soviet effort.[35]

On September 13, 1955, compelled by Senate Democrats, concerned citizens, and members of his own administration, Eisenhower approved National Security Council (NSC) Action No. 1433. The NSC document cautioned that "there would be the gravest repercussions on the national security and on the cohesion of the Free World, should the USSR achieve an operational capability with the ICBM substantially in advance of the United States" and directed that "the U.S. ICBM program [be] a research and development program of the highest priority above all others, unless modified by future decision of the President."[36]

Gardner wasted no time in using the momentum created by the president's decision to further speed the process of creating missiles. That same day Gardner established a team, the ICBM Administrative Procedures Evaluation Group, to streamline management procedures for ballistic missiles and ensure they were prioritized by the Air Force. Like the von Neumann Committee, the new group was often called the Gillette Committee after its chair, Hyde Gillette, the deputy secretary of the Air Force for budget and program management. Less than two months after they formed, the committee released its findings to Secretary Wilson, officially titled *The Air Force Plan for Simplifying Administrative Procedures.*

The Gillette Committee's plan reduced the number of agencies and offices that controlled ballistic missile decisions from forty-two to ten. It then consolidated the ten remaining approval organizations into two committees, one at Headquarters Air Force level, the Air Force Ballistic Missiles Committee, and another at Department of Defense level, the Office of the Secretary of Defense (OSD) Ballistic Missiles Committee, making them the only formal approval authorities for any item dealing with ballistic missiles. Gardner and Schriever also managed to garner a specific annex to the Air Force budget for the missile program that no one else could touch, creating resentment among Air Force leaders who were competing with them for money.

Political machinations worked both ways as the Air Staff used the Gillette procedures to block Gardner's ambitions, "real or imagined," to create another Manhattan Project by establishing special Air Force measures to integrate missiles into the Air Force. From either viewpoint, the procedures effectively bypassed the conventional Air Force and secretary of defense methods for coordinating the incorporation of new missions, infuriating many who were thereby avoided.[37]

These changes were significantly more important than the Gillette Committee's title reveals, as they granted Schriever authority only exceeded by the director of the Manhattan Project, even if it did remain in the Air Force. Although he still coordinated actions with the Air Research and Development Command, the Air Materiel Command, and others, Schriever was only responsible to the Air Force Ballistic Missiles Committee, which reported to the OSD committee. On December 19, 1959, after working with the system for a few years, the Ballistic Missile and Space Systems Panel of the Weapons Systems Management Working Group reported that establishing a separate organization with extraordinary power and authority did not solve the problem of Air Force bureaucracy but led to a division of responsibilities, duplication of functions, and conflict of authority.[38]

In addition to the administrative changes, the Gillette Committee also recommended establishing an initial operational capability for missiles that would be directed by the WDD. The division was to work with the appropriate commands to "develop a plan for employing the weapon in combat, prepare the associated logistics support plan, establish the first launching bases, and organize and train the first combat squadrons."[39]

While these recommendations would have been almost unthinkable just a few years before, they were not the only dramatic changes being considered to advance missiles. During its review, the von Neumann Committee had only been asked to study intercontinental missile programs, but the committee had warned that "there is . . . no current Air Force program for ballistic missiles of medium range (say, 200–1500 miles) [which] . . . should be considered by some qualified agency."[40] The Killian

Committee had also addressed this concern, reporting that "we believe the development of a medium range ballistic missile would be an easier development, more certain of success in a shorter time than that of the 5500 n[autical] m[ile] missile. Thus the Soviets could achieve a medium range ballistic missile capability sooner than the U.S. could achieve an intercontinental ballistic missile capability." The Killian Committee recommended that "the U.S. initiate a medium range ballistic missile program to increase the probability that the U.S. is first to achieve a ballistic missile capability."[41] The State Department agreed, first concluding in a study that, "should the Soviets be the first to develop a long range ballistic missile, this achievement would greatly reduce Free World confidence in American technological superiority and might lead several nations toward a 'third world orientation.'" The State Department then speculated that "if the United States managed to develop an IRBM [intermediate-range ballistic missile] at the same time that the Soviets demonstrated an ICBM, that feat would mitigate the problem."[42]

Schriever hated the very idea of a medium- or intermediate-range ballistic missile, believing it would harm the development of the Air Force intercontinental ballistic missile. He especially feared that the government would take the opportunity to "transfer . . . responsibility to another service or, because of the high priority of ballistic weapons, [establish] a separate management group for ballistic weapons directly under the DOD."[43] In February of 1955, when the Killian Committee agreed with the von Neumann Committee that the United States must immediately create an IRBM with a 1,500-mile range in parallel with the ICBM, Schriever's fears were realized.

The Army took its plans for a 1,500-mile IRBM to the Department of Defense, arguing that the service also required "the ability to attack targets with nuclear warheads at an extremely long range."[44] To make matters worse for Schriever, the Navy also offered two separate missile programs and a U.S.–U.K. cooperative program was presented. The Air Force, which had previously been given control of all missiles other than those replacing close air support or on water, responded to these perceived threats immediately. It first claimed that the IRBM would be a derivative of the ICBM and then offered a separate IRBM program. To determine which of the competing programs the Department of Defense would sponsor, the secretary of defense established a technical advisory committee, led by his deputy, Reuben Robertson.[45]

During this precarious time for the Air Force, on May 2, 1955, the Air Staff approved Gardner and Schriever's development of a second ICBM, later named the Titan, under the stipulations that they study the creation of an IRBM from this two-stage rocket and that it be produced in the central United States rather concentrating all missile development on the California seacoast. Neufeld reports that in July, the Robertson Committee determined that "the IRBM was not a natural derivative of the ICBM," knocking the Titan out of consideration for the Department of Defense's IRBM. Intriguingly, to accomplish this the Robertson Committee used studies Ramo-Wooldridge had conducted earlier, which revealed that "the longest range expected of this type of IRBM was approximately 700 nautical miles," a much shorter range than that of the Titan.[46]

Each service argued that it was most qualified to build the IRBM. In fact, the Army offered to combine the Air Force and Navy programs and build them at Redstone Arsenal, if needed. The services also argued over which branch should control the new shorter-range missile. Predictably, the Joint Chiefs of Staff were unable to agree. Finally, they recommended that the United States develop two IRBMs: an Air Force missile and a joint Army–Navy missile, with the latter "having the dual objective of achieving an early shipboard capability and also providing a land-based alternative to the Air Force program."[47]

The secretary of defense accepted this compromise on November 8, 1955, specifying, according to General White, that "an early operational capability will demand the utmost in cooperation between these programs." White noted that Secretary Wilson further "stated that not only is maximum technical and managerial coordination between the two IRBM programs essential, but maximum coordination among all of the ballistic missile programs is required."[48] General Twining complained that the IRBM would be more complicated than the ICBM, would take more time to deploy, would be "more vulnerable to the enemy, and more difficult to support," but Donald Quarles, interim secretary of the Air Force, rebuffed these concerns.[49]

That same day, the secretary of defense approved the Gillette Committee's recommended procedures. Six days later, he directed the Air Force chief of staff "to issue the appropriate directives which will implement the procedures and organizational arrangements contained in the plan." On November 18, General White, then vice chief of staff, charged the WDD with achieving an initial operating capability as soon as possible. White's order expanded the division's requirement from developing a working missile to creating, producing, manning, and basing the missiles. His directive did not dictate the required number of ICBMs or a timeline for its achievement, but he would provide these specifics the next month.[50]

Even though Eisenhower still had serious concerns about the efficacy of ballistic missiles, the willingness of the services to work together to develop them, and the technological expertise required to accomplish the two demanding tasks simultaneously, he conceded to the overwhelming political pressure. On December 20, 1955, a little over a month after the CIA produced a National Intelligence Estimate reporting significant improvement in Soviet bomber capability and during what historian Richard Leighton terms an abruptly chillier trend in the Cold War, "the President directed that the IRBM and ICBM programs should both be research and development programs of the highest priority above all others."[51]

Schriever and other like-minded ICBM advocates complained that establishing the creation of an IRBM as a program equal to that of the ICBM could slow or even prevent completion of the ICBM. Acknowledging these concerns, Eisenhower decreed that "mutual interference between these programs should be avoided so far as practicable, but if a conflict should occur in which strict application of paragraph a above would . . . cause major damage to the security interests of the United States, then the matter will be promptly referred to the President."[52]

The Air Force WDD—and the Army, given special permission to work with the Navy on the Jupiter IRBM—began to design and construct IRBMs while the Air Force retained the sole responsibility to develop the ICBM. Soon after, the Navy convinced the nation's leaders to let them work on the Polaris missile rather than the Jupiter since it could be launched from submarines, making it much less vulnerable to a nuclear first strike.[53]

Predictably, the services never achieved the required close coopera-tion. Each service viewed the task as a competition. They exchanged liaison officers, established delivery schedules for common components, and dis-cussed mutual use of facilities, but each realized the importance of success to their service. According to Richard Jacobson, an officer who worked on the Thor program, Schriever was surprised at the way that Thor became the linchpin of the Air Force's ICBM program. Jacobson concluded, "If Thor had been cancelled, there is no doubt in my mind that the Army would have gotten the ICBM." The Air Force established January 1960 as its initial goal for an operational IRBM capability.[54]

On December 28, 1955, a little over a month after his first direc-tive on missile initial operating capability, White added numbers and a timeline to his original requirements for operationalizing the missiles. He wanted to have one wing of 120 intercontinental ballistic missiles and sixty launching positions completed by January 1, 1960.[55] White specified that the wing should be divided equally between three support bases to be located on government property in the eastern, central, and western United States and the first ten missiles were to be operational by April 1, 1959. Once the wing was completed, White expected the new missileers to be capable of launching ten missiles from each base within fifteen min-utes of a warning alert, ten more within the next two hours, and the final twenty within four hours and fifteen minutes. This assignment required the WDD to not only construct the missiles, bases, and missile sites in this compressed timeframe but also to select and train the personnel who would operate the missiles.[56]

Schriever tasked Roy Ferguson to design an organization for the mis-siles. Ferguson remembered being given three or four days to complete the duty. After trying to compare the number of people required or the destructive capability to a standard Air Force unit, he discovered there was nothing to guide his decisions. Therefore, he decided to build the orga-nization in a way that would allow the Air Force to launch the first ten missiles in the required fifteen minutes. Because the Atlas guidance sta-tion could control three missiles, he organized the first missile squadron to have six missiles and two guidance stations. This decision provided each squadron missile with a primary and backup guidance station. While he admitted that the organization was completely arbitrary, no one had any better ideas.[57]

Concerned not only with retaining control of the new missiles and creating them before a potential enemy—foreign or domestic—did, but also about the impact of the new weapons on the service's flying mission, General White had also directed "the speediest possible integration of missiles and aircraft." This was not an idle threat, as Eisenhower, frustrated at the missile program's drastically increased costs, unsuccessfully tried to see if he could reduce defense expenditures by cutting technological development of the bomber force. Once he was informed that bombers would continue to be a critical part of the defense establishment until at least 1967, the president requested another review of the missile programs in order to reduce costs.[58]

This time Gardner was not available to influence the proceedings. Gardner and several other senior Air Force representatives had requested about $500 million in additional funding for fiscal years 1956 and 1957 but had been denied by the secretary of defense, who was trying to stay in line with the president's policy of frugality. Even though Gardner recognized that the ballistic missile program was not underfunded, he resigned in protest on February 10, 1956, proclaiming that other defense needs were not being met. Gardner had been a powerful force behind the development of the ICBM, and missile advocates keenly felt Gardner's absence soon after he left.[59]

In spite of the administration's pressure to reduce costs, General White and congressional Democrats continued the press to achieve operational status for the missiles as soon as possible. In March 1956 General White set the initial operating capability for IRBMs: one wing of three bases in England with 10 missiles ready by October 1958 and 120 missiles combat-ready by July 1, 1959.[60]

The pressure was too much for even Schriever, who worried that missiles built in this short time would not fly. After negotiations with General White failed to sway the vice chief of staff, Schriever requested help from his boss, the commander of Air Research and Development Command, Gen. Tommy Power, and from one of Schriever's arch nemeses, General LeMay, to help delay him. Power argued that White's timeline was so short that it would not allow Schriever to adequately test and produce the missiles, much less create training and personnel pipelines to generate the required operators. LeMay, one of the most powerful men in the Air Force at the time, backed Schriever and Power, contending that the compressed schedule would force contractors to produce the missiles before they had been adequately flight tested and would preclude required modifications.

In May the two sides agreed to a still-aggressive goal of 25 operational ICBMs by January 1, 1960, with 120 missiles (80 Atlas and 40 Titan) ready for launch by March 1961. The requirement for IRBMs had been pushed back as well, with only 30 IRBMs needing to be deployed by July 1, 1959, and the entire 120-missile wing postponed to July 1960. The new agreement reduced some of the pressure on the WDD.

Schriever should not have worried. The Air Force Ballistic Missile Committee, run by Secretary Quarles, refused to accept even the less compressed timetable due to financial concerns. On November 10, 1956, after all the negotiations were done, the Air Force reduced the ICBM force requirement to forty Atlas missiles and forty Titan missiles, to be in place by March 1961, with three launchers and six missiles prepared by March 1959. The IRBM schedule remained the same, with the first squadron to be ready by July 1959 and the fourth completed by July 1960, but the squadrons would now only possess fifteen missiles each, cutting the total number of missiles by 50 percent.[61]

During this same time Air Force missile proponents won another conflict. On November 26, 1956, the secretary of defense assigned "operational employment of the land-based Intermediate Range Ballistic Missile system [as] the sole responsibility of the U.S. Air Force." On the other hand, the secretary felt the need to document that "this does not, however, prohibit the Army from making limited feasibility studies in this area" and specifically mentioned that no decision had been made as to which missile, the Jupiter or Thor, would "be used for various missions in the armed services."[62] Less than two weeks later the solid-fuel Navy missile was added as a key defense priority because it could be safely launched from submarines, making it less vulnerable to a nuclear first strike. Therefore, on December 8, the Navy withdrew from the Jupiter program to develop its own missile, which it designated the Polaris. The competition between the services for control of ballistic missiles continued unabated.[63]

On January 11, 1957, President Eisenhower and the NSC approved the Air Force's initial operating capability plans, although Eisenhower warned that he might need to change the force's size or schedule. Two weeks later, the Air Force tried to launch its first Thor IRBM. The launch was a month behind schedule but still failed. On March 28, after coordinating with the British at the Bermuda conference, which was scheduled to improve relations between the two countries after a conflict over the Suez crisis, the president agreed to retain both the number and schedule of the missiles, although he changed the wording requesting the missiles from "the earliest possible date" to "the earliest practicable date."[64]

Then, during the summer of 1957, to prevent the national debt from rising over its authorized ceiling, the secretary of defense reduced the scheduled production of missiles—pushing the initial operational capability date back by months—and ordered the Air Force to cut overtime costs. On June 11 the Air Force attempted to launch an Atlas missile, but the attempt suffered the same fate as the Thor. While these failed launches were disappointing, they were not completely unexpected because the technologies used to create the missiles were so new.[65]

The reduced requirements and extended schedule created an opportunity for Eisenhower's critics to attack his defense policies, with Stuart Symington, a Democratic senator from Missouri who had been Truman's secretary of the Air Force, leading the pack, keeping politics firmly in the equation. Symington publicly "accused the administration of allowing the United States to fall behind the Soviet Union in the race for the 'ultimate weapon,' the guided missile, and of risking national security to save money."[66]

The Republican Party responded by contending that cuts during the Truman administration, when Symington was secretary of the Air Force, had stopped the initial work on the Atlas program. Over the protests of the Democratic congressmen and following his secretary of defense's advice, in July 1957, Eisenhower directed that the duplicative Titan program be prioritized lower than Atlas "in an effort to make substantial economies in this alternative development." He also asked the services to prioritize the IRBM programs so that they could focus on the Jupiter or Thor rather than on both of the competing projects. Therefore, Secretary Wilson reduced the priority of Titan and suspended production of both Thor and Jupiter until a single IRBM program could be selected for continuation.[67]

On August 6, General White, the missile advocate, who had become the Air Force chief of staff in July, appealed to the new secretary of the Air Force, James Douglas, to intercede against further cuts but, if the cuts could not be prevented, at least to allow the Air Force to determine where to take the cuts. The timing could not have been better for the missile advocates. Just two weeks later the Soviet Union launched its first ICBM, and within two months the Soviets' Sputnik satellite was orbiting the Earth. This put incredible political pressure on the U.S. to successfully launch their own missile.

On February 2, 1956, the Soviet Union had successfully launched an R-5M IRBM with a nuclear warhead, a feat made even more amazing since the engineers designing the missiles had not been allowed to talk to the scientists developing atomic weapons until late in 1954. Six months later, the military began deploying the new missile. However, the missiles did not have the range to reach the United States, so Soviet rocket scientists continued their quest to build a successful R-7 ICBM. Boris Chertok, one of the early designers, later exclaimed, "By early 1956, we had not yet performed the first test of a missile carrying a nuclear warhead, and just a year later, in 1957, we were already taking a stab at a missile carrying a thermonuclear warhead!"[68] Even though they had several failures, convincing some senior officials that they should shut down the ballistic missile program, on the morning of August 21, 1957, an R-7 ICBM smoothly lifted off of the launch pad and flew to the Pacific Ocean.[69]

Five days later, the Soviet news agency TASS reported that the Soviet Union had successfully launched an ICBM, proclaiming, "A few days ago, a super-long range, intercontinental multistage ballistic missile was launched. . . . The results obtained show that there is the possibility of launching missiles into any region of the terrestrial globe." If that did not convey the message clearly enough, the article continued, "The solution of the problem of creating intercontinental ballistic missiles will make it possible to reach remote regions without resorting to strategic aviation, which at the present time is vulnerable to modern means of antiaircraft defense."[70]

The story was quickly reported in the U.S. media, but Eisenhower downplayed the event, explaining that Soviet announcements were not particularly reliable, and a single missile was not militarily significant. He assured Americans that the U.S. missile program was progressing rapidly and, according to historian Robert Watson, "the public took their cue from these reassurances and showed little concern over the matter."[71]

Although no one in the United States knew it at the time, Eisenhower was correct. The missile was not as successful as the Soviets contended. Although the missile traveled about 6,500 kilometers, the warhead disintegrated before hitting the targeted area. Not until two years after the launch, on March 29, 1958, did Soviet engineers find a way to keep the nose cone intact as it returned from space. Even then they found that the missile was extremely inaccurate, missing the target by several kilometers.[72]

However, everything changed dramatically for both the Soviet Union and the United States less than two months after that first launch. On October 5, 1957, the top *New York Times* headline read, "Soviet Fires Earth Satellite into Space." The satellite was the 184-pound Sputnik. It circled the globe transmitting audio signals, ensuring that it could be both seen and heard by people around the world. The *Times* quoted unnamed military experts who said "the satellites would have no practicable military application in the foreseeable future" but also mentioned that "the study of such satellites could provide valuable information that might be applied to flight studies for intercontinental ballistic missiles."[73]

The Soviets quickly followed the announcement about Sputnik with a second story, a proclamation that they had successfully detonated a hydrogen bomb at high altitude. Tied to the launch of Sputnik just a few days before, the Soviets sent a clear message to America. Charles Jackson, an expert in psychological warfare and former advisor to President Eisenhower, privately declared the Soviets' launch of Sputnik, the almost simultaneous announcement of the hydrogen bomb test, and the predicted launch of a second, larger satellite—which the Soviets did launch soon after—a masterful piece of psychological warfare and "an overwhelmingly important event—against our side."[74]

Ironically, the event that allowed this "masterful piece of psychological warfare," the launch of Sputnik, almost did not happen. Vyacheslav

Malyshev, the director of the Ministry of Medium Machine Building, and a key Soviet leader overseeing the development of missiles, suspected that Korolev was only building his rockets for space exploration and argued strenuously that he should remain focused on military weaponry. However, Korolev used the growing Cold War competition to convince the Council of Ministers and Khrushchev to allow him to create an artificial satellite.[75]

In the United States, Eisenhower tried to retain his reduced defense budget in spite of a firestorm of negative public opinion and political pressure to respond to the Soviet achievements. On October 10 he told his National Security Council, "There's no reason for hand-wringing, just because the Russians got there first—they're to be congratulated. . . . But we've lost nothing of our national security, and we shouldn't change our scientific plan."[76]

However, this time the rest of the nation was not willing to accept his perspective. On October 10 the *Seattle Daily Times* declared, "in strikingly similar terms, several military-research officials privately described the sputnik as the opening battle of the Third World War." A little over a week later, on October 28, *Newsweek* reported that "most Americans are in favor of a crash program to put the U.S. ahead in the missile race. . . . There was concern but no panic. . . . Above all, they understood that catching up might well be a matter of survival."[77]

By November 3, when the Soviets launched Sputnik II, the much larger satellite they had forecast, some leading legislators were ready to call hearings to force Eisenhower to "'speed up our [missile] program' and to convert former target dates into much earlier deadlines for achievement in the development of missiles, satellites and rockets." Sen. Lyndon B. Johnson (D-Texas) declared that "target dates have been set for 1961 or 1965, while 'we ought to be talking about 1958 or '59, '60.'"[78] By the end of the month, when the congressional inquiry began, the *Washington Post and Times Herald* announced that the committee would "smash bottlenecks that could threaten 'national survival' in the space age."[79]

Once again, even Eisenhower's own advisors supported his political opposition. On April 4, 1957, facing a political firestorm and wanting to protect American civilians from nuclear attack, Eisenhower established the Security Resources Panel of the Office of Defense Mobilization Science Advisory Committee to determine if blast shelters should be built across the country. Although Eisenhower explicitly directed the Gaither Committee, as the group became known, to focus only on the use of blast shelters, when the team presented its report on November 4, its recommendations proved the members had not done so.[80]

The report asserted that "by 1959, the USSR may be able to launch an attack with ICBMs carrying megaton warheads, against which SAC [Strategic Air Command] will be almost completely vulnerable under present programs." The report further stressed that, under a "medium weight [attack]—divided between military and civilian targets . . . , about half of the population would be casualties." Among other things, it recommended that "an integrated program of Atlas and Titan [missiles], and an IRBM program including the achievement of a significant operational capability at the earliest possible date, should be given the highest national priority." In order "to lessen SAC vulnerability to an attack by Russian ICBMs (a late 1959 threat)," the report recommended that Eisenhower "increase the initial operational capability [IOC] of our IRBMs (Thor and/or Jupiter) from 60 to 240 . . . [and] increase the IOC of our ICBMs (Atlas and Titan) from 80 to 600." Finally, all the missiles "except for the initial Atlas group, . . . should incorporate hardening against the Soviet ICBM threat." While the Gaither Report acknowledged that to accommodate its recommendations would cost the nation billions, the authors still pressed strongly for their acceptance.[81]

Lyndon Johnson, as Senate majority leader, demanded access to both the Gaither Report and the Killian Report. The Gaither Report was classified, but on December 20, 1957, reporter Chalmers Roberts reported its key contents in a *Washington Post* story "Enormous Arms Outlay Is Held Vital to Survival" under the front-page banner "Secret Report Sees U.S. in Grave Peril." The story included a declaration that there was a "missile gap" that could not be closed before 1960 or 1961. Since he had access to intelligence from the U-2 reconnaissance aircraft, Eisenhower knew there was no missile gap but decided to debate the issue without disclosing that information rather than risk revealing the highly classified intelligence capability.[82]

Nonetheless, congressional inquiries and immense public pressure began to motivate Eisenhower's administration to revise its priorities again. Eisenhower increased the defense budget by $4 billion over the next two years and compromised in some other areas. Neil McElroy, who replaced Wilson as secretary of defense on October 9, convinced the president to accelerate the Jupiter, Thor, and Polaris IRBM programs. Even though Eisenhower correctly "feared that they would become obsolete quickly and have to be scrapped," he increased the number of planned ICBMs to 130 (90 Atlas and 40 Titans) and IRBMs to 180. McElroy had his new director of guided missiles, William Holaday, order the Army and Air Force to produce and deploy four squadrons each of the Thor and Jupiter missiles, with the first squadrons to be operational by December 31, 1958, and the last by March 1960. Soon after, Holaday approved an Air Force request to increase the number of Atlas missiles by five squadrons and to increase the rate of production in order to complete this task by March 1963. He also returned the Titan to operational status but did not agree to the Air Force request to double the production of that missile. These new demands intensified the pressure to select and train the new missileers. Eisenhower also authorized research to begin on the solid-fueled Minuteman, a missile that could be manufactured much more cheaply than the Atlas or Titan and was safer and more reliable than either.[83]

The political pressure to respond to the Soviet missile threat only got worse when, on December 6, the Naval Research Laboratory's Vanguard, a missile the administration touted as the U.S. response to Sputnik, with its own satellite, failed spectacularly after rising only a few feet in front of an assembled press. The first successful launch of the Atlas less than two weeks later, on December 17, did not significantly change the pressure on Eisenhower because the Atlas was a military missile, and its launch was not widely publicized. In addition, the Atlas only flew 530 miles and carried no satellite. In the same way, the successful launch of the Thor IRBM on September 20, 1957, was discounted because of its smaller range, even though Eisenhower argued that the U.S. IRBMs could be placed within range of the Soviet Union while the Soviet Union had no similar option for its IRBMs.[84]

Eisenhower declared space a separate and less important mission than military missiles, but many Americans felt so strongly about the issue that they kept up the political pressure to respond in some way. For this reason, the military continued substantial efforts to launch a satellite, finally succeeding a year later, on December 18, 1958, when an Atlas launched one into orbit, broadcasting a Christmas message from Eisenhower over short-wave radio for thirty-four days.[85]

In the meantime, the workers building the ICBM and IRBM labored at breakneck speed. Col. Richard Jacobson later remembered being told that they "were going to deploy [the Thor IRBM] as soon as you had something that would be a threat to the Soviet Union." When asked for clarification, he responded that the decision point to deploy the missiles was when 50 percent of the missiles would hit the Soviet Union—not a specified target within the Soviet Union but the country itself. This haste did not stop the political sniping, but the rush to quickly develop and deploy the new missiles, exacerbated by the political and interservice pressures, was creating havoc within the Air Force.[86]

CHAPTER 4

Making the Missile Operational

In his 1955 Air War College thesis, U.S. Air Force colonel Thomas McGehee contends that "in any race for qualitative weapons superiority the advantage gained is apt to be temporary and even lost if the weapon system is not operational almost simultaneously with its scientific development."[1] Many Americans, including political leaders, agreed with him. Thus, in November 1957, after the Soviets launched Sputnik and Sputnik 2, "a form of 'mass hysteria' coupled with frustration . . . spread rapidly over the political, military and scientific circles throughout this country. The public began to clamor for drastic emergency action in a desperate struggle to overcome our seemingly secondary position in technological development."[2]

This political pressure intensified the interservice rivalry over control of missiles. Following the Gaither Committee report, Secretary McElroy had turned to the Joint Chiefs of Staff for help determining clear ICBM requirements. Once again, the Joint Chiefs failed to find consensus. Gen. Thomas White pressed for more ICBMs while Adm. Arleigh Burke wanted to increase the number of the Navy's Polaris missiles. On the other hand, Gen. Maxwell Taylor, the Army chief of staff, declared that the military had too many nuclear weapons and needed to focus on nonnuclear forces.[3] Malcolm MacIntyre, undersecretary of the Air Force from 1957 to 1959, remembered: "Sputnik went off in October 1957 and there was great criticism about our missiles not being in place. As a matter of fact, around that time we had about six failures with the Atlas. There was a great cry to cancel the Atlas program [and give the ballistic missile program to another organization], which we [the Air Force] resisted."[4]

Due to the intense political and social pressure, the Air Force began the process of making the ballistic missile operational even though none had yet successfully completed a full-range launch. On November 27, 1957, the key leaders involved in the production and use of missiles (Thomas Power, now commanding Strategic Air Command [SAC]; Bernard Schriever; Edwin Rawlings of Air Materiel Command; Samuel Anderson, now commanding Air Research and Development Command; and Ben Funk of the Ballistic Missile Office) agreed that the Air Force should "transfer to SAC . . . all IOC training and operational responsibilities, units, and bases." This meant that the missiles would no longer be considered research and development. Instead, they were being treated as operational weapons. The Western Development Division, now called the Air Force Ballistic Missile Division

(AFBMD), transferred the new missiles and associated bases and personnel to the SAC.[5]

Thus, when a crew from the 576th Strategic Missile Squadron at California's Vandenberg Air Force Base (AFB) successfully launched an Atlas D missile about 4,300 miles into the Pacific Ocean on September 9, General Power pronounced the shot a "tremendous milestone." Then, less than two

Atlas 12D. The successful launch of this missile convinced Gen. Tommy Power, commander in chief of Strategic Air Command, to declare the Atlas missiles operational. *Air Force Historical Research Agency*

months later, on October 31, 1959, Power declared the Atlas missiles at Vandenberg to be the first operational ICBMs.[6]

Gary Alkire, a young lieutenant at the time, remembered that the Atlas was not ready to go. The Air Force, he contends, pushed Atlas into operational service because it desperately needed a squadron of missiles that the service could call operational.[7]

Power's declaration began a year of frustration for Air Force missileers. After the general deemed the Atlas operational, Schriever's team could not consistently replicate the successful launch. Maj. Benjamin Bellis, who worked for Schriever during this time, observed that when a missile was launched without problems, "we didn't have a record of how we made it successful. . . . So we were having random success, the worst thing that can happen to you because you know you got it right but you can't repeat it."[8]

Random success also created credibility problems for other Air Force missiles. As noted previously, the Air Force rushed the Thor and Jupiter IRBMs into operation, so these missiles, like Atlas, struggled with credibility issues. Col. Bill Large, a highly decorated pilot who was then serving as SAC's assistant commander-in-chief for missiles, recalled taking the members of a commander's conference to a Thor missile launch. After a leak in the missile system caused the launch team to cancel the operation, Large remembered that "all of the SAC guys said, 'We told you so. Missiles are no good, are not here to stay.'"[9]

Some missile crewmembers expressed similar concerns with the Atlas' capabilities, although they did not attempt to be so prophetic. Staff Sgt. Donald Glantz, who served as a missile guidance technician at Vandenberg from 1958 to 1964, remembered that the Air Force "eventually worked out most of the bugs and we had many successful launches, but it was not a reliable military weapon." He also believed "these missiles were more of a symbolic deterrent than a credible threat."[10]

The decision to place the Thor and Jupiter IRBMs in the hands of American allies created other difficulties as well. During the March 1957 Bermuda Conference, President Dwight Eisenhower and British Prime Minister Harold MacMillan agreed to deploy Thor missiles to England. Six months later, in September, the Air Force successfully test launched a

Thor from Cape Canaveral, Florida. A year after that, on September 19, 1958, the Air Force transported the first IRBM to England by air. However, the missile was not declared operational until December 16, nearly three months after the deployment, when a SAC crew successfully launched one from a site at Vandenberg. Even then, the Thor was not fully ready. The first squadron was scheduled to be operational in December 1958, the second in June 1959, the third in October, and the fourth in March 1960. Nevertheless, the Air Force did not turn over a complete Thor squadron to the United Kingdom until June 6, 1959, six months behind schedule.

The delays in Thor's operational status created friction between the United States and Great Britain, but this discord was nothing compared to the problems the Jupiter missile created with other American allies. The United States had originally planned to place Jupiter squadrons in several allied nations belonging to the North Atlantic Treaty Organization, including three in France, but Charles de Gaulle's government refused to accept the missiles on French soil despite the fact that France had previously requested U.S. nuclear missiles. Since the missiles were already designed and being constructed, the United States worked to coordinate new locations for the IRBMs in the Far East and on the European continent or North Africa.[11]

Concerned that the State Department might not find allies willing to accept the missiles on U.S. terms, the Department of Defense selected Elmendorf AFB, Alaska, as the fallback option. Diplomats finally worked out deals with Italy, in August 1959, and Turkey, in late October of the same year, to place Jupiter missiles in these countries, but political and technical struggles pushed back operational dates and further damaged the missiles' credibility.[12]

When historians asked several former SAC generals about integrating early missiles into the force, Gen. David Burchinal recalled, "We covered all their targets with manned airplanes initially; Thors and Jupiters, I think, were all backed up with manned airplanes." After Gen. Leon Johnson agreed, Burchinal continued, "One never counted on them as an independent strike force sufficiently reliable in themselves." Atlas did not fare much better in their minds. Curtis LeMay remarked, "The accuracy of the first missiles was nothing to jump up and down about." Gen. Jack Catton recapitulated the theme, "These idiots pulled me down into the basement there and started explaining to me that we were going to shoot this rocket, that was going to go 5,000 miles and it was going to be within . . . I guess about a mile of the target." Catton continued, "There you are, shooting a rocket like a cannon, and it is going to go 5,000 miles and be within a *mile* of the aiming point. That was just hard for me to comprehend. That makes you apprehensive. Then there was General LeMay's point about being tested fully, and being *sure* you know what you are doing." He did not say, but it was likely that all of the ICBMs were "backed up" by manned aircraft since most of LeMay's "bomber men" refused to trust missiles. Tellingly, in 1958 LeMay remarked, "Initially, strategic missiles will *augment* our offensive striking forces. As we learn more about them and know that they will be able to accomplish the job they are designed to do, they will replace a portion of our manned bomber force." He then revealed the Air Force's long-term perspective, disclosing that, "However, as far into the future as I can see, I feel we must have integrated forces of both piloted and unpiloted systems to give us greater flexibility in our operations."[13]

To make matters worse, Schriever had employed a concept he labeled "concurrency" to complete the missiles as quickly as possible. Previous work on aerodynamic missiles used what Major Bellis "called the three-step stage. We would do some handmade prototypes, and then we would come out with an experimental model. After we had demonstrated that, then we would go into a production prototype. What happened between the X version and the Y version is that we would take the new technology that was now available and incorporate it and literally create something new." Only after validating the concept would the engineers move on to production.[14]

Richard Jacobson, a veteran of Schriever's process, later explained how concurrency was different. "You develop and produce all at the same time, and you deploy as quick as you can though you may not have finished development."[15] Colonel McGehee explained the reasoning behind the change, contending that in aircraft development, "the maximum efficiency of the system is gained after a period of trial and error in which experience of personnel is increased, equipment is modified or augmented and operational concepts are tried and adopted or discarded." On the other hand,

McGehee argued, "in an ICBM system there is no opportunity for this trial and error period. The components of the system must be managed so as to guarantee simultaneous availability of missiles, warheads, operational and maintenance personnel, supplies and equipment, logistics concepts, launching sites and operational concepts and plans."[16]

Concurrency was not a new concept. According to Department of Defense historian Elliot Converse, the Army had tried the idea "to support the war in Korea and to ready the Army for a possible war with the Soviet Union . . . , but the acceleration complicated production and resulted in some inadequately tested systems that performed poorly in the field." The Air Force had used the concept as well, in World War II, with the B-24, the B-26, and the B-29 bombers, but Converse contends that "accelerated acquisition allowed little or no time for testing the system prior to the initiation of production. Changes to improve performance or correct deficiencies were made after production had begun or was completed, and special modification centers were established for this purpose."[17]

The initial iterations of concurrency involved known technologies produced en masse during a war but still struggled with problems. Major Bellis described how using concurrency for missiles created even more difficulties: "In the development part of the program, the problem of quality control was the harshest we had ever really gotten into because in the manned aircraft, the pilot can work it out. If the anomalies of the thing do not work out, we have a pilot to fix it; not so on ballistic missiles." He further admitted that, "the quality just has to be to a 'T', plus we had not set up a system test area to test the whole system. We had tested the propulsion system; we had tested the reentry; we had tested the subsystems, but we didn't have a system test area." After putting the system together, Bellis recounted, the designers found "that the subsystems looked fine, but wouldn't play [together] as the test system."[18]

When the Air Force began building the missile launch centers, the problem worsened. Contractors who were used to building to specifications defined in inches were now given standards measured in thousands of an inch. Since it was very unlikely that any of the construction workers had even seen a missile, they found it difficult to understand these tight tolerances. The workers' frustration with these exacting standards, added to complaints over the rushed timeline and sometimes perplexing leadership, led to conflicts between labor unions and government overseers, and several unions decided to strike over the issues.[19]

Another problem with concurrency was the ever-changing requirements. "The engineers kept finding new things in ballistic missiles that they wanted to make sure they got in that first operational site," Bellis recalled. "What we found was that we had been approving changes to go into the Thor from the test experience, from the development experience, from the technology advancement experience, and so we were directing the contractors to put changes into the program, into the missiles and then the corresponding changes into the ground support equipment," he commiserated. "All the testers and evaluators and controls and all those kinds of things that go with it, and the depot tooling, and the spare parts, and the tech manuals. You try to keep them all coming together. We found nobody was keeping it together."[20]

To resolve the difficulties, Bellis enacted what he later termed configuration control. "We went back and got into a specification program to define more specific detail so we could have a configuration baseline and then keep changing that baseline as we went along and know that the change was going to change at a certain numbered missile." The baseline allowed the Air Force to define "where the modification would be done and who was going to do it; the spare parts that had already been produced versus the new spare parts; and the tech manuals and the change sheets to the tech manuals, because we were going to have both configurations in the field at the same time. . . . Then you get changes on top of changes on top of changes on top of changes."[21]

Because this process still did not work as Bellis had hoped, he later amended the system to what he called configuration management but "found out we had no knowledge of what the status was with respect to all of these change decisions. We would find some change kits going in ahead of schedule because they had shorter leadtime [sic] than earlier approved changes. So we had stuff that wouldn't fit because the earlier change hadn't been put in that gave you the required fit." After many adjustments, Bellis' team was finally able to develop a more effective system.[22]

Nevertheless, Bellis found that the Atlas missile program struggled with the same problems he had seen in the Thor, except the situation was even more flawed. Because the Air Force decided to upgrade the Atlas at the same time as it placed the missiles at operational sites, the service began building three different configurations of Atlas missiles at the same time, compounding the problems.[23]

Bellis voiced this concern, "We had lost control of the Atlas. We were installing systems in Cheyenne at Warren Air Force Base for the Atlas D, which was [a] soft, horizontal [deployment] like a Thor. Now the E was a different configuration, and then the F was the hard silo vertical configuration." All were being placed into operation at the same time. What Bellis found astounded him. "We found the part numbers were wrong; we found the discipline of dash number—you have a part number and then the dash 1 or dash 3 or dash 5 tells you the change configuration. The log books were not up to date. They didn't even tell you what [change configuration or part] was there." This uncontrolled mishmash led to the random success that infuriated Bellis, further hurting the credibility of the missiles in the minds of many key Air Force leaders as well as those assigned to operate the missiles.[24]

The rush to put missiles on alert led to other problems as well, including the selection and training of personnel.[25] In early 1958 Col. Allen Stephens, the chief of staff for the 1st Missile Division, expressed the common worry from his organization that "all missilemen must be in the genius category." Many who were planning the missile enterprise for the Air Force had the same concerns. Lt. Col. Roy Ferguson once asked a group of General Schriever's missile planners, "Do we need a bunch of Ph.D's to fire this thing?" The response was not encouraging. Otto Glasser, program director for the Atlas quipped, "If you do, we've failed."[26] Initial crew requirements for each Atlas missile crew were set at thirty-one personnel, although this was quickly reduced to seventeen.

James Baar and William Howard, in *Combat Missileman*, quoted an unnamed Air Force officer as saying later, after the required numbers had dropped to nine, "Our research people and the factory people still wanted each crew made up of nine stars, every man [equal to] a Ted Williams," one of the greatest hitters in baseball history. The officer continued, "but you can't find nine Ted Williamses, and even if you could, you couldn't pay 'em. So we had a lot of give and take and ended up with some more reasonable requirements."[27]

After discussing the concern with Jim Dempsey, Convair's chief engineer for the Atlas program, Colonel Stephens was reassured that the Air Force was tailoring the missiles to meet the "personnel qualifications and limitations" of the thousands of airmen already serving to maintain and operate the current bomber fleet. Glasser agreed with Dempsey. "There is no real reason why the missile should be any more complicated than an airplane," Glasser said. "It isn't learning to fly that makes a good pilot. Learning to fly is easy. It's judgment that is important. It's who can make the right decision quickly. This is what you can't put into a machine, but what the combat missileman is going to have to be able to do."[28]

Glasser was right about judgment being necessary. The people selected to operate the new missiles would hold a position very different from any other. While they would hold the power to devastate large areas of land, killing or maiming almost everyone in the target area and destroying most of the buildings and natural habitat, they would also hold no authority to determine when their weapon was used and often were not aware of the target that their missile or missiles were aimed toward.

In addition, because of their isolation, missileers had little contact with the outside world and thus could not verify or prepare themselves for, other than through official channels, any situation leading to a launch command. Alerts were tedious—preparing for and awaiting a dreadful command that they hoped would never come but knowing that they must be prepared to respond to if it came. The bomber pilots held a similar responsibility but would at least have a few hours of flight time to reflect on their fearsome duty and ensure that their mission was ethical before launching their bombs.

General Power, in a message to the first missileers, expounded on the problem of finding the right people: "Not only because of the complexity of the weapon systems involved but primarily because of the unprecedented nature of combat missile operations, our main problem . . . is the manning of our rapidly expanding missile force with personnel who meet the stringent qualifications demanded of SAC missile combat crews."[29] Power detailed additional specifications required of the new missileers. "They must be thoroughly trained in the highly technical aspects of a revolutionary new science. They must possess the superior physical, mental and moral attributes required of the military man, especially in this day and age, and above all," he declared, "they must be imbued with an exceptional degree of maturity and dedication in order to be worthy of the unparraled [sic] responsibilities which are assigned to them."[30]

Since the Air Force focused its attention on "rated" flyers and since the pilots who had flown and fought in World War II and Korea had proven themselves capable in many of these aspects, as had the enlisted aircraft maintainers, SAC turned to them to fill the billets. Col. William S. Rader, the Air Force's first missile wing commander, strongly recommended this action, stating, "The operation of this mixed force [of manned and unmanned strategic weapons in the Air Force] will pose many problems. . . . Obviously, the man trained into missiles with the most experience and best background in the flying game should be the best qualified to solve these problems." Rader further advised, "These factors dictate a need for manning policies whose criteria provide for rated personnel in all key missile management functions and a minimum of 50% rated personnel for all officer positions exclusive of the combat support group and medical group functions."[31]

General Power levied the necessary airmen from the SAC units around the world. He requested volunteers, but volunteer status was not a requirement. The key requirement was "excellence," meaning that, for officers, the selectee had to be evaluated as "outstanding" or "very fine officer," the top half of a four-level rating system that the Air Force used at the time. Noncommissioned officers who were selected must have been assessed as above average and "demonstrated leadership and superiority." All volunteers were to be career servicemen, not in their first enlistment.[32]

This decision resolved one problem and a considerable one at that, but it created others. Taking large numbers of rated officers and qualified noncommissioned officers from the bomber fleet entailed losing valuable resources from what the Air Force considered their most critical mission—flying. Initially the Air Force planned to find "compatible [people], capable of accepting the most uniform behavior pattern" who would serve in missiles their entire career. Lt. Col. Anderson advised, "The launch officer will find his exercise of ingenuity largely restricted. The target is preselected. Weather is no longer a major factor. Where once military leaders implemented battle doctrine even at small unit level by varying their techniques, there is no requirement for this in ballistic systems. All this will mean a loss of the customary incentives." He further predicted, "The missile man will be a student of standard methodology. The highly individualistic personality, capable but unorthodox, loses his special value in this rigid situation. There is a new market for the compatible person, capable of accepting the most uniform behavior pattern. Monotony should flourish in this atmosphere." There was a concern that not many pilots would "flourish" in such a monotonous environment, which proved true.[33]

Instead of resolving the potential concerns, the Air Force moved flyers into the missile field, but only on a rotational basis to give the pilots career broadening experience, not as a new career. Moreover, because unit commanders selected the new missileers, it is doubtful that they sent their absolute best. SAC wanted good men in missiles, but the command's leaders would not consider losing volunteers to missiles as an excuse for a flying wing performing poorly on an exercise or inspection and the wing commanders who were selecting the new missileers knew this. Colonel Rader acknowledged this problem, complaining to his boss that "there have been cases where the officers were assigned primarily so that they, or a member of their families, might be in close proximity to a general hospital, . . . due to grounding action for physical reasons, . . . [and because an officer] was close to mandatory retirement."[34]

To prevent or at least reduce losing skilled rated and maintenance personnel from the SAC flying community, General Power's staff then decided that the flyers selected to rotate through missiles would come from overseas or school assignments, on their way back to the flying career field. Others were pulled from units with outdated aircraft that were intended to be deactivated. This way, the command retained many of their best flyers and maintainers in important operational units but were able to man the new missile units.[35]

Robert Kelchner, who retired as a chief master sergeant, reflected on his personal experience as a knowledgeable radar technician with more than two years remaining on his enlistment. "When I was identified for missile training in June 1961, I had been on active duty for over five years. The SAC personnel at Offutt AFB [in Nebraska were] in the process of fielding a huge weapons system. The Minuteman ICBM was to have at least six wings at six different bases. To man these bases, the Air Force had decided to shut down all the medium bomber B-47 wings." He then explained the reasoning behind the process, "The transfer of all these personnel to Minuteman was to get their experienced operations and maintenance people. It was a delicate balance of maintaining operational bombers until the Minuteman became operational."[36]

Concerned over losing such a large percentage of the flying force, even temporarily, the Air Force again revised the standards for selecting missileers. The service began to recruit young engineers to serve as deputy missile combat crew commanders, who would work under the guidance of a more senior crew commander.[37] The new engineers reduced the need for personnel with operational flying experience to serve in missiles, but the change did not imply that Air Force leaders no longer wanted rated missileers. Howard Tarleton, who began working in missiles in 1963 after seven years as a navigator, recalled, "They [SAC leaders] were trying to get people with operational backgrounds. Although many of the assignees were non-rated, they hoped to get experienced people (rated) to bring knowledge and leadership to the Minuteman program."[38] Leon Hojegian remembered that, at Plattsburgh AFB in New York, all key leadership positions were filled by rated officers, leaving no leadership opportunities for the nonrated missileers.[39]

The debate over whether missile units should be filled with rated officers or not raged for years. However, the Air Force never seriously considered making missiles a rated position, which would have presumably given missiles the same status in the Air Force as aeronautical positions, even if it never achieved the glamour of flying.[40]

Either way, the result was the same. Most rated officers who served in missiles did not consider themselves missileers. Rather, like Col. Floyd Wikstrom—the first wing commander at Malmstrom AFB, Montana, who "considered [himself] a rated officer with missile experience"—the flyers remained focused on flying.[41] The situation was made worse as all rated officers had to maintain their flight qualifications during missile duty, but missile leaders above the crew level were not required to be trained on missile operations. Thus, most Air Force personnel equated the leadership of missile units with that of commanding "support" units rather than operational units.

The overall impact of this unsettling standard was that many of those who did consider themselves missileers saw themselves as less viable for promotion than their flying peers—not an unreasonable view. In fact, Colonels William Brooksher and Jimmy Scott, in a survey of missileers conducted for a National War College study, discovered that "there is practically no demand for general officers who are not rated. Within the operations field in SAC, rated officers are a prerequisite for command. . . . As long as the operations command structure combines both missiles and rated organizations the demand for missile general officers will continue to be negligible."[42] While Lawrence Hasbrouck, a former missileer, pointed out that the complete hold on missile leadership positions by rated officers began to change in the early 1970s, the Air Force promoted very few non-rated missile officers to general for decades.

During this time the Air Force also developed and began giving aptitude tests to recent enlistees to weed out unproductive or undesirable personnel from the service. These new tests were also used to select enlisted personnel with backgrounds and aptitudes in electronics for important missile positions, meaning that test takers had to score in the top 20 percent of all enlistees on the electronics test to be placed in missiles. Several former missilemen remembered being given the tests during their basic training and being offered jobs in missiles after scoring highly in electronics.[43]

Once selected to work with the new weapons, the first missileers faced many difficulties. Duty with the Thor and Jupiter IRBMs presented the most frustrating duty. Because the IRBMs would be deployed on foreign soil, the U.S. government agreed to allow NATO allies to operate and maintain them, leaving U.S. SAC personnel responsible for the nuclear warhead but not the missiles. U.S. officers were expected to help launch the missile when authorized, but new evidence has revealed that the allied nations discovered ways to launch the missiles without U.S. support, so the U.S. officers really only served as figureheads.[44]

The initial state of affairs for missileers in the United States was not much better. The first missileers traveled to their new assignment to discover that the missiles they were to control had not yet been built. Moreover, the Air Force had not finalized plans for operations, so the service had no training program in place. For these reasons, many new missileers sat in the offices of their new squadrons for several months with no real mission. In some instances, they were allowed to visit the construction sites where their missile silos were being built, but this was not always the case.

The first missileers, whether assigned overseas with Thor or Jupiter or in the United States with Atlas or Titan missiles, all learned their profession by watching and listening to the engineers who were designing and building the missiles. When the Air Force did begin instruction, it paid Convair, Douglas, Burroughs, General Electric, and other missile contractors to conduct training programs at the manufacturers' factories. Douglas conducted initial Thor training in a World War II aircraft plant in Tucson, Arizona, while the AC Spark Plug Company trained missileers in a former brewery in Milwaukee, Wisconsin. Brig. Gen. Jerry Page explained that "while these conditions leave much to be desired from a training viewpoint, the concurrent phasing of research and operational developments dictates that the initial training be conducted as close as possible to the source of equipment and modifications."[45]

The instructors prepared training manuals as the courses progressed, updating them as the missiles evolved and changed. After the missileers spent up to three months at one or more of the plants studying the basics of how the missiles worked and the particulars of their duty position, they would be assigned to a crew. The crew was then assigned to work at Vandenberg AFB where they learned to operate the missile as a team.

Maj. John Merriman's experience illustrates the training that early missileers endured. A decorated bomber pilot with combat experience in both World War II and Korea, Merriman volunteered for missiles and was assigned to the Atlas program at Wyoming's F. E. Warren AFB. After traveling to the base, he was ordered to attend missile training at the Convair plant in San Diego. He found that the school was actually located in the former Bernard Street Grammar School.

Once in the school, Merriman worked to master the material, even attending the night classes held for the noncommissioned officers that would be working with him in addition to his own coursework. Still, Merriman struggled with the advice that one of his instructors gave him. "Everything that I'm telling you . . . will be true about the [training] missiles you will work [with] at Vandenberg [AFB]. But watch out. It won't be true necessarily about the [operational] missiles at Warren [AFB]." The Atlas that the students were working with every day was an A model, but the models they would be working with in the field would be the D model—for all practical purposes a completely different missile. Furthermore, because the missiles were being upgraded daily, the instructors could not keep up with the changes.[46]

Once the contracted instructors deemed the new missileers competent on the system itself, the graduates were assigned to a crew and transitioned to Integrated Weapon System Training at Vandenberg AFB. There the recently assembled crew learned how to operate and maintain the missile. Maj. James Brewer developed the training program for both the Thor and Atlas programs. He struggled with the same problem that the contracted trainers did—developing training for weapon systems that the Air Force was still modifying and still fitting into operational plans.

Before he was given this difficult assignment, Brewer was a pilot flying in England. He "understood that 'Missiles' had something to do with putting mice or dogs into capsules and launching them toward space." Arriving at Vandenberg, he was made chief of Thor Integrated Weapon System Training. He complained that he knew nothing about missiles or missile training, but Brewer recalled that his new boss replied, "Don't worry. No one else knows anything about missile training either. We are all learning here for the first time."[47]

Brewer quickly ascertained that "some eight different missile systems, each completely different but each with many missiles and extensive manning, [were] already in or planned for the [training] pipeline; and each missile had an inflexible deadline to become operational." His first duty was to instruct the launch crews and maintenance teams at Vandenberg.

These newly qualified missileers then trained the crews assigned to manage the Air Force's operational missiles. Brewer recalled that, under the concept of concurrency, "development step number fifty could not wait for number forty-nine to be completed—indeed not even for step nine." Consequently, "the inevitable problems and changes [did not] cause ripples—they cause[d] shock waves!" One of these shock waves included the missile blowing up during a training simulation, destroying the launch pad that Brewer had planned to use for future training. To ensure that personnel could become trained and proficient and that appropriate documentation would be prepared in spite of such problems, he and his two-person staff worked fourteen-hour days, seven days a week.[48]

Brewer's reward for creating a successful training program for the Thor missile was a second assignment to develop a missile training program—this time for the three Atlas missiles, models D, E, and F. The Air Force

An Atlas missile explodes on the launch pad. *Air Force Historical Research Agency*

now called the program Operational Readiness Training. Brewer discovered that, although the missiles all carried the name Atlas, "they were as different as any three different types of bombers." Since he was to create the three training programs concurrently, he was now allowed a staff of four—two captains, a sergeant, and a secretary. Brewer believed this number was not adequate to accomplish the job, so he coordinated with the Ramo-Wooldridge contractors to provide four additional personnel. As he had learned with the Thor program, "slow and painful progress was [often] wiped out in an instant by a change of design, change in priority for use of a facility, or a facility disaster."[49]

Since concurrency forced the Air Force to test and refine the missile systems during training launches, "on every launch the Launch Control Center (LCC) was crowded with [senior leaders] from SAC or some other headquarters, to the detriment of students and training." As a result, Brewer assessed his own training efforts as "nothing to brag about. There were simply too many people to be trained, too short a time, too few launch facilities available for training, and too many other demands and problems on the launch facilities available."[50] Thus, the decision to rush missiles into operation before they were ready continued to frustrate those who were trying to incorporate the new weapons into the Air Force.

Even after the new missileers moved to their operational squadrons, they faced unique problems with training. As previously noted, technical documentation was atrocious. Moreover, there were no qualified personnel to provide the continuous training and evaluation that the Air Force determined was required at the squadron level. Lawrence Hasbrouck remembered his first experience as a missileer in the 66th Strategic Missile Squadron at Ellsworth AFB in 1962. "I was selected as an instructor because I was told to 'pick a desk.' The one I chose was manned by a Lt. Colonel, who immediately said, 'Captain, welcome to the 66 SMW. You are an instructor!' I replied, 'Of what, sir?' He answered, 'Of this new weapon system.' My next question was, 'What if I had chosen one of the other desks?' If I chose the middle desk, I would have become an evaluator; [if] the last desk, just a crew member."[51] Because no one had any experience, instructors and evaluators were often chosen at random and had no better qualifications than the average crew member. This situation improved as the manning situation got better, but it presented another concern over the quality of training and the credibility as well as the capability of the overall missile program.

In their book *History of the Jupiter Missile System*, Army historians James Grimwood and Frances Stroud contend that the effort to create the training plan for Jupiter was even more grueling than either the Thor or Atlas. "Not only did the Agency have to struggle to get a training plan formulated, but they had to fight for the very life of the JUPITER program." Then, in 1959, when the United States decided to have allied forces control the missiles, the Army had to remove all restricted data, highly classified material that had been an integral part of the training, from the program and try to make the training comprehensible to nonnative English speakers.[52]

The rushed deployment and confusion caused by concurrency also wreaked havoc with the initial operations of the missiles. Staff Sergeant Glantz recalled that "the original Tech[nical] Orders and operational and maintenance procedures were so bad that new ones had to be written from scratch. It was a very lengthy, expensive operation with teams of engineers, tech[nical] writers and airmen working [twenty-four hours a day, seven days a week]."[53]

Ronald Bishop, a captain at the time, agreed that "in the early missile days . . . , 'growing' pains . . . included incomplete tech data, checklist errors, some evaluation issues resulting from the noted problems, a steep learning curve for not only the crew members but [also for] the squadron and wing senior staff officers who were aircraft oriented, and for all new SAC members, an initial shock at the standards that required mistake free performance."[54]

An early history of the 706th Strategic Missile Wing, the first Atlas wing, reveals that the rush to deploy the first ICBM squadrons created numerous difficulties there as well. In May 1956 the Air Force decided to place one and one-half of the four Atlas squadrons at Cooke AFB (renamed Vandenberg AFB on October 4, 1958), with the remainder to be assigned to the next base chosen. The next May, in 1957, the Department of Defense decided to redesignate the Army's Fort F. E. Warren as an Air Force base and to house the other two and one-half squadrons there. Shortly after this decision, the Air Force Ballistic Missile Division (AFBMD)—the renamed Western Development Division—wisely determined that dividing an operational squadron across a distance of over 1,500 miles was not as efficient or feasible as it first seemed. Since the Air Force chose to increase the number of Atlas squadrons at about the same time, the AFBMD just authorized Warren AFB to receive four complete squadrons rather than leaving a squadron divided.

The wing began preparing to build its first Atlas D missile site, as Major Ferguson planned, in what became known as a two by three design. In this configuration, the goal was to place everything the squadron needed in the same operating location, reducing logistics and maintenance problems. Two launch control complexes—where the missileers would control their missiles—were situated about seven miles from one another. Each launch control complex controlled three missiles that surrounded the control complex. The plan included storing four additional missiles nearby so that, after launching an attack, missileers would be able to place at least three additional missiles onto the launch platforms and prepare them for a second launch sequence. While the Army Corps of Engineers began building the missile site, the Air Force decided to cut costs by reducing the distance between the control centers to one thousand feet and consolidating some of the structures.[55]

Soon after, Air Force leaders grew concerned that placing the missiles so close to each other left them vulnerable to destruction from a single Soviet missile. Therefore, in May 1958, a year after the process began but before significant work on the first squadron's missile complex had even started, the Air Force changed the Atlas squadron configuration again. From that May on, all squadrons were to be built in a three by three concept: three launch control centers, built on separate sites, each controlling three missiles apiece. Therefore, each missile control center would be placed in an isolated plot of land, separated from the other launch control centers by fifteen to eighteen nautical miles. The new concept reduced the chances of the site's missiles being destroyed in a single attack but sacrificed the capability to provide a backup guidance facility for the missiles.

Although the reasoning is not documented, the Air Force chose to retain the original two by three orientation for the 564th Strategic Missile

Squadron, so SAC built the 564th's missile site as originally designed rather than reducing its size. Not long after, Air Force leaders determined that trying to deploy and launch a second round of missiles was unrealistic, so the extra missiles and support equipment for this purpose were consolidated with other wing assets instead of being placed with the 564th's missile site. Therefore, despite the fact that they controlled the same missiles, Warren AFB's first two missile squadrons were built to completely different specifications, controlled different numbers of missiles, and had differing operating procedures.

In another stunning change, the Air Force decided to begin colocating single Atlas squadrons with SAC bomber wings—the first near Omaha and Spokane—rather than continuing to build separate Atlas missile wings.

Maj. Gen. Charles McCorkle, assistant chief of staff for guided missiles, recommended that the Air Force disperse the Atlas to protect them as it was much cheaper to disperse them than to harden the missiles against attack. After the missiles were operational, he said, the Air Force could harden them. He also recommended that the Atlas sites be placed near SAC bases, but not near enough that a near miss would destroy the base and the missiles. Finally, McCorkle felt that incorporating the missiles into other Numbered Air Forces (a high level of command and control) would allow other Air Force personnel to become familiar with the capability during the transition period from aircraft to missiles.[56]

The 706th Strategic Missile Wing historians reflected their wing leadership's frustration, noting that "the concept of concurrency . . . was apparently causing a great deal of confusion. . . . Day to day changes in various projects were frequent. Pending actions were equally commonplace. In short, then, everything was in a rapid state of flux." Lt. Gary Alkire, assigned to the base as a civil engineer during this time, remembered that the change orders to the missile sites were as thick as the original contract.[57]

To continue the inadvertent trend of differentiating each squadron of missiles from the others, the Air Force decided to place a third Atlas squadron at Warren AFB but scattered the nine missiles of this squadron, the 549th Strategic Missile Squadron, hundreds of miles apart. The dispersal was not the only difference. The wing's first two squadrons used the initial Atlas D missile, but the third squadron was assigned the newly developed Atlas E missile. The new missile eliminated the need for the earlier missiles' radio towers and guidance buildings by means of a better guidance system, but once again considerably changed the operations and maintenance requirements.

The constant changes meant that each squadron had slightly differing operating methods and capabilities. The wing's first squadron stored its missiles horizontally in a "coffin-shaped" concrete structure and raised them for launch after sliding the roof of the coffin away from the building on steel railings. The second squadron's "coffins" opened more quickly as the roof separated in the middle and the two halves slid to the side before raising the missile. In the third, Atlas E squadron, the missiles remained horizontal but placed just underground so that the roof of their "coffin" was surface level. For the third squadron, the Air Force also upgraded the launch control center, placing it in a heavily reinforced underground room near the launcher rather than in an aboveground blockhouse like those in the original two squadrons.[58]

In late 1959 and early 1960 the lack of standardization became more problematic as the Air Force rushed the Titan and the smaller, solid-fueled Minuteman into production, even though neither had yet been successfully tested. In fact, "Minuteman facility drawings were in the hands of construction contractors before it had been proved that the missile could be fired from its underground silo."[59]

Bewilderingly, the service's leaders elected to place the four Titan squadrons, with missiles in hardened silos, near Lowry AFB in Colorado to ease logistical support from the contractor's plants rather than with other operational units. Consequently, even as the Air Force separated the Atlas squadrons, placing the units under the control of flying wings to assimilate them into the larger Air Force organization, it segregated Titan under a single leadership structure.

Then, in December 1961, the service upgraded the Atlas to the F model, the third iteration since the missile was declared operational twenty-five months earlier. The Atlas F allowed missileers to store the rocket propellant fuel (RP-1) in the missile rather than in nearby tanks. A concrete-lined cylindrical hole—an underground silo—now protected the missile and allowed it to remain upright even when it was below the surface, while a subterranean tunnel connected the missile to the nearby launch control center.

Each of these advancements helped to better protect the missiles and to improve their operational capability, but they also ensured that each squadron had unique requirements that prevented crew members from moving from site to site without retraining. The rush to place the missiles in operation as early as possible had prevented the Air Force from implementing these critical changes until after the first missiles were installed, thus costing missileers the benefit of standardized training and operations.

Jim Widlar, a missile mechanic on an Automated Programmed Checkout Equipment (APCHE) team for the Atlas D, provided more detailed information about the inability of technicians to work on differing Atlas versions, noting that propellant loaders and other people with related jobs could accomplish their tasks on any of the missiles, but the crewmembers were only trained and qualified to work on a specific version of the missile. Widlar also explained that while early Atlas D missiles required a seventeen-person crew, the number was reduced to eleven after the Air Force modified the missile system again in the early 1960s. The Air Force later reduced the Atlas D crew further still, trimming down the crew requirements to five.[60]

The constant changes, along with labor union strikes that slowed construction of the missile sites and other difficulties, delayed the deployment of the missile squadrons by up to six months. In part because of congressional concerns, General LeMay, now vice chief of staff of the Air Force, inspected the new missile sites in June 1960. He discovered a management nightmare. "Lines of authority crossed and recrossed in an administrative maze. There was no single recognized authority at any level. Construction contractors were receiving conflicting instructions from as many as seven separate agencies. Decisions that should have been made on the spot were in process for weeks." Stepping in decisively, LeMay established a Site Activation Task Force (SATAF) and placed each site under the control of a single Air Force colonel—a bomber pilot—to correct the problems. This resolved many of the worst issues, but missiles dropped further in the influential general's esteem.[61]

Both LeMay and Gen. Thomas Power (LeMay's successor as commander of SAC) had helped in the development of missile technology, Early on, LeMay was the Air Force's deputy chief of staff for research and development, and Power was commander of the Air Research and Development Command. Thus, both knew that the earliest missiles used untested technologies and were notoriously faulty, rarely reaching their target successfully. Therefore, both remained skeptical of missile capabilities even after the problems had been resolved.

LeMay explained, "We ha[d] never fired a missile with an atomic warhead on it. In other words we have never gone through the whole cycle. So there [was] always some question: will they work? We [had] done everything humanly possible to ensure they [would], and they probably will, but we have never done it." Remembering his experiences from World War II, he continued, "Here again, in the back of one's mind, is that first outfit going into combat the first time and screwing up the mission. We practiced in SAC. We ran our war plan time and time again. The crews spent hours and hours and made hundreds of bomb runs on their target in the trainer. So we had confidence, but we didn't have quite that same confidence in the missiles."[62]

Missiles were not alone in their struggle for credibility. The B-52 bomber, entering the inventory in 1955, suffered from structural failures during high-speed, low-level flights—the exact mission that the aircraft was intended to perform since the Soviets had built a strong antiaircraft system to defend against high-altitude attacks. Significant problems, both strategic and engineering, plagued the Air Force's other bombers as well, but the Air Force leadership, all pilots themselves, strongly supported the manned aircraft.

With the strategic bomber already struggling to hold its position as the crucial element of the nation's strategic nuclear component, the Air Force tried to develop a supersonic bomber capable of carrying nuclear weapons, the B-70. However, this created more friction with members of the Eisenhower administration, who supported missiles over the new bomber. George Kistiakowsky, Eisenhower's special assistant to the president for science and technology, argued that "it is not clear what the B-70 can do that ballistic missiles can't—and cheaper and sooner at that."[63]

Eisenhower was even more blunt. His staff secretary, Gen. Andrew Goodpaster, remembered that Eisenhower "was convinced that the age of aircraft for actual use over enemy territory [was] fast coming to a close. . . . [and the Air Force's leaders] were talking about bows and arrows at the time of gunpowder when [they] spoke of bombers in the missile age." Thus, while the Air Force leaders like LeMay, almost all "bomber men" themselves, struggled to keep and even increase the known capability of manned aircraft, many of their political leaders sided with missiles.[64]

Therefore, the rush to bring missiles to operational status, while politically imperative, threatened the status of the bomber and created more doubts about the efficacy of missiles in the minds of Air Force leaders. The decision to rapidly develop, build, and man the new weapon systems concurrently created unnecessary confusion and discord while the perceived political bias favoring missiles over the Air Force's beloved bomber caused long-standing enmity. Rated officers, temporarily thrust into missiles during the new weapon's stormy launch, struggled with erroneous and ever-changing guidance, variable standards, and a perceived loss of status. Thus, when LeMay became chief of staff of the Air Force in July 1961, many Air Force leaders who followed him into significant leadership positions were not supportive of the new weapons, causing enduring and negative repercussions.

CHAPTER 5

An International Crisis Foments Change

While the Air Force raced to build and staff the new ballistic missile units through the late 1950s and into the early 1960s, the political struggle that fueled the race continued well into the Kennedy administration. Politicians and journalists amplified the threat of Soviet nuclear missiles through the 1960 presidential election and insisted that the United States continue to build its own missiles to remain ahead of this existential threat, although the level of intensity began to drop once it became clear that the United States held a commanding lead in developing and producing nuclear armament.

Then, immediately following the Cuban Missile Crisis, the Kennedy administration's political will to use nuclear missiles radically diminished, leaving the missiles and missileers vulnerable to unsympathetic Air Force leaders who strongly preferred manned aircraft. Lyndon B. Johnson's administration, which included many members of the Kennedy administration, retained the postcrisis outlook on nuclear conflict. Without the strong political pressure to support the development and operation of missiles that had been applied during the late 1950s and very early 1960s, the promising potential of the Air Force nuclear missile community dissipated dramatically.

———

On October 10, 1958, in a speech to the Wood County, West Virginia, Democratic Committee, Sen. John F. Kennedy (D-Mass.) asserted, "We are rapidly approaching that dangerous period which General [James M.] Gavin and others have called the 'gap' or the 'missile lag period'—

a period, in the words of General Gavin, 'in which our own offensive and defensive missile capabilities will lag so far behind those of the Soviets as to place us in a position of great peril.'"[1] After defining "the most critical years of the gap" as 1960 to 1964, he continued the withering criticism of President Dwight Eisenhower's defense policies:

> Our peril is not simply because Russian striking power during the years of the gap will have a slight edge over us in missile power—they will have several times as many: intermediate range missiles to destroy our European missile and SAC bases; intercontinental missiles to devastate our own country installations, and Government; and history's largest fleet of submarines, and possibly long-range supersonic jet bombers, to follow up this advantage. If by that time their submarines are capable of launching missiles, they could destroy 85 per cent of our industry, 43 per cent of our 50 largest cities, and most of the nation's population.[2]

After Kennedy launched his candidacy for the 1960 presidential election on January 2, 1960, he continued the verbal assault on Eisenhower's record. The Democratic Platform Committee followed his lead, proclaiming that "our military position today is measured in terms of gaps—missile gap, space gap, limited war gap."[3] To resolve the "gaps," Kennedy promised to increase production of the Atlas missile; to accelerate the Titan program; to increase the numbers of the Minuteman missile, which was undergoing final testing at the time; to build more of the planned supersonic B-70 bombers; and to provide more of the Navy's Polaris missiles.[4] He tied these military increases, along with stronger conventional forces and enhanced airlift capabilities, into his Flexible Response security strategy.[5]

Eisenhower, maintaining his quest for a balanced budget, had argued that such increases were wasteful. In fact, in his 1959 State of the Union address, Eisenhower warned that "we must guard against feverish building of vast armaments to meet glibly predicted moments of so-called 'maximum peril.'" He reminded listeners that "in these days of unceasing technological advance, we must plan our defense expenditures systematically and with care. . . . The defense budget for the coming year has been planned on the basis of these principles and considerations."[6] Even so, as the second-generation Polaris and Minuteman missiles proved themselves more reliable and militarily useful and less vulnerable to a first strike from the Soviets, Eisenhower did increase the planned nuclear arsenal by authorizing more of these second-generation missiles.

Although the election was close, Kennedy won the presidency. During the campaign, he had convinced many voters that there was an existential nuclear threat to America. Therefore, after Kennedy's inauguration in 1961, these supporters expected him to quickly escalate defense spending, including the construction of new missiles.[7] Eisenhower left the new president with 12 operational Atlas ICBMs and 60 Thor IRBMs stationed in the United Kingdom but had directed the production of newer-model Atlas, Titan, Minuteman, and Jupiter missiles, all quickly moving toward operational status. In his proposed budget for 1962, Eisenhower had authorized over 1,100 ballistic missiles (255 Atlas and Titan missiles, 450 silo-based Minuteman missiles, 90 mobile Minuteman missiles, and 304 Polaris missiles to be placed on nineteen submarines, in addition to the 60 Thor and 45 Jupiter missiles stationed overseas). By contrast, the Soviets had 248 launchers in the summer of 1960, but these were all intermediate-range missiles, and none had a long enough range to hit the United States.[8]

Kennedy selected Robert McNamara, the former president of Ford Motor Company and a Republican, as his secretary of defense. In his memoir, *In Retrospect: The Tragedy and Lessons of Vietnam*, McNamara says he "immediately made it [his] top priority to determine the size of the [missile] gap and the remedial action required to close it."[9] McNamara felt that the new administration needed to review the Eisenhower administration's 1962 budget, but in order to appropriately appraise the Eisenhower defense strategy, he needed to know and take in consideration what the Soviets were doing. Within days of assuming his new position, McNamara requested a briefing on the situation. The Weapon System Evaluation Group quickly walked him through report #50, entitled "Evaluation of Strategic Offensive Weapons Systems." The evaluation, started in September 1959 and completed in December 1960, a "comprehensive report on the optimal U.S. strategic force structure . . . implicitly rejected the possibility of a missile gap."[10] McNamara and key aides also "spent days with the air force's assistant chief of staff for intelligence, personally reviewing hundreds of photographs of Soviet missile sites that had been the basis for the air force report."

McNamara became convinced by the available evidence that the missile gap actually favored the United States rather than the Soviet Union. When he informed reporters of this fact during a background interview on February 6, 1961, the press published the statement, creating quite a furor.[11]

By this time, Kennedy knew for certain that the missile gap did not exist. Nevertheless, after contending during the campaign that the Eisenhower administration was lax on national security precisely because it had allowed a "missile gap," Kennedy realized that immediately negating the gap would create a credibility problem and exacerbate concerns over his planned defense spending. Therefore, on February 8, Kennedy asserted in a news conference that "Mr. McNamara stated that no study had been concluded in the Defense Department which would lead to any conclusion at this time as to whether there is a missile gap or not."[12]

McNamara backtracked as well. On Friday, April 7, 1961, after Rep. George Mahan (D-Texas) defined "missile" as an intercontinental ballistic missile—specifically, Atlas, Titan, and Minuteman—and after "explicitly excluding POLARIS, MACE, SNARK, and any similar missile or weapon which the opponent or we may have" and limiting the information to that in official intelligence estimates, McNamara testified that, "based on the intelligence estimates available to me," there was a missile gap and "based on the intelligence estimates, there is evidence that a missile gap may exist up to and through 1963."[13]

After dispelling the public's questions over the reality of the missile gap, the Kennedy administration increased the 1962 defense budget by 10 percent. The president built up the conventional forces and enhanced the readiness of the Air Force bomber fleet, but he also strengthened the missile forces. Strategic Air Command (SAC) had successfully launched a Minuteman in early February 1961, and Kennedy found that the new missiles were much more reliable, less dangerous, and less vulnerable to surprise attack than the early iterations. Therefore, rather than increasing the number of Atlases or Titans as he had promised to do during the presidential campaign, Kennedy accelerated the production of the new Air Force Minuteman and Navy Polaris missiles. In fact, rather than speeding up the Titan program, he cut the last two squadrons of Titan missiles, using the funds planned for the Titans to double the production capabilities of

Minuteman missiles. He also increased the construction of Polaris subma-rines by ten, increasing the total submarines from nineteen to twenty-nine, even though the first of this new group was not scheduled for delivery until June 1963.[14]

The increases in the defense budget did nothing to reduce the continu-ing struggle with the Soviet Union. Kennedy met Soviet premier Nikita Khrushchev in early June 1961 at a summit in Vienna to reduce tensions between the two countries, but the conference failed to resolve the discord. Soon after the meeting, Khrushchev demanded that the United Kingdom, France, and the United States, which retained control of West Berlin after World War II, withdraw all Western troops from the city within six months or face war.[15] Khrushchev had made the same threat to Eisenhower but backed down when Eisenhower refused to respond. Knowing this, Kennedy, rather than backing out of Berlin, increased the size of the Army, the Air Force, and the Marine Corps and called up 150,000 reservists to prepare for war. This time, Khrushchev increased his military budget as well but, believing the Allies were militarily stronger and willing to fight, again dropped the threat of war. Instead, Khrushchev approved an East German plan to build a wall that would isolate the Western-occupied por-tion of Berlin. Construction began on August 13, 1961.

Concerned that Khrushchev might continue to threaten and cajole the United States as long as he thought Kennedy believed that the Soviet Union had a preponderance of nuclear weapons, the Kennedy administra-tion decided to reveal publicly that the missile gap did not exist. Kennedy selected Roswell Gilpatric, the deputy secretary of defense, to disclose the information since he was important enough to convince the Soviet leaders that he represented the Kennedy administration but not so important as to appear to be threatening to them.

In Gilpatric's speech, given to the Business Council in Hot Springs, Virginia, on October 21, he exclaimed that "Berlin is the emergency of the moment, because the Soviets have chosen to make it so. . . . But our real strength in Berlin. . . . is based upon a sober appreciation of the relative military power of the two sides." Gilpatric then explained: "Our forces are so deployed and protected that a sneak attack could not effectively disarm us. The destructive power which the United States could bring to bear even after a Soviet surprise attack upon our forces would be as great as—perhaps greater than—the total undamaged force which the enemy can threaten to launch against the United States in a first strike."[16]

In July 1962 Khrushchev responded in a way very few expected, coordinating an agreement with Fidel Castro of Cuba to place Soviet nuclear missiles in Cuba. These weapons not only provided a credible nuclear threat to the United States but also responded to the United States' failed attempt to overthrow Castro during the April 1961 Bay of Pigs debacle.[17] On May 24, 1962, the Soviet Defense Council approved Khrushchev's plan to place ballistic nuclear missiles and bombers, both capable of delivering nuclear weapons, along with supporting fighter planes, cruise missiles, and

Map 1. CIA map of the Soviet missile threat rings during the Cuban Missile Crisis. *John F. Kennedy Presidential Library and Museum*

ground forces in Cuba. Castro agreed to host the Soviets soon after. Unlike the American deployment to Europe of the Thor and Jupiter missiles, the Soviets planned to retain operational control of their missiles in Cuba, at least at the start of the deployment.

Khrushchev intended to deploy the arsenal quietly and announce their presence after the November elections in America. However, the United States had been spying on Cuba through photographic and electronic surveillance since the spring of 1962, monitoring the buildup of Soviet military capabilities on the island. Thus, on October 14, a U-2 aircraft flown by Air Force major Richard Heyser photographed what intelligence analysts identified the next day as "three Medium Range Ballistic Missile (MRBM) sites near San Cristobal[, Cuba]."[18] These missiles threatened every U.S. city south and east of a semicircle bounded by Washington, DC; Cincinnati, Ohio; and St. Louis, Missouri (see map 1). However, the CIA also revealed that the Soviets' longer-range IRBMs, presumed to be in Cuba as well, could reach almost as far as San Francisco, threatening almost every major city in the United States.[19]

Aghast at the implications, the president gathered several key advisors, a group he titled the Executive Committee of the National Security Council, or ExComm, to guide the nation's response. After considering and deciding against a surgical strike to destroy the missiles, ExComm recommended a naval blockade—renamed "quarantine" to sound less bellicose—to prevent the Soviets from shipping more missiles to Cuba. Then, on October 22, at 7:00 p.m. eastern time, six days after he learned of the threat, the president spoke to the nation, warning of the danger and reassuring both the American people and the world that he had a prudent plan to have the missiles removed. His actions initiated what became known as the Cuban Missile Crisis.[20]

Kennedy's speech was the first time many of the Air Force missileers heard about this new Soviet threat in Cuba. After reviewing a draft of the president's speech, Gen. Curtis LeMay, chief of staff of the Air Force, recommended that Gen. Maxwell Taylor, chairman of the Joint Chiefs of Staff, "direct [defense condition] DEFCON 3 worldwide at noon [on October 22] to place U. S. forces worldwide in an increased readiness posture" and "direct SAC to generate its forces toward a maximum readiness

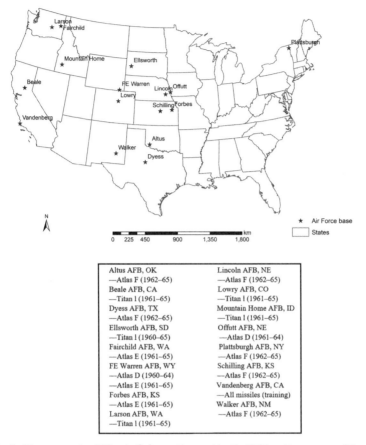

Map 2. First-generation U.S. missile bases. *Prepared by Cyril Wilson, Department of Geography and Anthropology, University of Wisconsin–Eau Claire*

posture, also at noon today." By doing so, LeMay explained, "the strategic air forces will be in maximum readiness by noon tomorrow, and the force generation should not be apparent until after the President's speech tonight." Furthermore, he declared, the action "comprises a clear warning to the Sino-Soviet Bloc and should serve as a powerful deterrent to any major counteraction. Additionally, such a posture will provide maximum flexibility to the President in choosing further actions, should Sino-Soviet belligerence or active counter-measures so warrant." General Taylor decided to direct the forces to DEFCON 3 when the president established the blockade.[21]

Map 3. Second-generation U.S. missile bases. *Prepared by Cyril Wilson, Department of Geography and Anthropology, University of Wisconsin–Eau Claire*

Gen. Thomas Power, who had replaced LeMay as commander in chief of SAC, responded prior to the directive's time frame. Two days before President Kennedy addressed the nation, Power ordered that all aircraft and missiles not ready for alert be covertly made ready. He also placed two bombers per squadron and the aircraft designated to refuel the bombers on standby status, ready for immediate launch. He ensured that his commanders and staff realized these actions did not mean a change in DEFCON status, although their actions would have been the same if it had.

Lt. Charlie Simpson was one of the first Air Force officers to respond. On October 20, while overseeing the testing of new Titan I missiles at Mountain Home AFB in Idaho, he received a call directing that the squadron "return the missile to alert immediately, no questions asked and no explanation." (See locations of U.S. Air Force bases with missiles in maps 2 and 3.) Then, over the weekend, his supervisors cancelled all passes and leaves and started planning for the maintenance shops to work twenty-four hours a day. He saw bomber and tanker aircraft deploying to predetermined dispersal locations but did not know why. On Monday, as the president delivered his speech, the Joint Chiefs of Staff ordered all U.S. forces worldwide to DEFCON 3, and Simpson's unit followed suit, upgrading to the higher level of readiness. The weekend's activities became clear.[22]

Sgt. Bob Kelchner, on a targeting and alignment team for the new Minuteman missiles at Vandenberg AFB, also received early notification of the new requirements. On Sunday, October 21, Kelchner's supervisor called to say that he was coming to pick up Kelchner for an emergency meeting on base. At the meeting, Kelchner remembered that they were briefed that SAC was preparing for "higher alert conditions," then sent home to wait "on 15-minute standby telephone alert."[23]

The next morning, each member who worked with Kelchner checked his equipment to ensure it was in top shape and, on October 23, the team traveled to the missile sites "with classified targeting tapes, side arms and orders not to return until our site was on 'alert.'" Kelchner reminisced that, before this crisis, the team "had never seen a loaded/live missile in the new launch facilities, nor an operational Guidance and Control System (G&C), nor a live reentry vehicle (RV)."[24]

Capt. Willard Stanley, who went by Stan, got the message as well. Working in the Air Force Ballistic Systems Division's Reentry Vehicle (RV) Directorate, he was ordered "to get as many MK 5 RV shells and fuzes to [the new Minuteman missile wing in Malmstrom AFB,] Montana in the shortest amount of time." He worked around the clock for the next several days to ensure the nuclear warheads were expedited to their operational location and able to be readied for launch. After he finished the stressful assignment, he recalled stopping at the officer's club for a stiff drink and watching "the 'super hyped' news anchors on the TV reporting."[25]

Not everyone heard about the crisis so quickly. Lt. Philip Moore, an Atlas F crew member stationed near Roswell, New Mexico, remembered learning that SAC had been ordered to DEFCON 3 two days after the event occurred, when he arrived on base for his next alert. He had been placed on telephone standby, meaning he had to remain near his phone twenty-four hours a day, ready to respond to a call, but had not known why. He recalled the tenseness in the air as crew members escorted maintenance teams around the missile site to fix critical equipment problems, now knowing they were at DEFCON 3.[26]

Airman 1st Class Michael Kenderes, of the Titan wing near Denver, Colorado, learned of the change while deer hunting. Returning to camp just before dusk, the hunters discovered a piece of paper on the truck's radio antenna. The paper read, "This is from the game warden! Report back to base immediately! This is NOT an exercise!" They returned home, and Kenderes called his supervisor, who informed him that the base had been ordered to DEFCON 3, and he needed to report for duty as soon as possible. He was also told to expect to be in the missile field for an indefinite time as the Soviets were "causing some trouble down in Cuba."[27]

Kenderes returned to Lowry AFB and learned that his mission was to keep the squadron's nine missiles on alert. He reviewed the unit's maintenance files to identify high failure items, then traveled to the supply building, where he picked up the items he believed he might need most. When ready, he gathered the security codes that allowed him access to the missile sites and drove to the missile site as the sun rose. After determining the missiles were all working fine, he took a quick nap to make up for the long night.

SAC quickly attained all DEFCON 3 requirements, primarily because General Power had directed the command to work toward the standards before the heightened state of readiness was ordered. The command also made shockingly rapid progress toward getting new missiles to operational status. The Air Force had declared their first missile operational only three years earlier, on October 31, 1959. From that time until January 1962, the service had only been able to bring another 22 missiles to alert status. However, by October 19, 1962, SAC had placed 112 missiles on alert. These missiles included 77 Atlas D, E, and F missiles and 35 Titan I missiles. Nevertheless, this phenomenal feat was nothing compared to the achievement accomplished over the next three days, as the command tried to achieve DEFCON 3 requirements. Pushed by the critical nature of the threat, SAC missileers, both those operating the missiles and those maintaining them, added another 20 missiles to the nuclear arsenal, bringing the number of operational missiles to 132— 91 Atlases and 41 Titans.[28]

The missileers accomplished this astonishing exploit in various ways. Some missileers, including Harry Birmingham, who conducted maintenance on the Atlas missiles near Walker AFB, New Mexico, labored through numerous twelve-hour shifts or longer, fixing critical problems that prevented missiles from operating correctly. Simpson's squadron, and others like it, stopped critical validation tests that required the missiles to be pulled off of alert status in order to ensure that their missiles were prepared for immediate launch. Some of the change, though, was brought about by teams struggling intensely to bring new missiles on alert. Airman Nelson "Pete" Turner recalled arming new Atlas missiles that "had only very recently been delivered to their respective silos and were only then being installed and debugged."[29]

Thus, only thirty-nine hours later, when President Kennedy imposed the naval quarantine and the Joint Chiefs of Staff directed the command to DEFCON 2, the highest level America's military has ever attained, the missileers stood ready. Once again, General Power had prepared SAC forces before the order was given, and the command accomplished the task swiftly but covertly, as ordered.

Airman 2nd Class John McLaughlin, serving on an Atlas F crew at Schilling AFB, Kansas, at the time, remembered "being directed to maintain a green 'ready to launch' status on the launch control console at all times in case a launch was ordered. . . . The briefings escalated in intensity and the messages over the Primary Alerting System from SAC headquarters seemed endless. When we went to DEFCON 2, it seemed like the next message could be coded in red."[30]

Patrick Spellman, a missile facilities technician for the 578th Strategic Missile Squadron, an Atlas F squadron near Abilene, Texas, remembered having a similar feeling. Away from the command console area when he heard the Primary Alerting System, he returned to see "the commander erasing the 3 [representing the current DEFCON] and replacing it with a 2." When he asked what was happening, his commander directed him to stand at his position and then began giving orders to the rest of the crew.

Spellman remembered everyone "standing by their positions and wondering what [was coming] next."[31]

Airman 2nd Class Lucius Morgan, working with the Atlas squadron at Dyess AFB, near Abilene, revealed the acts that made the time so harrowing. "When we reached DEFCON 2, Major [Truman] Grady told me to start the number 2 generator," he remembered. Then "he and Lt [Charles] Hancock took their guns out, cocked them and laid them on the launch console. Next, they took their keys and unlocked both [launch] buttons. The commander told us our job was to get the missile in the air. He said it was what we were trained to do and we would do everything in our power to do just that."[32]

Lt. Herb Gordon, the deputy missile combat crew commander at Atlas E Site 7 near Nunn, Colorado, recalled that "during our first duty shift following the DEFCON change, General Power . . . broadcast a message to all SAC bomber and missile crews. . . . He made it clear he wanted every effort to be made to launch all missiles [if the president directed]."[33] In the announcement, the general proclaimed,

> This is General Power speaking. I am addressing you for the purpose of reemphasizing the seriousness of the situation the nation faces. We are in an advanced state of readiness to meet any emergencies, and I feel that we are well prepared. I expect each of you to maintain strict security and use calm judgment during this tense period. Our plans are well prepared and are being executed smoothly. If there are any questions concerning instructions which by the nature of the situation deviates from normal, use the telephone for clarification. Review your plans for further action to insure that there will be no mistakes or confusion. I expect you to cut out all nonessentials and put yourself in a maximum readiness condition. If you are not sure what you should do in any situation and if time permits, get in touch with us here.[34]

Power did not exclude himself from the task of putting the command in "maximum readiness condition." On October 24, two days after Kennedy's speech signaled the beginning of the blockade and General Taylor ordered SAC to DEFCON 2, Power gained control over another thirty-six missiles. According to SAC historians, he accomplished this feat by invoking an agreement between the Air Force Systems Command

and Strategic Air Command that gave the latter operational control of all missile launch complexes "in which a missile could be launched on an E[mergency] W[ar] Order mission with strategic warning" if the Joint Chiefs declared DEFCON 2 or higher. Not one of the thirty-six missiles (nine test and training missiles at Vandenberg AFB and twenty-seven others being emplaced at four new missile sites) was prepared for immediate launch.[35]

Eleven other missiles at Vandenberg AFB remained under the control of Air Force Systems Command. Almost unbelievably, one of those eleven missiles, an Atlas D, was test-launched during the height of the crisis, at 4:00 a.m. (Pacific Time) on October 26, 1962, and a second was test-launched on November 14. Thomas Reed, who later became secretary of the Air Force, recalled the test launches, admitting "the fact that something important was going on in Florida and Cuba was lost on all of us. We continued to fire large thermonuclear weapons right through the missile crisis of late October, oblivious to the spurious signals we were sending into the most tense negotiations then in process half a world away."[36]

To ready the training missiles that had been transferred to SAC for wartime use, airmen like David Burcham rushed to attach live nuclear warheads to each missile that was deemed flyable. Then teams like the one Sergeant Kelchner served on realigned the missile's guidance system so that the missiles would launch north rather than west, allowing the missiles to be aimed toward authentic targets. Finally, the teams placed the new targeting data into the now operational Minuteman missiles.[37]

Staff Sgt. Rodolpho Armenta conducted similar work on the Air Force's Atlas training missiles. He recalled traveling to a missile site with a guidance control technician and a second lieutenant, who had just flown in with targeting information in a briefcase handcuffed to his wrist and a Colt .45 pistol strapped to his side. The technician tried to insert the card into the missile, but the process failed to work. Armenta remembered, "The technician yanked the card out, rubbed it on his pants, reinstalled the card and gave the [missile] a few hard taps to make sure it was seated. At this point, I looked over at the lieutenant and noticed the flap on his .45 pistol holster was now opened."[38]

"Because we had deviated from our stated installation procedures," Armenta clarified, "I immediately informed the guidance technician to stop his troubleshooting techniques, explaining my concern that the lieutenant was about ready to go Wyatt Earp on us. We then requested permission from the control center to install the card in slot 'B' to verify if the card was bad or if it was the slot." They received permission and accomplished the task, Armenta recalled joyfully, without the lieutenant adding "any notches on his gun."[39]

The twenty-seven new missiles that Power obtained from Air Force Systems Command required a similar level of effort to become operational. Capt. Melvin Driskill, a deputy combat crew commander at Plattsburgh AFB at the time, remembered that "because our squadron was just being activated in Fall of '62, there were only three sites alert qualified and only a handful of crews operationally qualified for alert."[40] His crew was on their first alert when President Kennedy declared the blockade. Thus, while some teams toiled feverishly to get the new missiles ready for alert, the operational crews controlling the new missiles "worked 24 hours on and 24 hours off for the first several weeks of the crisis" to ensure they could launch the missiles within minutes of notification.[41]

SAC leaders recognized the strain they had placed upon the Plattsburgh AFB missileers by adding the new missiles, with the official history acknowledging that "this unit's capability would have been marginal even without a crisis situation." For this reason, staff officers at SAC headquarters directed that Second Air Force temporarily send four combat-ready missile crews who were qualified to work on the Atlas F to the 556th Strategic Missile Squadron between October 29 and November 20 to alleviate the personnel problems. On November 1, the command temporarily moved five more crews to support the new squadron, including an instructor crew from Vandenberg AFB.[42]

The new Minuteman missiles transferred from Air Force Systems Command at Malmstrom AFB created their own difficulties. The Air Force had sent the missiles to the base in September but had not yet certified them for alert. Therefore, when General Power implemented the Emergency Combat Capability Plan, the agreement for Air Force Systems Command to surrender the missiles to SAC, the transfer ran into complications.

The field commander who controlled the missiles for Air Force Systems Command refused to transfer the missiles because Air Force Systems Command remained in DEFCON 3, not DEFCON 2 as he understood that the agreement required. Thus, the only way that the SAC wing commander was able to comply with his command's guidance to take control of the missiles was to sign waivers saying that SAC accepted responsibility for the missiles as they were, acknowledging that the Air Force Systems Command was no longer responsible for testing or validating the missiles.

Because the missiles had not been readied for launch, the systems still had several anomalies. Engineers had designed the Minuteman missile so that one crew could launch several missiles. However, to ensure the missiles were not launched without proper authorization, they had established a requirement for two separate crews to send launch commands from two separate control centers before launch. At the time of the Cuban Missile Crisis, only one launch control center was completed and ready for use, so the crew could not send two separate launch commands. For this reason, the wing leadership placed a second missile crew "on standby" with a second launch control panel. If directed to launch the missile, the on-duty crew would send a launch command with the original panel, and then the second crew would replace the installed panel with their "standby" panel and send the required second launch signal to fire the missile.[43]

In addition, because the site activation task force had never completed a required safety test on the new missiles, SAC kept each missile's safety control switch manually locked in the safety position, preventing the missiles from being launched without reconfiguring the switch. Chris Adams, an officer who served in the command for many years, retiring as a major general, acknowledged that crews and maintainers used workarounds to bring the weapons to alert. The workarounds resulted "in critical wiring and connection errors in emplacing the missiles in the silos and readying them for launch," thus necessitating the safe configuration, although this was not known at the time.[44]

The command used unofficial methods to get the crews to combat-ready status as well. SAC historians recorded that the 3901st Strategic Missile Evaluation Squadron "surveyed" the crews to determine if they were ready to man the missiles. If a crew had completed the two phases of initial training and passed a standardized test, the evaluators deemed them "capable." Sam Goodwin, a new captain at the time, illustrated his experience. "We went to Vandenberg AFB, CA, for crew training in October and had almost completed it when the Cuban Missile Crisis occurred. We quickly returned to Malmstrom AFB, MT. After a few sessions with the instructor crews, wing scheduling scheduled us for alert on Thanksgiving." He also recalled, "I soon heard from my squadron commander, Col Jim Farley, about going on alert prior to being evaluated and deemed qualified and without his knowledge."[45]

Other problems plagued the Air Force's effort to ready their missiles for employment. SAC had never prepared its entire missile force for war at one time. Therefore, on October 20, as the command placed several new missiles on alert and prepared them for launch, SAC leaders discovered the Air Force did not have enough liquid oxygen, one of the two vital ingredients used to fuel the Atlas and Titan missiles.[46] On October 21 the command quietly attempted to procure enough liquid oxygen to meet its requirements but found that the process would take twelve days, which the command did not have. The next day the command requested the federal government establish a national priority to provide the required liquid oxygen supplies to SAC missiles. The government responded immediately. Every government and commercial plant worked to provide the critical fuel. Finally, on October 25, SAC acquired the needed liquid oxygen to bring all of its missiles to mission-ready status.[47]

Through this phenomenal level of effort and sacrifice, SAC missileers increased the number of ballistic missiles ready for wartime service from 132 on October 22 to 147 on October 24. Astonishingly, by October 28, when Khrushchev notified the world that "the Soviet government . . . has given a new order to dismantle the arms which you [Kennedy] describe as offensive, and to crate and return them to the Soviet Union," the missileers had prepared 171 missiles for combat use.[48] When the Air Force missileers reached their peak readiness on November 4, sixteen days after General Power had begun preparing for war, the missile crews and maintainers had added 74 combat-ready missiles to their arsenal, increasing the number of nuclear missiles ready for launch from 112 to 186. During this same time, on October 10, the Navy added an additional ballistic missile submarine, carrying 16 Polaris missiles, to the six submarines that were operational at the beginning of the crisis and added a second less than a month later, on November 7. SAC historians emphatically note that "while SAC was in Defcon 2 posture, 92.5 per cent of its weapons systems were ready to launch within one hour."[49]

October 28 ended the most threatening part of the Cuban Missile Crisis, but the Kennedy administration retained both the quarantine and the heightened military alert status until November 20, when the Soviets said they had removed the missiles and Khrushchev agreed to also withdraw the nuclear-capable bombers that had been transported to Cuba. In fact, David G. Coleman, in *The Fourteenth Day*, reveals that even though Khrushchev assured Kennedy on November 20 that " 'all of the nuclear weapons have been taken away from Cuba,' . . . the tactical nuclear warheads [that threatened Guantanamo Bay rather than the Continental U.S.] did not actually leave Cuba until the following month." Coleman further contends that the Joint Chiefs "repeatedly raised the issue . . . between November 1962 and February 1963, arguing that the weapons were a threat to Guantanamo," but the Kennedy administration did not think they were that important.[50]

By November 15 the increased level of SAC operations had begun to degrade the capabilities of both the bomber and the land-based missile forces, so the command entered a "modified DEFCON 2" that allowed crews and maintainers to conduct critical maintenance and training. Then, as tensions began to ease further, on November 21, the Joint Chiefs directed the command to drop back to DEFCON 3. A week later, the command returned to normal operations and dropped its requirement for every missile to be continuously readied for launch.[51] Command historians declared the organization's effort to bring "ICBMs to alert status was eminently successful." They observed that the Cuban Missile Crisis had "provided the command a singular opportunity to determine exactly how far it had progressed toward an adequate missile capability. The results were encouraging."[52]

However, the event that was arguably the crowning success for the missileers caused them to become political pariahs and began their descent into perceived insignificance within the Air Force. Most people not associated with missiles were completely unaware of the remarkable level of effort the missileers exerted or the consequence they believed their missiles had. Doug Turner, a member of a Mobile Automatic Programmed Checkout Equipment team for the Atlas D missiles at Warren AFB, Wyoming, during the Cuban Missile Crisis, remembered that "although the crisis was receiving lots of attention in the news media, I think the local population saw our activities as business-as-usual since launch crews and maintenance teams continued to commute to and from the missile sites. We were directed not to do or say anything that might alarm the civilian community."[53] Capt. Jim Peck, a B-47 pilot at the time, acknowledged that even the command's pilots were not cognizant of the specific activities of the missileers. They knew that the missileers had attained a higher state of readiness, as the bomber pilots had, and were prepared to launch against their targets, but most did not know exactly what that entailed.[54]

Even more important to the future of missiles and missileers in the Air Force, General LeMay still refused to fully support the new missiles. In 1965 congressional hearings, he declined to accept Secretary of the Air Force Eugene Zuckert's statement that "we have achieved the point where our missiles, most particularly POLARIS and MINUTEMAN, can be depended upon to perform that part of the war plan our planners have assigned them." LeMay later contended that "like any machine, they don't always work" and that he did not think "that you are ever going to get to the point where you have the same confidence in the missile as you have in manned systems."[55]

Finally, the Kennedy administration, which had previously supported a robust buildup of missiles instead of bombers, began to question the value of missiles as actual weapons, rather than just a deterrent, and reduced its strong sponsorship of the new systems. Roger Hilsman, Kennedy's assistant secretary of state for intelligence and research, later contended that "one of the longer-range effects [of the crisis] was to change attitudes toward nuclear weapons."[56] This change allowed Air Force leaders like General LeMay to relegate the new weapons to a less significant role in the service's operations and to deemphasize their operations.

It is doubtful that Kennedy ever agreed with Eisenhower, who said in 1959 that "in ten years he saw missiles carrying the burden of warfare," especially since defense analyst Lawrence Freedman contends that "the basic guidelines for the strategic doctrines of the Kennedy administration were derived from the critique of the strategy of 'massive retaliation' as it had evolved during the 1950s."[57] In fact, it is possible that some members of the Kennedy administration never supported the use of nuclear missiles as strongly as they appeared to have. As early as 1945, key scientists from the Manhattan Project had banded together to warn against "any effort to formulate our [U.S.] foreign policy on the basis of a temporary superiority in atomic weapons" which they claimed would "force other nations as well as ourselves into an atomic armaments race, thereby creating a world of fear and hatred in which both great and small nations will face sudden destruction."[58]

Political scientist Nina Tannenwald argues that by the late 1950s, the Eisenhower administration's attempts to persuade Americans and their allies that tactical nuclear weapons should be treated as conventional weapons had failed. She writes, "Starting in 1954, American public opinion began shifting against initiating the use of nuclear weapons, where it has remained ever since. . . . In 1955, 67 percent of those asked supported the United States making an agreement with the Soviet Union that if war broke out the United States would not use atomic or hydrogen bombs if other countries did not."[59]

Daniel Ellsberg supported this mindset in his memoirs, contending that McNamara had decided not to use nuclear weapons before the Cuban Missile Crisis, "infer[ring McNamara's] position from the way he talked with me in a private lunch at his desk in 1961."[60] However, historian Lawrence Wittner warns that while some Kennedy advisors were more supportive of the antinuclear position than Eisenhower's staff, "the importance of this political transition [from the Eisenhower administration to the Kennedy administration] should not be exaggerated."[61] It is very likely that members of the administration were influenced against nuclear warfare at the same time as many of the nation's citizens, following the Cuban Missile Crisis, rather than before. Arthur Schlesinger, Kennedy's special assistant, later explained that "the Kennedy administration welcomed pressure from domestic arms control groups as an offset against the pro-arms-race pressure from Congress and the military, . . . [but] the administration valued these groups for political reasons rather than as a source of ideas."[62]

Kennedy had campaigned on Eisenhower's missile gap and entered office focused on reducing that gap and preparing a strong nuclear missile force. This engaged concentration only began to wane after the Cuban Missile Crisis as the administration reconsidered whether the United States could really effectively use nuclear missiles as weapons. In a message to Congress just seven months before the Cuban crisis, Kennedy argued that "in the event of a major aggression that could not be repulsed by conventional forces, we must be prepared to take whatever action with whatever weapons are appropriate."[63] On August 9, 1962, Gen. Maxwell Taylor reiterated the administration's position on the first use of nuclear weapons, warning, "In my judgment, if an attack on Western Europe comes, we must use whatever weapons and forces are necessary to defeat it. To meet a massive attack today, because of the lack of adequate conventional forces in the West, it would be necessary to resort to atomic weapons early in the conflict."[64]

McNamara, in a June 1962 commencement address in Ann Arbor, Michigan, said: "The U.S. has come to the conclusion that to the extent feasible basic military strategy in a possible general nuclear war should be approached in much the same way that more conventional military options have been approached in the past. That is to say, principal military objectives, in the event of a nuclear war stemming from a major attack on the Alliance, should be the destruction of the enemy's military forces, not his civilian population."[65] This counterforce doctrine required the United States to build enough missiles to destroy enemy offensive weapons since missiles could be better protected than bombers and launched more quickly. Paul Nitze, the assistant secretary of defense for international security affairs, explained further, "The President's first step was to strengthen our second-strike capability by accelerating our Minuteman and Polaris programs. . . . The effect of this decision . . . was to reduce dependence for survival of our strategic force on early warning and a quick response. While our B-52 bombers continued to rely on warning and alertness for their survival, our Minutemen in their hardened silos and Polaris missiles in their submarines, at that time, did not."[66]

Thus, while McNamara said during the same speech that he "look[ed] forward to the prospect that through arms control the actual use of these terrible weapons may be completely avoided," he continued to increase the number and quality of ballistic missiles. He also revised the Single Integrated Operations Plan (SIOP), the plan to use nuclear weapons, to make it less rigid and continued to prepare for nuclear war, including a first-strike capability. The revised SIOP, implemented in July 1962, focused U.S. nuclear attacks on Soviet military forces rather than its cities in order to limit the weapons able to be used against the United States, to convince the French that they did not need an independent nuclear force, and to convince the Soviets to do the same, but the plan's primary aim was still to win a nuclear conflict.[67]

However, by the end of the Cuban Missile Crisis, the key leaders of the administration had begun to change their perspectives on nuclear war. David Ormsby-Gore, the British ambassador to the United States and a friend of the president, recalled Kennedy bursting out during a private conversation they had during the crisis, "You know, it really is an *intolerable* state of affairs when nations can threaten each other with nuclear weapons. This is just so totally irrational. A world in which there are large quantities of nuclear weapons is an impossible world to handle. We really must try to get on with disarmament if we get through this crisis . . . because this is just too much."[68]

McNamara appeared to have a similar outlook, warning Kennedy during the crisis, "If one of these . . . things was launched against New York, Washington, or Miami . . . it would destroy so many people that you, Mr. President, would never want to accept the risk." He then mused, "If that was the case with one, think what a limited nuclear war would look like."[69]

Roger Hilsman, Kennedy's assistant secretary of state for intelligence and research in 1962, revealed the impact of that revelation on the members of the administration, stating that "before the Cuban missile crisis, most of the American officials who later participated in the crisis deliberations accepted Churchill's notion of a balance of terror." He explained,

"They assumed that to keep the peace all that the United States needed to do was to make certain that its nuclear forces were adequate, to maintain the will and determination to use those weapons if the worst came to worst, and to take appropriate steps to ensure that the other side understood all this." However, he continued, "For many people involved in the crisis the lesson . . . was that the risk of an inadvertent escalation during a crisis was unavoidable and that in a nuclear age such risk was unacceptable. The leaders of both the Soviet Union and the United States had gazed down the gun barrel of nuclear war and had shrunk back from the holocaust they saw there."[70]

Clark Clifford, Kennedy's chairman of the President's Foreign Intelligence Advisory Board, remembered that "after October 1962, . . . the leaders of both sides [Soviet and American] having experienced the bitter taste that comes from thinking the unthinkable, shied away from any repetition of that experience." In Clifford's mind, "The Missile Crisis had served the same function as an inoculation against a dread disease: there was never another confrontation as dangerous as that nuclear face-off between the two superpowers, which taught both sides how dangerous it was to go to the brink face to face, eyeball to eyeball."[71]

"The Cuban Missile Crisis marked the beginning of a long, slow trend away from the threat of nuclear war. War games, crisis planning, and a massive (and wasteful) military buildup on both sides would continue for another quarter century," Clifford asserted, "but after the Missile Crisis, even though the two sides continued their worldwide competition, neither side again flirted with a direct nuclear showdown."[72]

McGeorge Bundy declared similarly that "the preeminent meaning of the Cuban missile crisis, for participants and observers alike, and for the quarter century of history that followed, is that having come so close to the edge, the leaders of the two governments have since taken care to keep away from the cliff."[73] Even Henry Rowan, McNamara's deputy assistant secretary of defense for international security affairs from 1961 to 1964, recalled that McNamara's memorandums to the president on nuclear strategy abruptly shifted from the idea of fighting or controlling a nuclear war to the idea of deterring conflict.[74]

If there were any further doubt, McNamara himself cleared it up in his book, *Blundering into Disaster*, writing, "I do not believe we can avoid the serious and unacceptable risk of nuclear war until we recognize—and until we base all our military plans, defense budgets, weapons deployments, and arms negotiations on recognition—that nuclear weapons serve no purpose whatsoever." He continued, "They are totally useless—except to deter one's opponent from using them. This is my view today [in 1986]. It was my view in the early 1960s." He then clarified his outlook as secretary of defense: "At that time, in long private conversations with successive Presidents— Kennedy and Johnson—I recommended, without qualification, that they never initiate, under any circumstances, the use of nuclear weapons. I believe they accepted my recommendations."[75]

Paul Nitze noticed the change after the Cuban Missile Crisis, although he offered a different reason for it. In his revealing memoir, *From Hiroshima to Glasnost*, he argued that "the size of the budgetary requirement for a controlled and flexible nuclear strategic force oriented toward an effective counterforce capability soon cooled McNamara's ardor after the Cuban Missile Crisis of 1962. By then the danger of a nuclear confrontation with the Soviet Union appeared to have diminished and the costs of meeting it . . . were thought to be greater than he had originally assumed." Nitze continued, "Therefore, because of the requirements of building up our conventional forces and his concerns in 1963 that the country would not meet the cost of a ballooning defense budget, he [McNamara] changed his goals concerning our nuclear strategy and force structure."[76] Although Nitze did not agree with the change, McNamara's viewpoint prevailed.

Therefore, in December 1963, according to historian Andreas Wenger, McNamara advised Kennedy that "the central objective for the strategic nuclear forces was to assure U.S. ability to destroy, *after* a well-planned and well-executed Soviet surprise attack on U.S. strategic forces, 'the Soviet government and military controls, plus a large percentage of their population and economy.'"[77] The Kennedy administration then significantly revised both its war plans and military arsenal, including the cache of nuclear ballistic missiles, switching from the counterforce strategy to mutual assured destruction.[78]

McNamara called his nuclear strategy Mutually Assured Destruction to show the futility of nuclear conflict.[79] Although his source is not documented, he may have borrowed the concept from the book *The Ultimate Weapon*, edited by Bernard Brodie in 1946. In Brodie's book, Arnold Wolfers contends, "In the atomic age the threat of retaliation in kind is probably the strongest single means of determent. Therefore, the preparation of such retaliation must occupy a decisive plan in any over-all policy of protection against the atomic danger." He then applied it to the situation that McNamara faced: "Neither we nor the Russians can expect to feel even reasonably safe unless an atomic attack by one were certain to unleash a devastating atomic counterattack by the other."[80] Brodie agreed, proposing,

> If the aggressor state must fear retaliation, it will know that even if it is the victor it will suffer a degree of physical destruction incomparably greater than that suffered by any defeated nation of history, incomparably greater, that is, than that suffered by Germany in the recent war. Under those circumstances, no victory, even if guaranteed in advance—which it never is—would be worth the price. The threat of retaliation does not have to be 100 per cent certain; it is sufficient if there is a good chance of it, or if there is a belief that there is a good chance of it.[81]

Historians Gerard Clarfield and William Wiecek contend that Mutually Assured Destruction was McNamara's admission that fighting a limited nuclear war within defined boundaries, a key goal of the Flexible Response and counterforce strategies, was impossible.[82]

The change in perspective on nuclear war was not limited to the Kennedy administration. Khrushchev, too, changed his rhetoric, telling Norman Cousins, the leader of the Committee for a Sane Nuclear Policy, in mid-December 1962, "Peace . . . is the most important goal in the world. If we don't have peace and the nuclear bombs start to fall, what difference will it make whether we are Communists or Catholics or capitalists or Chinese or Russians or Americans? Who could tell us apart? Who will be left to tell us apart?"[83]

American citizens also recognized the change in relations between the two superpowers. In October 1961 Snell Putney and Russell Middleton conducted a study of college students' attitudes toward war. At that time,

72 percent of respondents agreed that "the U.S. must be willing to run any risk of war which may be necessary to prevent the spread of Communism," while only 34 percent agreed that "the U.S. has no moral right to carry its struggle against Communism to the point of risking the destruction of the human race."[84]

After the Cuban Missile Crisis, though, American citizens "emerged from the crisis like convicted felons who received a reprieve after being strapped into the electric chair: they sighed with relief but could not shake the near-memory of sudden death."[85] For a few months after the crisis, people remained concerned. However, by April 1963 the percentage of people who believed a world war would occur in the next five years dropped to the lowest point recorded in the 1950s and 1960s, and by July 1964 only 1 percent of respondents responded to a Gallup poll question on "the most important problem facing the country today" with communism or communist infiltration, while 34 percent mentioned racial discrimination / civil rights and integration, and 17 percent mentioned unemployment. Just two months later, when asked if the Russian leaders would refuse to risk launching a nuclear war *no matter what the U.S. did*, a surprising 29 percent agreed.[86]

McNamara's Mutually Assured Destruction policy appears to have continued into the Lyndon Johnson administration, along with Kennedy's secretary of defense and foreign policy advisors. Johnson himself, in a September 16, 1964 speech at the Peace Arch in Seattle, Washington, proclaimed, "We have worked consistently to bring nuclear weapons under careful control, and to lessen the danger of nuclear conflict. . . . I do not want us to fight a war that no one ever meant to begin." He continued, noting that his administration had "expanded and modernized our conventional forces . . . [so] we do not need to use nuclear power to solve every problem."[87]

McGeorge Bundy, Johnson's national security advisor, proclaimed that "by 1964 he [Johnson] was entirely clear in his own mind that he would have no interest whatever in ordering the use of even one [atomic] bomb, ever, except in the context of some overwhelmingly dangerous and direct confrontation with open Soviet aggression." Johnson, Bundy believed, saw atomic weapons as "a danger so much greater that one must think of any use of it not in the terms of a battle or a campaign, or even a war won or lost, but rather in terms of the long-term effect of any such use on the survival of man. It is not wrong, I believe, to conclude that for Johnson the use of the bomb in Vietnam was quite literally unthinkable."[88]

Johnson's decisions during the Vietnam conflict prove this to be accurate. Political scientist Nina Tannenwald contends that because "the United States sustained large losses in men, money and materiel at tremendous political cost [and] U.S. officials repeatedly declared that the United States could not tolerate the loss of Southeast Asia to Communism, and that the war was vital for American interests, prestige, and security," she believes, "one of the remarkable features of the Vietnam War is how little serious consideration US leaders gave to nuclear options. Although they made some veiled nuclear threats, top political leaders did not come close to using nuclear weapons." Tannenwald argues persuasively that "while nuclear weapons might have been militarily useful in the war, it was clear that, by the time the war was fought, they were politically unusable, and for some officials, even morally unacceptable."[89] This remarkable change in attitude toward nuclear conflict among influential American leaders and politicians had significant and long-term influence on U.S. defense posture and allocations for military forces after 1963, particularly on Air Force missiles and missileers.

CHAPTER 6

Freefall

The first casualties of the Kennedy administration's new attitude toward nuclear conflict were the Thor and Jupiter IRBMs.[1] It is doubtful that Allied leaders on either side of the Atlantic ever considered these missiles as a long-term defense capability, as they were created to be a stopgap measure until the Atlas missile could become operational. Following the Cuban Missile Crisis, the United States quickly removed both types of IRBMs from Europe, planning to upgrade them in the future with improved land-based medium-range ballistic missiles when the new weapons were ready to fulfill their mission.

Thus, when presenting the fiscal year 1963 defense budget to Congress, McNamara included funds for "the development of 'a new mobile, quick reacting, medium-range ballistic missile,' which would fill the range gap between the Pershing and the ICBM's. The missile was to be adapted for transport on a road net; in other words, it would be truck transported instead of rail transported as in the case of the mobile Minuteman." When congressional leaders asked him why he proposed this missile, much like the mobile version of the Minuteman, which the Department of Defense had just abandoned, he responded "that the [mobile medium-range ballistic missile] MMRBM was in response to a requirement for an all-weather attack capability in overseas theaters. Since this weapon would be small enough to be hauled in a furniture van, it would be much cheaper than the mobile Minuteman; it would also have a high degree of survivability, great accuracy, a nuclear warhead and could be fired quickly from any point."[2]

However, McNamara apparently changed his mind as, in a separate briefing to Congress, McNamara said the Thor missiles were British, so the United States had nothing to do with their replacement. In February 1963 Gen. Curtis LeMay testified before Congress that the British "never were very enthusiastic about Thor as a weapon system . . . [and] felt they would rather put their money into something else." The British appear to support this perspective. During the height of the Cuban crisis, on October 26, British prime minister Harold MacMillan told Kennedy that he would dismantle the Thor missiles in England in a quid pro quo for the Cuban missiles.[3]

Either way, the Department of Defense never built the new medium-range ballistic missiles. Instead, the Navy filled the gap with submarine-launched Polaris missiles, increasing the number of Polaris submarines from twenty in 1964 to forty-one in 1967, where it stayed until 1979. The first Thor squadron was closed early in 1963, and the last shut down in August of the same year.[4]

The Kennedy administration's new perspective on potential nuclear conflict quickly sealed the fate of the Jupiter missiles as well. In the spring of 1961, even before the squadrons in Italy and Turkey had become operational, Department of Defense representatives consulted with NATO authorities about the need to replace the missiles, which they deemed obsolete. Therefore, in January 1963, soon after the crisis over Cuba was settled, the United Kingdom, Italy, and Turkey announced that they would be phasing out their IRBMs.[5]

In late February 1963, in response to a congressional question on why he was removing the missiles so quickly, McNamara contended that the Jupiters were too vulnerable and expensive. He testified: "Our invulnerable or near invulnerable missile force, of course, is expanding very rapidly, and as it expands, it seems unwise to us to maintain these highly vulnerable weapons subject to sabotage, subject to attack, which are costing us substantial sums to maintain." He further exclaimed, "It costs us roughly $1 million per year per missile simply to maintain the missile in Turkey, and we pay that, and we see no need to continue that expenditure for such an ineffective weapon." Less than two months later, in April 1963, the Air Force had dismantled the last Jupiter squadron.[6]

A month later, in May 1963, McNamara decided to remove the liquid-fueled Atlas and Titan I missiles from the Air Force inventory as well. These weapons suffered from some of the same problems as the Thor and Jupiter. They were extremely hazardous as the large missiles required thousands of gallons of liquid oxygen to launch the warhead. The liquid oxygen reacted explosively to contact with organic materials, so if the missile crews and maintainers did not keep the missile area completely clean, any released oxygen tended to cause fires or explosions. Furthermore, the fuel had to be stored in insulated tanks at −297 degrees Fahrenheit and could not be loaded into the missiles until shortly before launch. Missiles loaded with liquid oxygen could not remain on alert for an extended time as, at room temperature, the liquid oxygen would return to its gaseous state and "burn off." These dangerous and volatile conditions caused several accidents during training and operations, including four accidents at operational sites during 1963 and early 1964, costing millions in damages.[7]

Tests of the integrated Atlas system showed that the frenzied development caused several hundred problems in the missiles. The Air Force conducted an eight-month retrofit program to correct the known problems but still only hoped to achieve 50 to 75 percent reliability. For this reason, in the spring of 1963, an Air Staff study group recommended that the Air Force retire the Atlas D and E models, along with the Titan I. The Department of Defense also grew concerned over the poor showing of the Atlas F, a missile even less reliable than its predecessors since it had been rushed into production for the Cuban Missile Crisis.[8]

Thus, when the new Minuteman missile proved safer, cheaper, and more dependable than the old, notoriously unreliable liquid-fueled missiles, defense officials decided to replace the old missiles with the new Minuteman. The new missiles could also be launched more quickly, making them safer against a sneak attack.

An additional benefit for the Kennedy administration was that the new missiles carried much smaller warheads than the earlier missiles. Kennedy was facing election, and nuclear security was still a topic that congressional opponents could use against him, especially since Kennedy had come into office vehemently accusing Eisenhower of weakening national security. Relations between the Kennedy administration and Congress, especially Rep. Carl Vinson (D-Ga.), the respected chairman of the Armed Services Committee, were extremely poor because of the administration's refusal to fund the proposed B-70/RS-70 nuclear-capable bomber. Therefore, replacing the older, larger missiles with Minuteman allowed the administration to contend that they were building larger numbers of missiles without actually increasing the real detonating power.[9] Consequently, in May 1964 McNamara decided to retire all liquid-fueled missiles. By July 1964 the Air Force had begun replacing Atlas and Titan I missiles with Minuteman missiles, and thirteen months later they were gone.[10]

McNamara's decision to retire the Atlas and Titan I missiles so quickly had a sudden and harsh impact on the missileers, especially the enlisted personnel. A single crew of two officers could oversee ten of the new Minuteman missiles while the older missiles each required a larger crew, including several enlisted members. Therefore, when the Air Force retired the Atlas and Titan I missiles, over five thousand Atlas and Titan I crew members, primarily enlisted personnel, were told to retrain to another career field, return to their previous occupation years behind their peers,

Early Minuteman crew performing crew duty. *Air Force Historical Research Agency*

or separate from the Air Force. The only enlisted positions that remained in missile operations were two posts per crew on the fifty-four Titan II missiles, along with a small number of instructors and evaluators.[11]

The situation was only slightly better for the officers serving on Atlas and Titan I crews. Many World War II pilots were retiring, and younger pilots were separating to join the growing and high-paying civilian airline industry, so the Air Force grew concerned about pilot retention. Therefore, in March 1964 the Air Force directed 1,700 qualified pilots working in nonrated assignments back to aviation duties. The pilots were reassigned to flying billets over the next year through the normal assignment process rather than all at one time, similar to what had happened to the bomber personnel transferred into missiles during the previous three years. Those who remained had to retrain into the very different Minuteman and Titan II weapon systems, leave the career field, or separate from the Air Force. In consequence, the nascent missile career field lost almost all of its experienced cadre.

In 1964 and 1965 the conflict in Vietnam began to command more attention, making the personnel problems even more challenging for missile operations. In August 1964, after a Navy destroyer reported being fired upon in the Gulf of Tonkin, President Lyndon Johnson requested congressional support to begin conventional military operations in Southeast Asia. The Johnson administration, including McNamara, proscribed the use of nuclear weapons during the conflict in Vietnam, so the Department of Defense focused its attention on developing and augmenting its conventional forces.[12]

Struggling with nearly overwhelming requirements, the Air Force decided that providing combat support to Vietnam was more important than manning missiles with experienced personnel, a significant change in perspective, and transitioned many missile officers who had worked in other fields back to their previous duties rather than retraining them to work in the growing Minuteman arsenal. By 1965 the Air Force had returned about 75 percent of pilots working in nonrated positions like missiles back to their cockpits. Two years later, the number of pilots working in nonrated positions dropped even further, from about 15,000 in 1965 to about 5,000. By 1969 the number was reduced to about 2,700.[13]

To fill the gaping holes in the missile field created by the wholesale transfer of personnel to Southeast Asia during the height of the buildup of the new Minuteman missiles, the Air Force began assigning newly commissioned officers, many from Air Force ROTC detachments, to missiles. Consequently, in just a few years, the missile community changed from a notable group of mostly rated, midlevel officers with years of combat experience to a very junior group composed almost entirely of nonrated officers with less than four years in the Air Force. While the service also recruited many new pilots for service in Vietnam, Col. Vance Mitchell acknowledged that "even in 1967, after most of the World War II pilots had retired, only 20 percent of the pilots were under thirty, while nearly 40 percent were over forty."[14] Meanwhile, Donovan Bowe, in a 1969 research report, documented that the rate of second lieutenants, the most junior rank in the officer corps, rose from 5 percent of the Minuteman crew force in 1963 to 47 percent in 1968. He further asserted that by 1969, 75 percent of Minuteman missileers were lieutenants and almost all of the other 25 percent were junior captains, the vast majority of whom were under twenty-six and had been in the Air Force less than five years.[15]

The new Air Force attitude toward this new cadre was a drastic change from Lt. Col. William Anderson's 1957 directive that "the missile crew must be brought to realize that it is the foremost element in the defense structure."[16] Many missileers who had not realized it before now understood that the Air Force did not consider them as valued warfighters, much less the future of the Air Force.

The missileers were further demeaned by the increased automation of the Minuteman missile system because the new system left little opportunity for ingenuity or innovative thought. Chaplain Arthur Engell asserted in a 1964 Air Command and Staff College thesis that "as we approach perfection in the push-button stage of our weapons system, with less and less effort required for maintenance and operation, the more difficult it becomes to provide useful and meaningful activity that will motivate and keep a man on the job."[17] Capt. Pierce Smith agreed: "As improved missile systems were phased into our strategic forces, advanced technology made crew duty much less demanding. This is especially true in the Minuteman system, where sophisticated equipment has greatly simplified crew duties."[18]

In other words, the missileers' daily work routine became more tedious, but the tedium did not mean the job was easy. Maj. Thomas Gilkeson, citing *Strategic Air Command Manual* 55-66, vol. 1, and *Strategic Air Command Manual* 23-9, revealed that "the primary responsibility [of a missile crew member] . . . is to be fully proficient in the use of the E[mergency] W[ar] O[rder] Documents, checklists, and procedures necessary to implement the SAC EWO. In addition," he continued, "missile crews must be on alert, monitoring the safety, security, and reaction capability of their weapon system until receipt of an execution order, upon such receipt they must properly interpret, authenticate, and react to effect a proper launch."[19]

Pierce Smith further described actual duty for the command's Minuteman crew members: "The average work week for a missile crew is far in excess of the normal 40-hour week. They average at least 300 hours per month. . . . The duty and tasks performed during the actual alert tour . . . are to monitor and report the status of the ten missiles in their flight by observing an array of color-coded lights on electronic panels." He added, "This routine of monitoring and reporting is continued throughout the tour, interrupted occasionally by practice launch messages or other routine calls over the communications network. These . . . functions are closely regulated by various publications and directives."[20]

Maj. Donald Sherman, in a research report for the Air Command and Staff College, explained how the directives made the daily tasks difficult: "There [was] no room for initiative or applying an individual's own systems knowledge in solving malfunctions or even in accomplishing the most routine tasks. . . . The most serious discrepancy a crew member can make is deviating from prescribed procedures."[21] This was not just an opinion. Most guidance, including Air Force Technical Order 21M-LGM25C-1 "Model LGM-25C Missile Weapon System Operations" specifically clarified: "Unusual operations or configurations are prohibited unless specifically covered herein. Clearances must be obtained from the authorized commander before attempting any operation not specifically permitted in this manual, other technical orders, or SAC CEM manuals. All crew functions must be performed as specified in this manual or other technical orders."[22] Sherman then revealed that some crew members chose to obey incorrect guidance because they "may blow up the missile by following technical data as prescribed, but at least [they] won't be court-martialed for not following it."[23] Not everyone followed this mindset, but the pressure to conform was constant and intense.

Continuous evaluations increased the stress that missile duty imposed on the missileers. The Air Force determined that evaluating each crew by launching a missile was too expensive, so SAC tested its missile crews through written exams and simulations. The command demanded perfection, which translated to scores of 100 percent on several specified monthly tests and scores of at least 90 percent on all others—although perfection was expected on these as well. Evaluations occurred several times each month, adding additional pressure to an already stressful profession and removing any opportunity to excel, leading Col. Max Henney, vice commander of the 341st Strategic Missile Wing, to report in 1964, "The combat crew lives in an artificial environment—strict, tight, closely controlled. They face rigorous examinations regularly on which they have to make perfect scores, and yet the tests are not really challenging, just demanding. Some of the men can't do it. A few have simply resigned their commissions and left the Air Force."[24]

Any discrepancies were resolved through immediate corrective action, and an individual who failed to display the required excellence or showed a chronic weakness was removed from the missile assignment and, often, the Air Force. The pressure was even more intense during performance assessments since evaluators conducted these tests at operational missile sites, forcing the crews to determine whether to prioritize real-world status or the simulated status.

Several students at Air War College or Air Command and Staff College quoted James Baar and William Howard, in *Combat Missileman*:

> If a missile combat crew commander makes an improper decision while in charge of his launch complex, or if he fails in one of the many evaluations to which he or his crew are subjected, the consequences may be serious. Failure to execute an Emergency War Order during an Operational Readiness Inspection satisfactorily not only invariably brought instant removal from command, but also generally ended all hope of a successful career in the Air Force. There were no second chances. As a system it was hard. It was unfailing. It was barely human. But it was very effective.[25]

In at least one case, this decision caused an entire wing to fail an inspection, an extremely rare and catastrophic event that ended the careers of all of the wing's leadership. The continuous pressure actually led to stress related diseases for some of the missileers.

Yet another factor increased stress and reduced morale for missile personnel. The Air Force intentionally situated the Minuteman missile wings away from populated areas and placed the missile sites miles away from their supporting Air Force bases. The isolation amplified the missileers' frustration and boredom as they spent much of their days driving through rural terrain or sitting alone in the missile launch facility. Because missile squadrons were often undermanned, the missileers were tasked with additional work, magnifying these concerns and dissatisfaction.[26]

Col. Donovan Bowe summarized the situation in a 1969 research report: "Arduous duty, isolated work environment, lack of glamour, inability to see the fruits of productivity, and lack of opportunity for the challenging work that produces job satisfaction are all factors that combine to make missile combat crew duty less than a rewarding experience." E. S. Ewart had identified many of these problems as far back as 1958, before the first missile was declared operational, in his study, "A Survey of Potential Morale, Motivation, and Retention Problems at Ballistic Missile Sites," but eleven years later, they remained critical concerns.[27]

Author Robert Rodwell also acknowledged that "nobody has yet come forward with a palliative for what we feel will be a basic root of discontent with future service life, that is the sense of complete frustration that life in a missile force will engender among its personnel." He then defined the primary problem: "Basically, inactivity will be the cause of this frustration—not inactivity in the sense that there will be little to occupy the serviceman's working day, but the inactivity of the force as a whole. It will be a sterile, static force, prevented by its very nature from ever being fully exercised."[28] Rodwell predicted what was readily apparent by the early 1960s: "There will be no indication to officers or airmen [in missile units] that their combined efforts are achieving anything. They will be denied the satisfaction derived from a job well done." In its rush to deploy the missiles as quickly as possible, the Air Force had chosen to ignore these concerns about morale as they arose, presuming that somehow the situation might resolve itself.[29]

The extremely negative impact of the problems remained hidden for several years. From October of 1959 through the end of 1961, the Air Force had only placed twenty-seven ballistic missiles in operational units. Thus, 1962 was the first year that numerous airmen began working with missiles, primarily in Atlas and Titan I units. The first missileers were almost all volunteers and saw themselves as the vanguard of a new concept in military operations. The enlisted missileers maintained the missiles and support equipment but were designated as operational personnel, a rare honor in the Air Force. Since the early missiles were rife with problems, this provided the missileers with constant work, and they were able to see the fruits of their labor. Almost all of the officers were rated personnel who were temporarily reassigned to missiles from flying units. These early missileers retained their aeronautical status and, in addition to their operational responsibilities, they guided and supervised the enlisted personnel, similar to their duties in the flying community.[30]

Even when the Air Force began recruiting some nonrated personnel into the career field, in 1962, missileers still had reason to believe that ICBMs were the future of the Air Force. The Air Force, under political pressure, terminated all new long-range bomber production in October of that year—the beginning of fiscal year 1963. This was the first year that the Air Force did not have a bomber in production since 1946 and senior leaders from the service were desperate to obtain new bombers for a "mixed force."[31]

Therefore, although manned bombers formed the bulk of Air Force strategic power until April 21, 1964—the first time there were as many missiles on alert as bombers—the new missileers were willing to deal with the hardships of missile life, believing conditions would improve once missiles replaced bombers as the primary weapon system of the Air Force.[32]

However, the missileers did not foresee the impact of the administration's new focus on limited war. As Mike Worden noted in *Rise of the Fighter Generals*, "the apex of SAC and bomber influence within the Air Force coincided with signals of a dimmer future," since fighter pilots—not missileers—would replace the bomber pilots as the leadership of the Air

Force. While McNamara refused to procure new bombers, he requested and received approval to increase the Air Force's tactical fighter wings from sixteen to twenty-one, and to increase reconnaissance wings from fourteen to twenty.[33]

At the same time, McNamara increased missiles, but not necessarily of his own volition. Despite the Kennedy administration's decision to scale back its reliance on nuclear weapons, in 1963 congressional pressure forced them to continue purchasing strategic missiles. David Halberstam reveals that, in early 1961, "the United States had 450 missiles; McNamara was asking for 950, and the Joint Chiefs of Staff were asking for 3,000." Halberstam remembers Kennedy asking, "Why the nine hundred and fifty, Bob?" to which McNamara responded, "Because that's the smallest number we can take up on the Hill without getting murdered." Thus, for the next several years ballistic missiles continued to increase in overall numbers and in comparison to nuclear-capable bombers. However, comprehensive nuclear power still began to decrease as the Air Force began to replace the expected purchases of more powerful Atlas and Titan missiles with the more reliable but much smaller Minuteman warheads while it made significant cuts to the bomber force.[34]

Air Force bomber pilots faced the same dilemma over limited war and the increasing influence of fighter pilots as they had with the development of missiles. The Army, frustrated with what they saw as a lack of support for ground forces from the Air Force, had established the Howze Board to investigate whether it should create its own tactical air force. In light of this Army threat and not perceiving fighter aircraft as a risk to Air Force's strategic mission, the bomber generals, led by LeMay, helped to build their service's tactical air force. Since politicians were focused on building the tactical capability, the bomber pilots used this opportunity to reduce the strength and influence of missiles within the service.[35]

Therefore, only in 1965—as Air Force leaders pulled pilots, navigators, and more senior support officers for assignments to Southeast Asia and replaced them with newly minted lieutenants or those who failed out of flight school—did this disdain for ballistic missiles become obvious. By then most of the early missileers had left the career field, and the few who remained required retraining to enter the new Minuteman or

Titan II systems. Thus, it cost the Air Force very little to replace them with new officers if the experienced officers separated from the service.[36]

Missileers struggled with another stigma. Even though sizable numbers of pilots and navigators had been pulled from operational missile jobs, the rated officers continued to be assigned to command and senior leadership positions in missiles, positions that many missileers did not believe these officers were qualified to fill. Maj. Robert Luckett, a former missileer studying at Air Command and Staff College, contended, "High level command and key staff positions in the missile wings were occupied by rated personnel. No one questioned the need for these personnel initially. However, they were not attuned to the problems and irritants of their assigned personnel." Luckett continued, "Some of these same people had not visited a launch control center since it became operationally ready. Not a single commander or staff member had ever spent a full alert tour at a control center to witness and experience firsthand what crew members were trying to convey when airing complaints [about the stresses of the assignment]."[37]

The situation was even more frustrating to the missileers since it violated a long-standing belief in the Air Force flying community—that "operators," those who conducted the operational mission of the Air Force, would only be led by someone who held the same qualifications. Col. Lloyd Brauer, in a 1956 *Air University Quarterly Review* article, acknowledged that the Air Force "established a . . . policy requiring that all Air Force activities having flying as their primary mission be commanded by a rated pilot. That the rated pilot who is serving or may serve in command and operational positions must continue active flying to maintain the 'cockpit viewpoint' has been argued exhaustively." Brauer further contended that "regardless of current assignment an officer expected to command or control flying activities must stay abreast of aviation advances, know the capabilities and limitations of the flyers and their machines, and most important of all, gain and maintain the respect and confidence of the men he is to lead."[38] Melvin Deaile, a former SAC pilot, put it more succinctly, "leaders flew and fliers led." Yet Air Force leaders chose not to apply a parallel policy in the case of missiles.[39]

By 1967, because the Department of Defense had focused on building fighters while retiring a significant portion of the bomber force and replacing the large Atlas and Titan I missiles with larger numbers of the smaller Minuteman missiles—decisions made in the late 1950s and early 1960s—there were more than two times as many missiles as there were bombers in the U.S. Air Force.[40] Nonetheless, the Air Force still granted the key leadership positions to the flyers either by regulation or fiat. Thus, the nonrated missileers became convinced that they were needed to operate missiles but would never be offered upward mobility as the promotable positions were almost all designated for rated personnel. Furthermore, because the new missile officers were entering missile duty as young lieutenants, they finished their assignment in missile operations as young captains.

Unlike their pilot contemporaries, only those designated as the very best were even able to get potentially promotable staff positions, while the rest were placed in local jobs with little promotion potential or transferred out of the career field. In 1971 there were "only twenty-one missile staff positions authorized on the Air Staff, a ratio of one staff position for every 159 field authorizations. This [was] one of the lowest Air Staff to field representations within the Air Force."[41]

Since the Department of Defense uses an "up or out" promotion policy for retention, most of those assigned to jobs with minimal potential would eventually be forced to leave the service because their jobs were not as prestigious and they could not compete well for limited promotions. Thus, when 625 missileers from five bases responded to a survey on morale in 1971, "40 percent of those surveyed considered missile duty a 'dead-end' for career progression, while only 14 percent viewed it as a positive career opportunity."[42]

The lack of career potential was demoralizing, but another action taken by the Air Force infuriated the missileers just as much. Colonels William Brooksher and Jimmy Scott conducted a survey of current and former missileers, who responded that the Air Force practice of labeling missile personnel as support personnel in "statistical reports, such as promotion analyses, and other publications detract[ed] from both the prestige and image of the career field. To them," exclaimed the colonels, "it is inconceivable that personnel charged with one-third of the Triad [the title for the three legs of U.S. nuclear defense: ICBMs, bombers, and submarine-launched missiles] could be considered or listed as 'support' personnel for any reason. As one officer put it, 'Who do we support? . . . Missile operations officers are *not* support officers!' "[43]

A midlevel officer in the study contended, "M[issileers] should receive as much recognition as other AF combat specialties. That would be vastly more than they receive now. It appears to be AF policy to classify them [missile combat crew members] as support troops." Another officer, a senior leader of a missile wing, argued that "the missile combat crew member is generally looked upon by his non-missile combat crew contemporaries as the dumbest 'wienie' in the force and, as such, he is considered to be an inferior breed. . . . His flight officer contemporary receives his flight [pay and benefits] in addition to his normal military pay for doing a similar job, while his non-rated, non-missile contemporary is working his good old eight to five job, five days a week and is not betting his career about four times a month."[44]

The study revealed that missileers believed they were "treated as second class citizens compared to rated personnel. This applie[d] to prestige, pay, [and] considerations around the base."[45] In one example of blatant discrimination, Lt. Leon Hojegian remembered trying to enter the Plattsburgh AFB Officers Club in his missile uniform, as he had seen numerous pilots do in their flight suits. Nevertheless, he was turned away, told that missileers could not enter the club in their duty uniform.[46]

The Air Force policy toward the missileer's badge and request for special pay also reflected this discrimination. Even before the Air Force had become a separate service in 1947, Army Air Force pilots were awarded badges that represented their aeronautical status.[47] This tradition became a symbol of pride and was transferred to the Air Force. As the Air Force formed new missile units, missileers began to request their own badge. On April 28, 1958, General White ordered the service to devise a new badge for the missile operators. However, unlike the flyer's "wings," which were specifically designed to show the exact type of aeronautical rating that a flyer held (pilots, navigators, flight engineers, bombardiers, flight surgeons, and other aircrew members), the Air Force designed a single

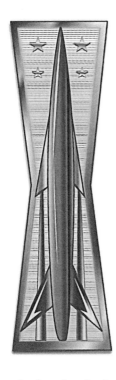

Fig. 2. The Air Force missile badge as designed in 1958. *Defense Media Activity, San Antonio (image created by Corey Parrish)*

badge for everyone associated with the new field (see fig. 2). That same day, the Air Staff directed that "the design [was] not to include wings of any type. . . . It should be no larger than the pilot wings and some smaller designs are requested."[48]

On May 23, 1958, Air Force Regulation 35-5 was published, authorizing a missile badge for wear by any person "with a direct and distinctive role in the command, maintenance, operation, or guidance of the missile and/or its related ground equipment . . . [or] to a position with primary duty directly associated with guided missiles."[49] Thus, all of the personnel that oversaw, guided, developed policy for, or worked closely with missiles were authorized to wear the badge, including the rated commanders, whether they had operational experience with missiles or not. Further, an airman only needed to perform duty associated with the new weapons for three months before earning the badge. The explicit differentiation between the standards of the two badges frustrated the operations personnel, who believed they deserved a specific badge for their operational experience, like that of their rated peers. This may seem a trivial concern, but it underscored and reflected the accumulating perception of discrimination against missile operations.[50]

A similar frustration developed over the Air Force's refusal to provide missileers with additional pay to compensate for their difficult duties. Once more, the missileers compared their situation to their flying brethren and questioned why the pilots not only earned aviation incentive pay but also received other bonuses related to flying as well as promotion and other benefits. The missileers reminded the Air Force that Congress had authorized responsibility pay as part of the Military Pay Act of 1958, designated for officers occupying positions of unusual responsibility. Since they controlled one-third of the nation's nuclear capability and, with it, held the capability to destroy significant portions of any enemy's territory, people, and infrastructure, the missileers believed they had earned the pay for unusual responsibility. Colonel Henney, a fighter pilot who served as the vice wing commander at Malmstrom, agreed, remarking, "In the history of warfare, in the history of the world, no junior officers have ever before been called on to take such responsibility."[51] Still, the Air Force, while arguing strenuously to continue aviation incentive pay, never authorized any additional pay for missileers until 2014.[52]

In 1973 Brooksher and Scott quoted another midlevel missileer as saying, "Most of the crew members, I believe, are crying out for recognition. Nothing sticks in my throat more than 'The mission of the Air Force is to fly and fight and don't you forget it.' With the missile fleet carrying the portion of the SIOP [Single Integrated Operations Plan—the nuclear war plan] load that it does it would seem they are vastly underrated and [under]recognized."[53]

Howard Tarleton, an active navigator for seven years before he joined the missile career field, acknowledged that the perception was real: "I sensed the operational [flying] part of the Air Force thought the ICBM mission really belonged to the Army. They believed that ICBMs were necessary but the strategic mission was best carried out by aircraft bombardment and airborne missiles."[54] Therefore, even though the Air Force had struggled bitterly with the Army to control ballistic missiles from the service's beginning in 1947 until the transition of the Jupiter missile to Air Force control in 1956, after the service had secured complete control of the new weapons and the missiles no longer threatened the service's strategic bombing mission, it chose to treat the exceptionally powerful weapons and those who controlled them as secondary at best.

Study after study tied the abject frustration of the missileers with their perceived neglect to poor retention rates, concerning the Air Force leadership greatly, but the service's leaders refused to respond in any meaningful way to the missileers' concerns. The situation only grew worse as fighter pilots, who had won recognition for conventional warfighting in Southeast Asia, began to earn positions of leadership and influence. These flyers, frustrated over years of their own neglect from SAC bomber pilots, denigrated all nuclear operations, especially missileers, who could not show what novelist Thomas Wolfe called the "code of the right stuff: . . . courage, skill, coolness, and eagerness for combat."[55]

The Air Force did make incremental improvements to the Minuteman missile, as long as the costs did not reduce funding for flying operations. However, technologies designed and deployed in the late 1950s and early 1960s remained the backbone of missile operations for the next five decades. In fiscal year 1963, the Air Force began researching an advanced ICBM. Some concepts considered for use in the new missile included a "cold launch," whereby compressed gases would expel the missile from its silo before the missile's rockets ignited, and an improved guidance system. Congress authorized $15.5 million in 1964 and $15 million in 1965, but Secretary of Defense McNamara, by then focused heavily on conventional fighting in Vietnam and averse to anything that would increase the risk of nuclear conflict, reduced actual allocations to $8 million and $3 million, respectively. The new technologies appeared promising, but none were actually used for two decades. In 1965 the Air Force determined that the Minuteman missiles would need to be replaced by 1973. Advanced development of the next missile did not begin until late 1973, and the missiles, known as the Peacekeeper, did not become operational until 1986, considerably after the time frame of this study. Even then, only fifty Peacekeeper missiles were ever deployed, and these remained operational only until 2005, when the last one was deactivated under the terms of the Strategic Arms Reduction Talks. Thus, the U.S. Air Force ballistic missile force in 2018 consists of 450 Minuteman III missiles, designed and built in the early 1960s.[56]

In 1957 Brig. Gen. Charles McCorkle, the Air Force's assistant chief of staff for guided missiles, had warned the Air Force that "even without a great deal of study it becomes apparent that we cannot treat the command and control of missiles as though we were simply integrating additional bombers into our forces."[57] The Air Force complied with McCorkle's advice, although not in the manner he intended. As long as the service feared that political leaders would take the Air Force's long-range strategic mission from the bombers and give it to missiles, its senior leaders worked vigorously to show that they were quickly and efficiently incorporating the mission into the service. However, it was evident that Air Force leaders never fully accepted the new weapon, seeing it as a threat to the flying mission they loved. Therefore, once McNamara and other political leaders stopped pressing the service to quickly incorporate and integrate missiles into operations, service leaders placed the bulk of their money, personnel, and emphasis back in the areas they preferred—flying and mission support for flying operations. As political and service attention became more devoted to limited war, Air Force missiles entered a long tenure of benign neglect.

Conclusions

D uring the 1950s, when scientists and engineers designed and created ballistic nuclear missiles, the new capability was marketed as the ultimate weapon, the future of warfare. A unique confluence of several critical events, including the incorporation of the thermonuclear bomb into the ballistic missile, the beginning of the Cold War, and the creation of the U.S. Air Force and the Department of Defense, combined to provide the nuclear ballistic missile with seemingly unlimited potential.

However, many in the Air Force feared the new mission, remembering the start of their own service only a decade before the creation of the nuclear missile. To best contend for a new service, the early airmen had prioritized a core mission—strategic bombing, rather than several cohesive and cooperative roles for air power, such as air support to ground forces, transporting critical supplies, or even defending control of the airspace. For this reason, by 1942 instructors at the Air Corps Tactical School, the primary school for military aviation, "began to graft the concept of the primacy of the bomber onto the concept of air warfare and strategic air operations."[1]

The invention of nuclear bombs only heightened the importance of the bombing mission, since the Air Force's heavy bombers were initially the only effective delivery system for atomic weapons. President Dwight D. Eisenhower, apprehensive that establishing a large defense structure would damage the U.S. free market economy and turn the nation into a garrison state, decided to build his defense structure around the nuclear bomb and the Air Force's strategic bombers. Based on this decision, by the end of its first decade, the Air Force was the preeminent military service, dominating

U.S. security policy. It received almost half of the nation's defense budget and held the key to national defense policy—the nuclear bomb.[2]

Since many believed the ballistic missile would be more capable than bombers of performing the strategic air mission, the weapon was an existential threat to the new service. Thus, several U.S. Air Force leaders and their supporters struggled mightily to control the new weapon system, even though many of the service's pilots wanted nothing to do with it. The differing perspectives about missiles led to a struggle within the Air Force between those who saw the potential of the new missiles and those who saw them only as a threat to manned strategic air operations.

Once the Air Force gained responsibility for the new missiles, the service's missile proponents quickly built a substantial force, concurrently designing, building, deploying, and manning the new weapons. The rush to build the "bomber's replacement" further incited those who worried about the future of manned aircraft. The haste of construction created problems with the first missiles' reliability and standardization and generated concerns over personnel selection and training. Many of these troubles were overcome as the Air Force built the second iteration, but some problems inherent to missile duty remained unresolved: isolation; sterile, monotonous, and tedious work; an inability to see the results of one's labor; and the stressful, exacting standards that held no benefit to the crewmember or the mission. Although the Air Force leadership recognized many innate problems with missile crew duty, they chose to downplay these in the hurry to put missiles into operation.[3]

As long as national political and social pressure continued to promote missiles, Air Force leaders strove to publicly assimilate the new weapon into the Air Force, no matter what their personal attitudes toward the weapons were. Service leaders created missile squadrons and placed them into operation. They also assigned pilots temporarily into the missile squadrons to conduct the modified strategic air operation—and to ensure that the new missileers adopted the strategic air mindset and cultural traditions. Soon the Air Force had a strong and viable missile force that grew to be as potent as the manned bomber force.[4]

After the Cuban Missile Crisis, the political leaders who led the buildup of nuclear missiles determined that the United States should move away from atomic weapons. As the nation became enmeshed in the Vietnam conflict and the focus of the political leaders transitioned to limited war, the service replaced their operationally savvy missileers with inexperienced second lieutenants. Air Force leaders and the rated officers in command of the new missile wings continued to ignore the festering concerns of the new missileers. Believing they had effectively eliminated the threat to the service, they focused on reinvigorating the mission of strategic bombing and manned flight.

For decades the missile field remained unchanged. Therefore, missileers took a very different lesson from their experience in SAC. Rather than valuing operational experience controlling the missiles, the commanders of missile units began to behave as if those who served in the missile field were less capable than those who did not. Those who were deemed the best and brightest were removed from the weapon system as soon as possible, while those whose future was not as bright were left to atrophy in the operational environment. Although the practice changed in 2014, for nearly fifty years the leaders of missile units selected their instructors and evaluators from very inexperienced crew members. These personnel spent very little time operating the missiles but were then promoted into leadership positions while those who had remained in operational positions were held in lower esteem and often were forced out of the missile community or the Air Force itself.

The devaluation of experience actually operating the missiles meant that missileers had to be differentiated in some other way. The differentiator became monthly test scores. Lt. Gen. James Holmes, while vice commander of Air Education and Training Command, revealed in a "Report of Commander-Directed Investigation" that

> all MCCMs [missile combat crew members] receive periodic training to maintain the operational readiness required to perform their alert missions. This training consists of classroom and simulator instruction and is given on a monthly basis. Every month, a missileer must attend recurring classroom training in weapon system . . . , codes handling . . . , and E[mergency] W[ar] O[rder operations]. Additionally, every month a missileer must take and pass a 20–30 question knowledge test in each of those three subjects—with a minimum passing score of 90 percent on each test.[5]

However, these tests had become the single differentiator between success and failure. Holmes' investigation revealed that "leaders placed too much emphasis on monthly test scores. Although the required passing score is 90 percent, crewmembers felt pressured to score 100 percent on each and every test. Leaders lost sight of the fact that execution in the field is more important than what happens in the classroom." Daniel Sharp, a missileer at Warren AFB in 2014, concurred, explaining, "When I first came here leadership that was in place told me that the minimum passing score for my test was a 90 percent, but if I was making 90s I was a D student. And I would be treated that way."[6]

In 2014 Secretary of the Air Force Deborah Lee James expressed alarm over this poor leadership, stating, "The drive to always score a hundred percent on exams when 90 percent was the standard, and the use of these scores in some cases as the sole differentiator on who got promoted and who didn't, just seemed inappropriate to me," so she changed the standard.[7] This standard had applied to missileers all the way back to at least 1964, when Col. Max Henney, vice commander of the 341st Strategic Missile Wing, reported to an *Esquire* writer, "The combat crew lives in an artificial environment—strict, tight, closely controlled. They face rigorous examinations regularly on which they have to make perfect scores."[8]

Other frustrations expressed by missileers in 2014 reflected similar ones revealed by their predecessors from the 1950s and 1960s. Author R. Jeffrey Smith, in a 2014 article, wrote that the missileers' "day-to-day enemy, for decades, has not so much been another superpower, but the unremitting boredom of an isolated posting that demands extreme vigilance, while also requiring virtually no activity. . . . paired with the military's sky-high expectations for their workplace performance."[9] This complaint resembled those addressed by numerous missileers, including Pierce Smith, who described missile crew duty in 1965 as "long, monotonous hours in an isolated environment, a high degree of tension and stress, and (in the Minuteman system) greatly simplified tasks to perform."[10]

These decisions not only produced a dysfunctional missile community that struggled with low morale, little sense of mission, and operationally inexperienced leadership, but contributed to a resolute and uncompromising Air Force focused singularly on perpetuating piloted aircraft. The experience taught the service to first gain control of any politically supported mission that threatened the dominance of manned flight and then to devalue it once political attention was directed elsewhere.

The Air Force's flying leadership learned an important but detrimental lesson from their experience with nuclear missiles. During its formative years, the early years of the Cold War, the Air Force focused almost solely on the strategic nuclear air assignment. Pilots who flew fighters and other aircraft struggled unsuccessfully to expand this single-minded focus.[11] Then discerning and farsighted leaders like Henry "Hap" Arnold, Thomas White, and Bernard Schriever—generals who all spent the majority of their careers in nonflying assignments—attempted to broaden the service's focus by expanding into missiles, a mission they perceived as critical to the future of the service as well as U.S. defense capabilities. With the political support and oversight of men like Assistant Secretary Trevor Gardner, Sen. Henry Jackson (D-Wash.), and Sen. Clinton Anderson (D-N.M.), the Air Force moved quickly and forcefully into the new enterprise. The Air Force desperately fended off efforts by the other services to share or take the assignment, but it never lost its resolute focus on strategic air. Therefore, when the Air Force leaders saw the opportunity to reduce the service's attention on missiles and return its primary focus to strategic air operations, they believed that they had defeated the Department of Defense's attempt to expand the service's mission in any meaningful way.

The next contest was not long in coming. As the national focus changed from nuclear preparation to the conflict in Vietnam, Air Force leaders attempted to use the same methodology to defeat what they perceived as the new threat to strategic air. Within three months of his promotion to chief of staff of the Air Force, LeMay had replaced all of the fighter generals in senior leadership positions in the U.S. Air Forces in Europe and in Tactical Air Command with bomber pilots. By October 1, 1957, most of the air staff leadership and all major operational commanders were LeMay's bomber protégés. To meet the increasing need for pilots to support the ongoing conflict, SAC pilots were trained to fly fighters, transports, and other aircraft and sent on tours to the combat zone.

This time the results differed from the missile experiment. As pilots flying missions over Vietnam gained combat experience, the pilots most capable of flying fighters earned respect, medals, and promotions based on their combat exploits, just as the bomber pilots of World War II had, while those who perceived themselves as bomber pilots returned to nuclear alert. Thus, the fighter pilots began to move into key leadership positions after LeMay retired, positioning themselves to take over the Air Force in the decades to come. Although the victors were different, the lesson learned was the same. The fighter pilots retained the singular focus on a particular undertaking—this time, fighter operations—and the Air Force established a trend of focusing on a single primary mission rather than several cohesive and cooperative assignments. Charles Gabriel, a fighter pilot, became chief of staff of the Air Force in 1982. A decade later, all nuclear forces were transferred to the newly created Air Combat Command, run by fighter pilots, and SAC was disestablished. By 2001, even though fighter pilots constituted only 5.3 percent of the Air Force, they occupied two-thirds of the Air Force's four-star general positions and commanded the same percentage of the service's major commands.

The impact to the long-term health of the Air Force was the same as when the bomber pilots had controlled the service. The senior leaders of America's newest military branch continued to focus on a single mission to the detriment of all other capabilities. Early theories in aviation created a reflexive drive to have an aviator in a cockpit rather than allowing leaders to consider new concepts to best to control the airspace. When a new and politically supported defense commitment appeared to threaten the Air Force flying mission, the Air Force took immediate action to incorporate the capability into the service. Once the Air Force leaders effectively gained control of the new capability, they tied it closely to manned flight and then, as political oversight waned, assimilated it as a subsidiary of the flying mission. Other Air Force aviators have seen this trend as well and have speculated on when—or even if—a new breed of flyers will take the helm of the Air Force.[12]

A second example of this mindset is the remotely piloted aircraft (RPA) or unmanned aerial vehicle (UAV) program. Secretary of Defense Robert Gates complained that in 1992, while he was the director of the CIA, "the Air Force would not co-fund with CIA a vehicle without a pilot."[13]

Nevertheless, as had occurred with missiles, interservice rivalry created Air Force interest. The Office of the Secretary of Defense created the Predator UAV, then offered both the Air Force and Navy the opportunity to operate the new capability in Bosnia in 1995. Both services refused, so an Army military intelligence battalion flew operations over the Balkans. "Suddenly, the Air Force made an all-out bid to be the 'lead service' for Predator," Thomas Ehrhard declared, because "combat operations over Bosnia had caused a stir and had crystallized Congressional support. Air Force Chief of Staff [Ronald] Fogelman could see that due to its success in Bosnia, Predator was going to be fielded and he wanted to control the UAV for doctrinal reasons."[14]

Fogelman successfully gained control of the newly revealed weapon system, with the Army Chief of Staff ceding the mission after Air Force assurances that they would respond effectively to Army requirements. On April 9, 1996, the secretary of defense approved the Air Force as the lead service for UAV operations and, less than six months later, on September 2, 1996, the Air Force took control of Predator operations over Bosnia with experienced pilots who were transferred to the 11th Reconnaissance Squadron.

By June 2011 congressional and defense leaders had to remind the Air Force to take care of their new mission as it was still critical to ongoing defense operations. Promotion rates to major for the pilots who flew the service's RPA had fallen from 96 percent to 78 percent, well below that of other airmen. Secretary Gates "directed the Air Force to 'increase opportunities for highly skilled members of the UAS [unmanned aircraft systems] military community to reach senior leadership positions,' emphasizing that 'General Officers originating from this community are critical to our institutional goals.'"[15]

By 2015 the Air Force had not effectively addressed Gates' requests. Struggling to retain its qualified RPA pilots, the Air Force lost about 240, or 25 percent, each year. The Air Force acknowledged that the low retention numbers added incredible stress to the lives of the RPA pilots, who were required to serve, on average, fourteen-hour days, six days a week, but the pilots expressed another concern as well—the humiliation of being scorned by other Air Force pilots who viewed them as second-class citizens. Brandon Bryant, a former RPA pilot, explained in an interview with *Democracy Now*, "Everyone else thinks that the whole program or the people behind it are a joke, that we are video-game warriors, that we're Nintendo warriors. And that's—that's really not the case. And these—the people that do the job are just as legit and just as combat-oriented as anyone else."[16]

The RPA pilots were not alone in their frustration. The missileers did not escape their experience of entering the Air Force unscathed either. While the pilots who ran the Air Force demanded that an experienced pilot lead other pilots and looked upon extensive flying experience as a badge of honor, they chose not to apply a similar standard to missile units. At first there were no Air Force leaders with missile experience to place into these leadership positions, but even after the first midlevel officers finished their missile crew experience, the Air Force chose to continue placing rated pilots in the key leadership positions.

Finally, missileers, like the RPA pilots, reached the conclusion that the Air Force designated them as second-class citizens. Complaints heard from both missileers and RPA pilots after 2010 sounded strongly like those expressed by missile crew members from earlier decades. After news reports surfaced revealing problems in the missile career field, Charlie Simpson reminded missileers that "there have been periods where those of us who were missileers felt we were the 'second class' part of the Air Force," especially when all of the leaders wore wings.[17]

Once fighter pilots disestablished SAC in 1992 and then replaced it with the less influential Global Strike Command in August 2009, missileers expressed uneasiness that the Air Force reduced the top nuclear commander from a four-star general to a three-star, a significant reduction. In 2014 Secretary James upgraded the position to four stars, like the other major operational commanders. The person that she sent to fill the position was not a missileer though—he was a fighter pilot. James dismissed the concern, emphasizing, "I think he is just the ticket. . . . It would have been great if he also had the nuclear experience, but in this case we didn't have somebody immediately in the wings who was ready to take that on at that level, who had the experience."[18] Thus, nearly sixty years after

Gen. Thomas Power declared the first Atlas missile operational, pilots remained in command of missiles, confirming William Brooksher and Jimmy Scott's findings from 1973 that "as long as the operations command structure combines both missiles and rated organizations the demand for missile general officers will continue to be negligible."[19]

In 1957, as the first ballistic nuclear missile sat on alert, many Americans thought its potential—and that of the men who would control it—was limitless. Less than ten years later, the nation had returned to non-nuclear, limited war and the missileers were relegated to secondary status in their own service. In part, this drastic change resulted from the missile being oversold as the "ultimate weapon" during the early Cold War, when many Americans believed that a nuclear war was not only likely but preferable to domination by the communist Soviet Union. That the missiles' development also occurred as the newly established Air Force was at the height of its power ensured that the Air Force would struggle strenuously to take on the new capability, if for nothing else than to ensure that the missile did not replace the strategic bomber. Finally, the Kennedy administration's decision to return emphasis to conventional conflicts and away from the ballistic missile allowed the Air Force leadership to push the missiles and their missileers into relative obscurity. Problems with missile duty that were recognized in the late 1950s were left to fester into the early twenty-first century while the Air Force maintained a singular focus on its flying mission.

NOTES

Introduction and Historiography

1. Robert McNamara, draft "Remarks by Robert S. McNamara before UPI Editors and Publishers," 8, National Security File, Agency File, Box 12, Defense, Department of—August 1967, Volume V [2 of 2], Lyndon Baines Johnson Presidential Library and Museum, Austin, Texas.

2. NSC Action No. 1484, accessed November 6, 2014, http://www.foia.cia .gov/sites/default/files/document_conversions/18/1960-08-19a.pdf.

3. While the Combined Bomber Offensive in Europe and the aerial campaign against Japan both had pilots engaged in killing large numbers of people, their attacks were conducted sequentially and could have been called off after the attack had begun. A missile launch, however, once begun, cannot be recalled.

4. Jacob Neufeld, phone interview with the author, May 2014.

5. Archie DiFante, archivist at the Air Force Historical Research Agency, conversation, December 2013. See also John Darrell Sherwood, *Officers in Flight Suits* (New York: New York University Press, 1996), 9; and Edmund Beard, *Developing the ICBM: A Study in Bureaucratic Politics* (New York: Columbia University Press, 1976), viii and iv.

6. Kenneth F. Gantz, ed., *The United States Air Force Report on the Ballistic Missile* (Garden City, NY: Doubleday, 1958).

7. Bernard Brodie, *Strategy in the Middle Age* (Princeton, NJ: Princeton University Press, 1971).

8. Herman Kahn, *On Thermonuclear War* (Princeton, NJ: Princeton University Press, 1960).

9. James Baar and William E. Howard, *Combat Missileman* (New York: Harcourt, Brace and World, 1961).

10. Roy Neal, *Ace in the Hole* (Garden City, NY: Doubleday and Company, 1962).

11. Ernest G. Schwiebert, *A History of the U.S. Air Force Ballistic Missiles* (New York: Praeger, 1965).

12. Jacob Neufeld, *The Development of Ballistic Missiles in the United States Air Force, 1945–1960* (Washington, DC: Office of Air Force History, 1990).

13. Beard, *Developing the ICBM*.

14. Christopher Gainor, "The United States Air Force and the Emergence of the Intercontinental Ballistic Missile, 1945–1954" (PhD dissertation, University of Alberta, Edmonton, 2011).

15. Desmond Ball, *Politics and Force Levels: The Strategic Missile Program of the Kennedy Administration* (Berkeley: University of California Press, 1980).

16. Neil Sheehan, *Fiery Peace in a Cold War: Bernard Schriever and the Ultimate Weapon* (New York: Random House, 2009).

17. David Spires, *On Alert: An Operational History of the United States Air Force Intercontinental Ballistic Missile Program, 1945–2011* (Colorado Springs, CO: U.S. Space Command, 2012).

18. James P. Tate, *The Army and Its Air Corps: Army Policy toward Aviation, 1919–1941* (Maxwell AFB, AL: Air University Press, 1998).

19. John Lewis Gaddis, *The Cold War: A New History* (New York: Penguin Press, 2005).

20. Carole Fink, *Cold War: An International History* (Boulder, CO: Westview Press, 2014).

21. Norman Friedman, *The Fifty-Year War: Conflict and Strategy in the Cold War* (Annapolis, MD: Naval Institute Press, 2000).

22. Michael Dobbs, *One Minute to Midnight: Kennedy, Khrushchev, and Castro on the Brink of Nuclear War* (New York: Knopf, 2008); David Coleman, *The Fourteenth Day: JFK and the Aftermath of the Cuban Missile Crisis* (New York: Norton, 2012); and Robert Kennedy, *Thirteen Days: A Memoir of the Cuban Missile Crisis* (New York: Norton, 1969).

23. David Holloway, *Stalin and the Bomb: The Soviet Union and Atomic Energy, 1939–1956* (New Haven, CT: Yale University Press, 1994).

24. Boris Chertok, *Rockets and People*, 4 vols. (Washington, DC: NASA, 2006); Asif Siddiqi, *Challenge to Apollo: The Soviet Union and the Space Race, 1945–1974* (Washington, DC: NASA, 2000); and Asif Siddiqi, *The Red Rockets' Glare: Spaceflight and the Soviet Imagination, 1857–1957* (New York: Cambridge University Press, 2010).

25. Pavel Podvig, ed., *Russian Strategic Nuclear Forces* (Cambridge, MA: MIT Press, 2001).

Chapter 1. The Atomic Bomb

1. Albert Einstein to Franklin D. Roosevelt, letter dated August 2, 1939, Franklin Delano Roosevelt Presidential Library and Museum, accessed February 21, 2014, http://www.fdrlibrary.marist.edu/archives/pdfs/docs worldwar.pdf. Dr. Alexander Sachs testified to Congress that the letter was given to President Roosevelt. Hearings Before the Special Committee on Atomic Energy, U.S. Senate, 79th Congress, 1st Session, November 27, 1945 (HRG-1945-AES-0001), 10.

2. Henry L. Stimson and McGeorge Bundy, *On Active Service in Peace and War* (New York: Harper, 1948), 613.

3. Holloway, *Stalin and the Bomb*, 76–86.

4. Kenneth McRae, *Nuclear Dawn: F. E. Simon and the Race for Atomic Weapons in World War II* (Oxford: Oxford University Press, 2014), 120–21.

5. Leslie Groves, "General Grove's Report on 'Trinity,' July 18, 1945," in *Now It Can Be Told: The Story of the Manhattan Project* (New York: Harper and Brothers, 1962), appendix VIII. See also Robert C. Williams and Philip L. Cantelon, eds., *The American Atom: A Documentary History of Nuclear Policies from the Discovery of Fission to the Present, 1939–1984* (Philadelphia: University of Pennsylvania Press, 1984), 48–49.

6. Groves, "General Grove's Report on 'Trinity,' July 18, 1945."

7. Groves, *Now It Can Be Told*, 254.

8. Sidney Shalett, "First Atomic Bomb Dropped on Japan; Missile Is Equal to 20,000 Tons of TNT; Truman Warns Foe of a 'Rain of Ruin,'" *New York Times*, August 6, 1945, 1.

9. A. Lavrent'ieva in "Stroiteli novogo mira [Builders of a New World]," *V mire knig* [In the world of books], 1970, no. 9, 4, as quoted in David Holloway, "Entering the Nuclear Arms Race: The Soviet Decision to Built the Atomic Bomb, 1939–1945," *Social Studies of Science* 11, no. 2 (May 1981): 183.

10. Semen Al'tshuler, "Tak my delali bombu," *Literaturnaia Gazeta*, June 6, 1990, 13, as quoted in Holloway, *Stalin and the Bomb*, 204.

11. A. P. Alexandrov, "Kak delali bombu," *Izvestiia*, July 22, 1988, 3, as quoted in Holloway, *Stalin and the Bomb*, 132.

12. Holloway, *Stalin and the Bomb*, 213–16.

Chapter 2. Creating a Working Missile

1. Lawrence Freedman, "The First Two Generations of Nuclear Strategists," in *Makers of Modern Strategy from Machiavelli to the Nuclear Age*, ed. Peter Paret (Princeton, NJ: Princeton University Press, 1986), 736.

2. Curtis LeMay, interview with Edgar F. Puryear Jr., November 17, 1976, Call #K239.0512-1450, IRIS #01053318, AFHRA, [142]. LeMay was the Army's only deputy chief of air staff for research and development. He held the position from December 1945 to September 18, 1947, when the Air Force became a separate service. For further information on the position of deputy chief of Air Staff for research and development, see Elliot V. Converse II, *Rearming for the Cold War, 1945–1960* (Washington, DC: Historical Office, Office of the Secretary of Defense, 2011), 215.

3. Robert H. Goddard, "A Method of Reaching Extreme Altitudes," *Smithsonian Miscellaneous Collections* 71, no. 2 (1919): 1–69, accessed February 20, 2014, http://www.clarku.edu/research/archives/pdf/ext_altitudes.pdf. Konstantin Tsiolkovsky described multistage rockets fueled by liquid propellant in his 1903 paper, "Exploring Space with Reactive Devices," *Scientific Review* (in Cyrillic; this is a Russian journal), but it is unlikely that anyone in the United States was aware of this in 1919, and Goddard's studies were the first to result in a working rocket.

4. Horst Boog, Gerhard Krebs, and Detlef Vogel, eds., *Germany and the Second World War*, vol. 7, *The Strategic Air War in the West and East Asia, 1913–1944/5*, trans. ed. Derry Cook-Radmore (Oxford: Clarendon Press, 2006), 438.

5. Gregory P. Kennedy, *Vengeance Weapon 2: The V-2 Guided Missile* (Washington, DC: Smithsonian Institution Press, 1983), 76.

6. Steven J. Zaloga, *V-2 Ballistic Missile 1942–52* (Oxford: Osprey Publishing, 2003), 21.

7. Zaloga, 21.

8. John L. Chapman, *Atlas: The Story of a Missile* (New York: Harper, 1960), 26. Eric Burgess explains that the "V-2 was the first of the long-range ballistic missiles. It depended upon a large-thrust, liquid-propellant rocket engine to accelerate a payload of about one ton of the high-explosive Amatol to a speed of about 3,500 miles per hour. . . . The vehicle rose about 100 miles above the earth's surface before falling back along the downward leg of an elliptical trajectory to impact on a target about 200 miles from the launching point." Burgess, *Long-Range Ballistic Missiles* (New York: Macmillan, 1962), 6.

9. Arnold, quoted in Neufeld, *Development of Ballistic Missiles*, 35.

10. Part of a microfilmed collection of documents that were in the personal collection of General Henry H. Arnold, MICFILM 43804, IRIS #01102996, AFHRA.

11. E. Michael Del Papa and Sheldon A. Goldberg, *Strategic Air Command Missile Chronology, 1939–1973* (Offutt AFB: Office of the Historian, HQ

Strategic Air Command, 1990), unpaginated, [7]; and part of Arnold collection. Max Rosenberg reveals that General Arnold assigned overall management authority to the Air Communications Office. Rosenberg, *The Air Force and the National Guided Missile Program, 1944–1950* (Washington, DC: USAF Historical Division Liaison Office, 1964), 12.

12. Part of Arnold collection. For background on the JB-1, the JB-2, and the JB-10, see Neufeld, *Development of Ballistic Missiles*, 12–13.

13. For further information, see Annie Jacobsen, *Operation Paperclip: The Secret Intelligence Program that Brought Nazi Scientists to America* (New York: Little, Brown, 2014). See also "Early History of the Soviet Missile Program (1945–1953)," *Cryptologic Spectrum* 5, no. 3 (Summer 1975), Secret, NSA FOIA, accessed November 17, 2014, http://www2.gwu .edu/~nsarchiv/NSAEBB/NSAEBB278/17.PDF.

14. Lt. Gen. Joseph McNarney, Deputy Chief of Staff, to Commanding General, Army Air Forces, memo dated October 2, 1944, RG 341, HQ USAF DCS/O, Assistant for General Military, Box 408, "War Department General Military Policies," File 319.1, NARA-MD.

15. McNarney, memo October 2, 1944.

16. "First ICBM Order Went out in 1945," *Air Force Times*, December 7, 1957, M16; and Beard, *Developing the ICBM*, 50–51. *Encyclopedia Britannica* defines a turbojet engine as "a turbine engine that passes all the air through a combustion chamber." It further notes that the "turbojet is far simpler than a reciprocating engine of equivalent power, weighs less, is more reliable, requires less maintenance, and has a far greater potential for generating power." Accessed June 1, 2015, http://www.britannica.com/ EBchecked/topic/11014/airplane/64163/Jet-engines.

17. For a list of the forty-eight missile projects that were begun and "cancelled, terminated, or re-oriented" between June 1943 and December 1958, see H. R. Logan, Deputy Comptroller for Budget to the Undersecretary of the Navy, the Assistant Secretary of the Army (FM), and the Assistant Secretary of the Air Force (FM), memorandum dated November 5, 1959, and attachments, RG 340, A1 1F, Box 406, File 386-59 Guided Missiles (General), NARA-MD.

18. Memo from Brig. Gen. R. C. Coupland, AC/AS-4 to AC/AS-3, Guided Missiles Division, dated March 6, 1946, File "AAF GM Policy 1946," Box "A-7 Catapults," HQ USAF, DCS/D, GM Branch, NARA, as quoted in Beard, *Developing the ICBM*, 29.

19. Michael H. Gorn, *Harnessing the Genie: Science and Technology Forecasting for the Air Force, 1944–1986* (Washington D.C.: Office of Air Force History, 1988), 29.

20. Guyford Stever oral history, Call #K239.0512-1752, IRIS #01095219, AFHRA, 25.

21. President's Air Policy Commission, *Survival in the Air Age* (Washington, DC: U.S. Government Printing Office, 1948), 84.

22. Donald L. Putt, interview with James C. Hasdorff, April 1–3, 1974, Call #K239.0512-724, IRIS #01001024, 01001025, 01001026, 01001027, 01001028, 01001029, and 01001030, AFHRA, p. 150.

23. Beard, *Developing the ICBM*, 56, quoting a letter from General Chidlaw, Engineering, AMC, to Commanding General, Army Air Forces, attention AC/AS-4, dated May 12, 1947.

24. Memorandum for the Commanding General, Army Air Forces, from Gen. Thomas S. Power, Deputy Assistant Chief of Staff of Air Staff Operations, Commitments and Requirements, dated June 12, 1947, RG 341.10, File 319.1, Box 408, HQ USAF, DSC/O, Assistant for GM, NARA-MD.

25. Tate, *The Army and Its Air Corps*, 2–3. See also William Mitchell, *Winged Defense: The Development and Possibilities of Modern Airpower— Economic and Military* (New York: G. P. Putnam and Sons, 1925), viii. Mitchell was not alone in his remonstrations. Maj. Gen. Mason Patrick, chief of the Air Service in the 1920s, when testifying before the President's Aircraft Board, claimed the Army's leaders were hidebound Neanderthals who failed to recognize the potential of airpower. "United States President's Aircraft Board, Testimony of General M. M. Patrick, Maj. W. J. Hilner, Maj. T. G. Lamphier and others before Morrow Board," September 21, 1925, 53, Call #248.211-61V, IRIS #00159949, AFHRA.

26. Sherwood, *Officers in Flight Suits*, 51. While Sherwood writes primarily of fighter pilots, he states a common perception that "when the student pilot finally graduated from Advanced training, he gained more than the title of Air Force 'pilot,' he gained immeasurable status as well. Only he had the 'rated' title; all other officers were 'nonrated,' in other words, insignificant" (66).

27. "Army-Air Force Agreements: As to the Initial Implementation of the National Security Act of 1947," compiled by the Offices of the Deputy Chief of Staff and the Deputy Commander Army Air Forces, 11. This portion is in Section IV, Agreements on Organization, Mobilization and Training Functions, Combined Arms Research Library Digital Library, accessed March 5, 2014, https://server16040.contentdm.oclc.org/cdm4/ item_viewer.php?CISOROOT=/p4013coll11&CISOPTR=1974&CISOB OX=1&REC=5.

28. Del Papa and Goldberg, *Chronology*, [12–13]. See also Neufeld, *Development of Ballistic Missiles*, 17 and 53–56. Neufeld contends that, in

the first Joint Chiefs of Staff study, "although the JCS omitted to mention long-range surface-to-surface missiles, it was understood that, so long as the Air Force retained responsibility for strategic bombardment, it remained the logical user" (53).

29. Harry S. Truman, "Statement by the President on the Hydrogen Bomb," January 31, 1950, online at *The American Presidency Project*, ed. Gerhard Peters and John T. Woolley, accessed March 17, 2014, https://www.presidency.ucsb.edu/documents/statement-the-president-the-hydrogen-bomb.

30. A naturalized citizen born in Belgium in 1904, Bossart was the driving force behind the creation of the Atlas missile. He entered the United States in the late 1920s to conduct graduate work in aeronautics at the Massachusetts Institute of Technology. By 1945 he was the chief of structures at Convair, where he became intrigued by the possibilities of long-range missiles. He is credited with conceiving the pressurized fuel tank, which dramatically reduced the weight of the missiles, and the gimbaled rocket engines, which allowed the missile to maneuver while in flight. David N. Spires includes a full-page biography of Bossart in *On Alert*, 6.

31. *Encyclopedia Britannica* defines a ramjet engine as an "air-breathing jet engine that operates with no major moving parts. It relies on the craft's forward motion to draw in air and on a specially shaped intake passage to compress the air for combustion. After fuel sprayed into the engine has been ignited, combustion is self-sustaining. As in other jet engines, forward thrust is obtained as a reaction to the rearward rush of hot exhaust gases"; accessed June 2, 2015, http://www.britannica.com/EBchecked/topic/490671/ramjet.

32. Del Papa and Goldberg, *Chronology*, [13]. Joint Publication 1-02 defines the CEP as "the radius of a circle within which half of a missile's projectiles are expected to fall." Joint Publication 1-02, *DOD Dictionary of Military and Associated Terms*, 12 April 2001, as amended through 9 June 2004, p. 86. See also Donald MacKenzie, *Inventing Accuracy: A Historical Sociology of Nuclear Missile Guidance* (Cambridge, MA: MIT Press, 1993), 114.

33. Richard D. Curtin, interview with Neil Sheehan, June 16, 2000, 15–16, Box 15 of 21, Sheehan Papers (accession 23821), Manuscript Division, LOC. See also Neil Sheehan, notes from a telephone interview with Richard D. Curtin, August 5, 1957, Box 15 of 21, Sheehan Papers (accession 23821), Manuscript Division, LOC.

34. Curtin interview.
35. Gill Robb Wilson, "The Public View of the Air Force," *Air University Quarterly Review* 6, no. 4 (Winter 1953–54): 3.
36. Personal collection of Gen. Henry H. Arnold.
37. "The USAF Policy on Missile Development and Employment," attachment to Memorandum for Members of the Armed Forces Policy Council, November 26, 1956, Subject: Clarification of Roles and Missions to Improve the Effectiveness of Operation of the Department of Defense, an attachment to "AMC Participation in the AF Ballistic Missiles Program— Vol. II, Supporting Documents Nos. 1–64 (1953–1956) (Unclassified)," Call #K215.18 August 1954–December 1957 V.2, IRIS #0476795, AFHRA.
38. The reference to pilotless aircraft is from Jamie Wallace, interview with Neil Sheehan, notes from a phone interview on December 13, 1999, Box 4 of 21, Sheehan Papers (accession 23821), Manuscripts Division, LOC; and Neufeld, *Development of Ballistic Missiles*, 66–67.
39. Claude E. Putnam, "Missiles in Perspective," *Air University Quarterly Review* 10, no. 1 (Spring 1958): 10.
40. Irvine is quoted in "The USAF Reports to Congress: A Quarterly Review Staff Report," *Air University Quarterly Review* 10, no. 3 (Spring 1958): 39.
41. John Lonnquest, "The Face of Atlas: General Bernard Schriever and the Development of the Atlas Intercontinental Ballistic Missile, 1953–1960" (PhD diss., Duke University, Durham, NC, 1996), 41.
42. Harry C. Jordan, Memorandum: Notes transcribed from an interview conversation with Colonel Ray E. Soper, Vice Comdr Ballistic Systems Division, November 29, 1966, Call #K239.0512-783, IRIS #1000339, AFHRA.
43. Roy Ferguson, interview with Neil Sheehan, April 26, 2002, Box 15 of 21, Sheehan Papers (accession 23821), Manuscript Division, LOC. Ferguson retired from the Air Force as a lieutenant colonel.
44. Henry M. Narducci, ed., *SAC Missile Chronology, 1939–1988* (Offutt AFB, NE: Office of the Historian, Strategic Air Command, 1990).
45. John Sessums, interview with Edmund Beard, quoted in Beard, *Developing the ICBM*, 133.
46. Robert L. Perry, *The Ballistic Missile Decisions* (Santa Monica, CA: RAND, October 1967), p. 9 footnote; and Del Papa and Goldberg, *Chronology*, [13].

Chapter 3. Race to the Finish

1. Roswell Gilpatric, Undersecretary of the Air Force, to the New Secretary and Undersecretary of the Air Force, memo dated December 31, 1952, p. 12, RG 341, Box 12, folder 321.1, Organization and Policy, NARA-MD.

2. Roy Ferguson, interview with Neil Sheehan, April 26, 2002, 3–4, Box 15 of 21, Sheehan Papers (accession 23821), Manuscripts Division, LOC.

3. Ray Soper, interview with Neil Sheehan, September 10, 1997, Sheehan Papers (accession 23821), Manuscript Division, LOC.

4. Eugene Callahan, Colonel, USAF, to Samuel Brentnall, Major General, USAF, Subject: Guided Missile Policy, dated November 3, 1953, citing a January 1953 letter from Partridge to White, 1–2, RG 341, Air Force Office of Guided Missile (AFCGM) Records (accession 61A1643), Box 2, Folder "Organization—1953," NARA-MD.

5. "Month by Month: Highlights of the National Defense," *Ordnance* (May–June 1955); and *American Aviation Daily*, June 10, 1955, as cited in Richard M. Leighton, *Strategy, Money, and the New Look, 1953–1956*, vol. 3, *History of the Office of the Secretary of Defense* (Washington, DC: Historical Office, Office of the Secretary of Defense, 2012), 391. Gardner's position was equivalent to an assistant secretary of the Air Force; in fact, by 1955 the position was renamed assistant secretary of the Air Force for research and development, and Gardner was confirmed as such in August 1955.

6. Max Rosenberg, *Plans and Policies of the Ballistic Missile Initial Operational Capability Program* (Washington, DC: USAF Historical Division Liaison Office, 1960), 14, Call #K2624, IRIS #480640, AFHRA.

7. Harry Jordan Memorandum, November 29, 1966, 4, AFHRA; Soper interview with Sheehan, LOC.

8. Members of the committee were Dr. John von Neumann, Clark Millikan (aeronautics professor at Caltech), Charles Lauritsen (physics professor at Caltech), Louis Dunn (director of the Caltech jet propulsion lab), Hendrik Bode (director of mathematical research at Bell Labs), Allen Puckett (head of Hughes Aircraft's aerodynamics department of the Guided Missile Laboratory), George Kistiakowsky (chair of the National Academy of Science's Committee on Science, Engineering, and Public Policy), Jerome Wiesner (director of MIT's Research Laboratory of Electronics), Lawrence Hyland (vice president and general manager of Hughes Aircraft), and Simon Ramo and Dean Wooldridge, who had left Hughes Aircraft to start their own company, Ramo-Wooldridge, which would be closely associated with the Air Force's development of missiles.

9. "AMC Participation in the AF Ballistic Missiles Program through December 1957," vol. 1, Narrative, p. 4, Call #K215.18, IRIS #476794, in the USAF Collection, AFHRA.

10. "Recommendations of the Strategic Missiles Evaluation Committee," 2, attached to Charles M. McCorkle, Deputy Asst Chief of Staff for Guided Missiles, to Director of Air University, undated letter, Call #K168.15-75, IRIS #1027472, AFHRA. In an appendix to the report, Simon Ramo, the author, attributed the first quote to "Professor von Neumann" and admitted that it had not been coordinated with the other committee members due to a lack of time. See appendix A, Recommendations of the Strategic Missiles Evaluation Committee, attached to Simon Ramo to Trevor Gardner, letter dated February 10, 1954, included in Neufeld, *Development of Ballistic Missiles*, appendix 1, 262–65.

11. "Recommendations of the Strategic Missiles Evaluation Committee," 7–8.

12. Bruno Augenstein, *A Revised Program for Ballistic Missiles of Intercontinental Range* (Santa Monica, CA: RAND, 1954), accessed September 20, 2014, http://www.rand.org/pubs/special_memoranda/ SM21.html. For more information on the Von Neumann Committee using "the RAND report as source material for its own study," see Beard, *Developing the ICBM*, 142.

13. H. E. Talbott to General Twining, memo dated March 19, 1954, Subject: Acceleration of the Intercontinental Ballistic Missile Program, quoted in Beard, *Developing the ICBM*, 164–66.

14. "The Air Force Ballistic Missile and Space Program Chronological Highlights," February 5, 1960, 3, Bernard Schriever Papers, Box 87, Folder 6, Manuscripts Division, LOC. Beard, on page 168, quotes memorandum dated September 1955 from the assistant for programming, Weapon Systems Division, to Maj. Gen. Ben Funk, which states that the Air Force agreed "in order to prevent the establishment of another Manhattan Project."

15. Peter Stache, *Soviet Rockets*. Foreign Technology Division Translation. FTD-ID(RS)T-0619-88 (from unnamed source). Wright-Patterson AFB, Ohio. November 29, 1988. This is a translation of Peter Stache, *Sowjetischer Raketen* (Berlin: Militarverlad der DDR, 1987) as quoted in Siddiqi, *Challenge to Apollo*, 78.

16. Nikita Khrushchev, *Khrushchev Remembers*, ed. Strobe Talbott (Boston: Little, Brown, 1970), 45–46. Italics in original.

17. Khrushchev, 46.

18. Siddiqi, *Challenge to Apollo*, 132.

19. David M. Fleming, interview with Robert Mulcahy on April 5, 2001, 3, Call #K239.0512-2395, IRIS #01143416, AFHRA.

20. Anthony Krieg to Gen. Ben Funk, memorandum September 1955, Subject: SM-65 Missile (Atlas), attachment to "AMC Participation in the AF Ballistic Missiles Program," vol. 2, Supporting Documents Nos. 1–64 (1953–1956) (Unclassified), 1–2, Call #K215.18 August 1954–December 1957 v. 2, IRIS #0476795, AFHRA.

21. "The Air Force Ballistic Missile and Space Program Chronological Highlights," Schriever Papers, LOC.

22. Krieg to Funk, memorandum, AFHRA. Krieg's memorandum stated that the directive was written by the deputy chief of staff, matériel, but does not mention his name. Conversely, Neufeld, in *Development of Ballistic Missiles*, 107, claims that General Putt, the deputy chief of staff, development, authored the document. Edmund Beard, in *Developing the ICBM*, appears to take both sides of the issue, quoting Krieg's memo on page 168 and then declaring on page 171 that the decision was made by General Putt. Putt's support for the ballistic missile is well known, and his position would have placed him in an appropriate position to have written the guidance, but without further documentation, I have chosen not to take a side. Intriguingly, Krieg and Beard agree that the decision was made because the Air Staff was concerned about Gardner, but Neufeld, in *Development of Ballistic Missiles*, 104, concludes that Gardner "envisioned" and recommended the organization. All references indicate friction between Gardner and members of the Air Staff and it is likely that there was considerable maneuvering over the organization before someone finally made the decision.

23. Jamie Wallace, telephone interview with Neil Sheehan on December 13, 1999, Sheehan Papers (accession 23821), Manuscript Division, LOC.

24. "The Air Force Ballistic Missile and Space Program Chronological Highlights," February 5, 1960, p. 4, Bernard Schriever Papers, Box 87, Folder 6, Manuscripts Division, Library of Congress. The requirement for a second system appears to stem from disagreements between Gardner and Schriever with Convair over bringing in another company, Ramo-Wooldridge, run by a close friend of Gardner, to oversee the contract. For more information on the Gardner–Ramo relationship, see Beard, *Developing the ICBM*, 157–58.

25. Beard, *Developing the ICBM*, 170; "AMC Participation in the AF Ballistic Missiles Program," 1:10–12; and Converse, *Rearming for the Cold War*, 493.

26. "AMC Participation in the AF Ballistic Missiles Program," 1:175–80. For further information on the aircraft industry frustration with the process, see Neufeld, *Development of Ballistic Missiles*, 119. For more information on the Robertson Committee, see Neufeld, 136–37.

27. "AMC Participation in the AF Ballistic Missiles Program," 1:183–84.

28. "AMC Participation in the AF Ballistic Missiles Program," 1:184–85.

29. U.S. Army Aviation and Missile Life Cycle Management Command, "Redstone Missile," accessed January 1, 2015, https://history.redstone .army.mil/miss-redstone.html; and James Grimwood and Frances Strowd, *History of the Jupiter Missile System* (Redstone Arsenal, AL: History and Reports Control Branch, Management Services Office, U.S. Army Ordnance Missile Command, 1962), 2–3, accessed January 1, 2015, http://heroicrelics.org/info/jupiter/jupiter-hist/History%20of%20the %20Jupiter%20Missile%20System.pdf.

30. CONARC (Continental Army Command) to OCRD (Office of the Chief of Research and Development), memo dated April 2, 1955, Subject: Surface-to-Surface GM Requirements for Support of Corps and Larger Units, cited in Department of the Army (DA) Pamphlet 70-10, "*Chronological History of Army Activities in the Missile/Satellite Field, 1943–1958*," 38; and Grimwood and Strowd, *History of the Jupiter Missile System*, 4–6, 10.

31. For information on Lee DuBridge's recommendation, see Valerie L. Adams, *Eisenhower's Fine Group of Fellows: Crafting a National Security Policy to Uphold the Great Equation* (Lanham, MD: Rowman and Littlefield, 2006), 109.

32. "Brief of the Report to the President by the Technological Capabilities Panel of the Science Advisory Committee," February 14, 1955, accessed November 5, 2014, https://history.state.gov/historicaldocuments/frus 1955-57v19/d9.

33. Joint Committee on Atomic Energy, *Findings and Recommendations Concerning the Intercontinental Ballistic Missile*, June 30, 1955. White House Office, Office of the Staff Secretary, Box 4, Dwight D. Eisenhower Presidential Library, Abilene, Kansas (hereafter cited as Eisenhower Library).

34. Thomas R. Phillips, "The Growing Power of the Soviet Air Force," *Reporter* (June 30, 1955), 16.

35. Rosenberg, *Plans and Policies*, 15–18. For further information on the request to meet Eisenhower, see Arthur S. Flemming to Secretary Wilson, letter dated July 5, 1955, Subject: "Briefing on the Status of the ICBM Program," Special Assistant to the President for National Security Affairs, NSC Series, Briefing Notes, Box 13, Missiles and Space Programs, Eisenhower Library.

36. NSC Action No. 1433, accessed November 6, 2014, http://www.foia.cia .gov/sites/default/files/document_conversions/18/1960-08-19a.pdf. The Millikan Committee report gives the date that Eisenhower assigned "highest national priority" as September 8, 1955. It is likely that he verbally approved the prioritization on the eighth, signing the NSC action on the thirteenth. Final Report of the SECAF "Management Study Committee," dated January 29, 1960, Call #K243.012-57 V.10, IRIS# 00919678, AFHRA.

37. Harry Jordan memorandum, 4.

38. Converse, *Rearming for the Cold War,* 496; Ballistic Missile and Space Systems Panel, "Weapon Systems Management, The Decision-Making Process," December 19, 1959, Headquarters, United States Air Force, Washington, DC, 12, as cited in Donald Lepard, "Missiles, Men, and Management: Do USAF Policies and Directives Insure Adequately Trained Personnel to Maintain and Operate the Missile Force?" (master's thesis, Air War College, Maxwell AFB, 1963), 6.

39. "AMC Participation in the AF Ballistic Missiles Program," 1:12–13; see also Sheehan, *Fiery Peace,* 300–301.

40. "Recommendations of the Strategic Missiles Evaluation Committee," 3.

41. W. M. Holiday to Mr. Fred M. Dearborn Jr., memorandum dated October 29, 1957, Subject: Chronology of Significant Events in the U.S. Long Range Ballistic Missile Program, Harlow Records, Box 1, File: Missiles: Chronology of Long Range Ballistic Missiles (10-29-57) (2), Eisenhower Library.

42. Draft Memorandum of Understanding, dated December 6, 1955, as quoted in Neufeld, *Development of Ballistic Missiles,* 147.

43. Neufeld, 115.

44. CONARC, memo dated April 2, 1955, p. 38. See also Grimwood and Strowd, *History of the Jupiter Missile System,* 5–9 (quote on p. 6).

45. Grimwood and Strowd, *History of the Jupiter Missile System,* 5–9.

46. "AMC Participation in the AF Ballistic Missiles Program through December 1957 (Unclassified), Vol. 1—Narrative," 130, AFHRA. See also Neufeld, *Development of Ballistic Missiles,* 130, 145.

47. Thomas White, Vice Chief of Staff, to Commander, Air Research and Development Command, letter dated November 18, 1955, Subject: Priority of the ICBM and IRBM Programs, Supporting Document #314 to Call #K220.01 V.6, IRIS #477049, AFHRA. For more information, see untitled paper from SECAF to CSAF, Attn: Gen Brentnall, dated March 2, 1956, on the long-range ballistic missile program, File 471.6, Box 20 General Files 3340C—Country Files—Cuba 471.6, 1957, Top Secret Folder for Retirement by ISA/R&C, 44B, Entry UD-UP, RG 330, NARA-MD.

See also and Grimwood and Strowd, *History of the Jupiter Missile System*, 11–13; and Neufeld, *Development of Ballistic Missiles*, 146.

48. White to Commander, Air Research and Development Command, November 18, 1955, AFHRA.

49. NSC Action No. 1484, accessed November 6, 2014, http://www.foia .cia.gov/sites/default/files/document_conversions/18/1960-08-19a .pdf. See also Chief of Staff, USAF to Commander, ARDC, letter dated November 18, 1955 (appears to have been transmitted January 23, 1956), attached to Chief of Staff, USAF to the Deputy Chiefs of Staff, dated December 2, 1955, Subject: Responsibilities for ICBM and IRBM Programs, Call #K220.01 V.6, IRIS #477049, AFHRA; and Neufeld, *Development of Ballistic Missiles*, 151.

50. Quoted in "AMC Participation in the AF Ballistic Missiles Program," 1:13.

51. Leighton, *Strategy, Money and the New Look*, 16–17; see also unsigned Eisenhower memo to Secretary of Defense Wilson, dated December 21, 1955. Eisenhower Diary, Papers as President (Ann Whitman File), Eisenhower Library, quoted in Leighton, *Strategy, Money and the New Look*, 677; and NSC Action No. 1484. For information on the National Intelligence Estimate, see Peter Roman, *Eisenhower and the Missile Gap* (Ithaca, NY: Cornell University Press, 1995), 24.

52. NSC Action No. 1484.

53. Andreas Wenger, *Living with Peril: Eisenhower, Kennedy, and Nuclear Weapons* (Lanham, MD: Rowman and Littlefield, 1997), 152–53; and C. E. Wilson, Secretary of Defense, to the Secretary of the Army and Secretary of the Navy, Memorandum dated November 8, 1955, Subject: Management of the IRBM #2 Development Program, in appendix 2 of Neufeld, *Development of Ballistic Missiles*, 307.

54. Richard "Jake" Jacobson, interview with Neil Sheehan, April 20, 1997, Sheehan Papers (accession 23821), Manuscripts Division, LOC.

55. Air Force Instruction 38-101, "Air Force Organization," March 16, 2011, defines the organizational entities of the Air Force as follows: "Squadrons are the basic 'building block' organizations in the Air Force, providing a specific operational or support capability.... A squadron has a substantive mission of its own that warrants organization as a separate unit based on factors like unity of command, functional grouping and administrative control, balanced with efficient use of resources." A Group is the "level of command between wings and squadrons. Groups bring together multiple squadrons or other lower echelon units to provide a broader capability." The instruction also explains that "a wing is usually composed of a primary mission group (e.g., operations, training) and the necessary

supporting groups. By pulling together the mission and support elements, a wing provides a significant capability under a single commander."

56. Max Rosenberg, "USAF Ballistic Missiles, 1958–1959," USAF Historical Division Liaison Office, July 1960, Secret, Excised Copy, National Security Archives, accessed November 6, 2013, http://www2.gwu.edu/~nsarchiv/nukevault/ebb249/doc01.pdf, pp. 7–8; Neufeld, *Development of Ballistic Missiles*, 143; Air Force Instruction 38-101, "Air Force Organization," dated March 16, 2011, defines a wing as having "a distinct mission with significant scope. A wing is usually composed of a primary mission group (e.g., operations, training) and the necessary supporting groups. By pulling together the mission and support elements, a wing provides a significant capability under a single commander. . . . Wings will have a minimum adjusted population of at least 1000."

57. Ferguson, interview with Sheehan, April 26, 2002, LOC.

58. Neufeld, *Development of Ballistic Missiles*, 141–42. This latter concern remained a key Air Force concern for years. When pondering the impact of unmanned missiles and space vehicles, Leslie Bray Jr., in "The Role of the Rated Group in the Missile and Space Era" (master's thesis, Air War College, Montgomery, AL, 1959), 3, asks, "Is it likely that within a relatively short period of time, Military Air Transport Service will be all that will remain of the United States Air Force?" For information on Eisenhower's review of weapon systems, see Wenger, *Living with Peril*, 152–53.

59. Leighton, *Strategy, Money and the New Look*, 619–20. Neufeld, in *Development of Ballistic Missiles* (151), mentions two possible other reason for Gardner's resignation: "duplicative and competing missile programs in all of the military departments" and "disappointment at not being named the OSD Special Assistant for Guided Missiles."

60. Rosenberg, "USAF Ballistic Missiles," 7–8; and Neufeld, *Development of Ballistic Missiles*, 152.

61. Rosenberg, "USAF Ballistic Missiles," 8; and Neufeld, *Development of Ballistic Missiles*, 154–55.

62. Secretary of Defense to Members of the Armed Forces Policy Council, letter dated November 26, 1956, Subject: Clarification of Roles and Missions to Improve the Effectiveness of Operation of the Department of Defense, Supporting Document 336 to Call #K220.1 V. 6, IRIS #477049, AFHRA. See also A. G. Waggoner, Acting Director of Guided Missiles, Memorandum for the Secretary of the Army, Subject: Jupiter Program, File 1306-58, IRBM/ICBM Deployment of Squadrons and Units, Box 280, A1 1F, RG 340, NARA-MD; and "Wilson Gives USAF Lead Role For Missiles Development, Use," *Air Force Times* (December 1, 1956), 45.

Del Papa and Goldberg, *Strategic Air Command Missile Chronology*, [20], also reveals details of the decision.

63. Grimwood and Strowd, *History of the Jupiter Missile System*, 34–36; and Wenger, *Living with Peril*, 152–53.

64. Eisenhower, quoted in Rosenberg, "USAF Ballistic Missiles," 9. For more on the Bermuda Conference, see Matthew Elderfield, "Rebuilding the Special Relationship: The 1957 Bermuda Talks," *Cambridge Review of International Affairs* 3, no. 1 (1989): 14–24.

65. Neufeld, *Development of Ballistic Missiles*, 166.

66. William White, "Ike Letting Missiles Lag, Asserts Symington as Democrats Attack," *Atlanta Constitution*, February 11, 1956, 1. See also "Democrats Protest 'Secret' Budget Cut," *Dallas Morning News*, July 14, 1957, 3.

67. For information on the Republican party's response, see "Notes," Harlow Papers, Box 2, File: Missiles, Misc. Papers [1957–1968] (2), Eisenhower Library. Quote from Memorandum of NSC meeting, August 1, 1957, *Foreign Relations of the United States, 1955–1957*, 19:535–58, as cited in Wenger, *Living with Peril*, 152–53.

68. Chertok, *Rockets and People*, vol. 2, *Creating the Rocket Industry*, 289.

69. Saddiqi, *Challenge to Apollo*, 161.

70. "Report on Intercontinental Ballistic Missile" (English translation). Pravda. August 27, 1957, quoted in Saddiqi, *Challenge to Apollo*, 161.

71. Robert J. Watson, *History of the Office of the Secretary of Defense*, vol. 4, *Into the Missile Age, 1956–1960* (Washington, DC: Historical Office, Office of the Secretary of Defense, 1997), 123.

72. Saddiqi, *Challenge to Apollo*, 161.

73. "Soviet Fires Satellite into Space," *New York Times*, October 5, 1957, 1; and "Soviet Satellite Visible with Binoculars; Will Reflect Sun's Rays, Scientist Says," *New York Times*, October 5, 1957, 2.

74. C. D. Jackson to Mr. Luce (presumably Henry Luce, Jackson's former boss at *Time* magazine), memorandum dated October 8, 1957, C. D. Jackson Papers, Box 69, Log-1957 (4), NAID #12086487, Eisenhower Library, accessed November 19, 2014, https://www.eisenhowerlibrary .gov/sites/default/files/research/online-documents/sputnik/10-8-57 -memo.pdf. Sputnik II was launched November 3 and was significantly larger, approximately 1,120 pounds, and carried a dog. See "Sputnik II and Pioneer Rider," *Life*, November 18, 1957, 43.

75. Saddiqi, *Challenge to Apollo*, 129; and Steven J. Zaloga, *The Kremlin's Nuclear Sword: The Rise and Fall of Russia's Strategic Nuclear Forces, 1945–2000* (Washington, DC: Smithsonian Institution Press, 2002), 44.

76. Minutes, October 10, 1957, 339th Meeting of the National Security Council, AWF, National Security Council Series, Eisenhower Library, as quoted in Yanek Mieczkowski, *Eisenhower's Sputnik Moment: The Race for Space and World Prestige* (Ithaca, NY: Cornell University Press, 2013), 59.

77. "Sputnik May Spur U.S. Research," *Seattle Daily Times* (October 20, 1957), 16; and "The U.S., Ike, and Sputnik," *Newsweek*, October 28, 1957, 30.

78. "Senate Quiz on Missiles Opens Today: Defense Hearings Start with Teller as First Witness," *Washington Post and Times Herald*, November 25, 1957, A1.

79. Albert Riley, "Russell, Johnson to Call Hearings on Missiles Lag," *Atlanta Constitution*, November 6, 1957, 1; and "Stage Set for Missile Inquiries: to Probe Absence of Real War Plan," *Atlanta Constitution*, November 23, 1957, 1.

80. Mieczkowski, *Eisenhower's Sputnik Moment*, 114.

81. Security Resources Panel of the Science Advisory Committee, "Deterrence and Survival in the Nuclear Age," November 7, 1957, 6, 14, 20, 26, Special Assistant to the President for National Security Affairs, National Security Council Series, Policy Papers Sub-Series, Box 22, National Security Council Files 5724 (2), Eisenhower Library, accessed November 20, 2014, http://www2.gwu.edu/~nsarchiv/NSAEBB/NSAEBB139/nitze02.pdf.

82. Chalmers Roberts, "Enormous Arms Outlay Is Held Vital to Survival," *Washington Post*, December 20, 1957, 1, 19. The story continues on page 19 under the title "U.S. in Gravest Danger, Gaither Report Holds." For Eisenhower's decision not to release the classified information, see Mieczkowski, *Eisenhower's Sputnik Moment*, 116.

83. David Snead, "Eisenhower and the Gaither Report: The Influence of a Committee of Experts on National Security Policy in the Late 1950s" (PhD dissertation, University of Virginia, 1997), 212; Memorandum of Discussion at the 363rd Meeting of the NSC, April 24, 1958, 2, Folder: 363rd Meeting of NSC, April 24, 1958, Box 10, National Security Council Series, Dwight David Eisenhower Papers, Eisenhower Library; and "Aerospace Talk 2—Minuteman" notes, Call #K416.861-4 1964–1966, IRIS #00502558, AFHRA.

84. For details of the Vanguard failure, see Mieczkowski, *Eisenhower's Sputnik Moment*, 116. For the successful launch of the Atlas, see Chapman, *Atlas*, 132–33; Sheehan, *Fiery Peace*, 399; and Schwiebert, *History of the U.S. Air Force Ballistic Missiles*, 222. Although the Thor had been successfully launched on September 20, 1957, the launch was not significant because it was an IRBM rather than an ICBM.

85. Periodic History of the Air Force Missile Test Center, July 1, 1958–December 31, 1958, Call #K241.01 V.1, IRIS #00484484, AFHRA, xiii and 170. See also "ICBM Fired Successfully," *Air Force Times* (December 6, 1958), 14. The message was on an endless loop by short-wave radio that played for thirty-four days from an onboard tape recorder.

86. Jacobson to Sheehan, notes from an interview on April 20, 1997, Sheehan Papers, LOC.

Chapter 4. Making the Missile Operational

1. Thomas McGehee, "The Case for a Separate USAF Guided Missiles Command" (master's thesis, Air War College, Montgomery, AL, 1955), 17.

2. Noel T. Cumbaa, "Training and Training Facilities for Strategic Missile Forces" (master's thesis, Air War College, Maxwell AFB, AL, 1958), 3. See also John B. Hudson, "The ICBM Race" (research paper, National War College, 1960), 1, who contends: "To say that the U.S. was shocked is a gross understatement. The overall psychological impact was such that it was probably a pleasant surprise to the people in the Kremlin who never for a moment lose sight of their political and psychological objectives." Both Cumbaa and Hudson were colonels in the U.S. Air Force when they authored their studies.

3. Taylor's attitude reflected the concepts of flexible response that he later refined in his book *The Uncertain Trumpet* (New York: Harper, 1959), as he discusses in chapter 5, note 5.

4. Malcom A. MacIntyre, interview by George M. Watson Jr. on September 26, 1983, USAF Oral History Program, MacIntyre, Malcolm, Box 1, File Air Force Oral History 1985, Eisenhower Presidential Library, Abilene, Kansas, 12. According to his military assistant, Eisenhower had considered taking the ballistic missile out of the military altogether and creating another Manhattan Project–like organization because of the earlier interservice rivalry. See Andrew Goodpaster, "Memorandum of a Conference with the President: October 8, 1957," in *Foreign Relations of the United States, 1955–1957,* vol. 14 (Washington, DC: U.S. Government Printing Office, 1990), 613.

5. Max Rosenberg, *Plans and Policies for the Ballistic Missile Initial Operational Capability Program* (USAF Historical Division Liaison Office, February 1960), 93, Call #K2624, IRIS #480640, AFHRA. Although many attribute this decision to the desperate need to have an operational mission (see beginning of chapter 4), Maurice "Cris" Cristadoro believed there was a more sinister motive, claiming that "ARDC [Air Research and Development Command] was to run the operational aspects of missiles

until LeMay decided he wanted to control them—when Schriever started to get into the target assignments." Maurice Cristadoro, interview with Neil Sheehan, Box 15 of 21, Sheehan Papers (accession 23821), Manuscripts Division, LOC. Cristadoro, who served under Schriever as the program director for Atlas, remained focused on engineering and development until his retirement from the Air Force as a brigadier general on February 1, 1970.

6. John Bohn, *Unclassified History of SAC from 1946–1971* (Offutt AFB, NE: Office of the Historian, Strategic Air Command, 1972), 77, Call #K4318, IRIS #502339, AFHRA.

7. Gary Alkire, interview with the author on January 28, 2015. Alkire continued serving in the Air Force for thirty-three years, retiring in 1990 as a major general.

8. Bellis is quoted in Sheehan, *Fiery Peace*, 407. Bellis rose through the ranks to become a lieutenant general, serving in both research and development and leadership positions, including command of the Electronic Systems Division. He entered the Air Force in 1946 and retired in 1981 as the vice commander in chief of U.S. Air Forces in Europe.

9. William Large, interview with Neil Sheehan, May 26, 1998, Box 14 of 21, Sheehan Papers (accession 23821), Manuscripts Division, LOC. Large became the first wing commander of the 706th Strategic Missile Wing.

10. Donald Glantz, email to the author, May 2, 2014. Staff Sergeant Glantz served as a missile guidance technician in the 576th Strategic Missile Squadron until he left the Air Force after his six-year enlistment.

11. For information on placing IRBM wings in Europe, North Africa, or Asia, see Donald Quarles, Memorandum for the Secretary of Defense, Subject: Air Force Requirements for Intermediate Range Ballistic Missile (IRBM) Bases in the U.K., Box 3, A1 1F, RG 340, NARA-MD.

12. For more information on the decision to use Elmendorf as an alternate location, see W. M. Holaday, Director of Guided Missiles, Memorandum for the Secretary of the Air Force, Subject: Future Deployments of the JUPITER IRBM Squadrons, dated May 9, 1958; and Charles McCorkle, Maj Gen, Assistant Chief of Staff for Guided Missiles, Coordination Sheet Subject: IRBM Deployment Site in Alaska, dated June 17, 1958, both located in File 1306-58, IRBM/ICBM Deployment of Squadrons and Units, Box 280, A1 1F, RG 340, NARA-MD. For more information on the deals with Italy and Turkey, see Grimwood and Strowd, *History of the Jupiter Missile System*, 93–104.

13. Quoted in Richard H. Kohn and Joseph P. Harahan, eds., *Strategic Air Warfare: An Interview with Generals Curtis E. LeMay, Leon W. Johnson,*

David A. Burchinal, and Jack J. Catton (Washington, DC: Office of Air Force History, U.S. Air Force, 1988), 102–3. During the time in question, Burchinal served as chief of staff for the 8th Air Force; deputy director of operations on the joint staff, and deputy director, then director of plans for the Air Staff. Leon Johnson, who was awarded the Medal of Honor during World War II, was the air deputy to the Supreme Allied Commander Europe. LeMay was commander in chief of Strategic Air Command, then vice chief of staff of the Air Force. Jack Catton served as chief of staff for 8th Air Force, commander of the 817th Air Division, and then commander of the 822nd Air Division. "The Big Hanger," *Air Force Times* (April 19, 1958), 8.

14. Benjamin Bellis, interview with David C. Ladd, January 10–11, 1985, 64, Call #K239.0152-1629 CY. 1, IRIS #01070943, AFHRA.

15. Richard "Jake" Jacobson, interview #4 with Neil Sheehan, April 20, 1997, Box 14 of 21, Sheehan Papers (accession 23821), Manuscripts Division, LOC. After working for Schriever, Jacobson continued his career with the Air Force, retiring at the rank of colonel.

16. McGehee, "The Case for a Separate USAF Guided Missiles Command," 24. See also "Missiliers [*sic*] Trained Concurrently with Development of the Weapon," *Air Force Times* (December 8, 1962), 26.

17. Converse, *Rearming for the Cold War*, 171, 233.

18. Bellis interview, 90.

19. Harry Goldsworthy, "ICBM Site Activation," *Aerospace Historian* 29, no. 3 (Fall, September 1982), 160. Goldsworthy's comments have additional credibility as he was not a historian but one of the original Site Activation Task Force commanders. He served for thirty-three years before retiring as a lieutenant general from the position of Air Force deputy chief of staff for systems and logistics.

20. Bellis interview, 90–91.

21. Bellis interview, 91.

22. Bellis interview, 92.

23. Bellis interview, 93.

24. Bellis interview, 93. See also "ICBMs Held Least Tested of All Top U.S. Weapons," *Air Force Times* (May 15, 1963), 3.

25. In terms dealing with nuclear weapons, a missile on alert refers to a missile armed with a nuclear warhead that is prepared for launch upon valid orders from the national command authority (the president).

26. Allen Stephens, "Missilemen—Present and Future," *Air University Quarterly Review* 10, no. 3 (Spring 1958): 16. The article was incorporated as chapter 6 of Gantz, ed., *The United States Air Force Report on the*

Ballistic Missile, 99–108. The Ferguson and Glasser quotes are from Baar and Howard, *Combat Missileman*, 37. Glasser was a lieutenant colonel or colonel at the time of the conversation.

27. Baar and Howard, *Combat Missileman*, 55.

28. Stephens, "Missilemen—Present and Future," 16; and Glasser, quoted in Baar and Howard, *Combat Missileman*, 37.

29. Gen. Thomas Power, unclassified message, 301500Z ZFF6, "For all missile combat crews," in the personal collection of John M. Kiereck, Rochester, New York. Airman Kiereck served as an electrical power production technician in the 550th Strategic Missile Squadron in Schilling AFB, Kansas, from April 1961 to July 1964 and obtained the message while on missile duty.

30. Power message.

31. William Rader, letter to Lieutenant General Archie Olds, September 18, 1959, attachment to 706th Strategic Missile Wing Program Progress Report for the month of November 1959, Vol. 2, Call No. K-WG-706-HI V. 2, IRIS #0459767, AFHRC.

32. "Missile 'Handful of Men' Myth Hit," *Air Force Times* (September 7, 1957), 1, 12; and Baar and Howard, *Combat Missileman*, 57–58.

33. William Anderson, "Organizing and Manning Ballistic Missile Units," *Air University Quarterly Review* 9, no. 3 (Summer 1957): 81, 85. Anderson served as the deputy director of personnel, 1st Missile Division. The article was incorporated as chapter 4 of Gantz, ed., *Report on the Ballistic Missile*, 81–90. In "Fewer Mistakes Now in Picking Missilemen," *Air Force Times* (September 18, 1963), 24, the Air Force acknowledged that "pilots used to going places and doing things found it hard to adjust to the relatively stable life of the missile crew."

34. In his second article on the topic (see note 32 for the first article), William Anderson strongly recommended the use of transitioning rated personnel through missiles and back to the cockpit to give pilots and navigators experience. Anderson, "Officers and Missiles," *Air University Quarterly Review* 10, no. 3 (Spring 1958): 73–81. He contended on page 78 that such a transitional force would provide future staff officers with a knowledge of missiles without creating "a fissured officer corps. This could be doubly unfortunate, since interim missile developments may be quite uncharacteristic of the future." He did acknowledge, on page 77, that "actual missile operation does not require a rated officer" but believed it "essential to consider the role of the rated officer above the crew level of missile operations." Howard Tarleton, a navigator for seven years before entering missiles, recalled in an email to the author

on October 17, 2014, that "when I entered the missile force in 1963, we had very little expectation of remaining in the missile force as most of us were there to receive our MBAs." Military exercises and inspections are methods the military uses to practice its planned operations for combat. Rader, letter to Olds, September 18, 1959, AFHRC.

35. Jerome Martin, Command historian, USSTRATCOM, phone call to the author, December 12, 2014. The information was based upon historical Strategic Air Command meeting minutes in the USSTRATCOM archives. See also Baar and Howard, *Combat Missileman*, 58.

36. Robert Kelchner, email to the author dated January 19, 2015. Chief Master Sergeant Kelchner, who served in the missile field from 1962 to 1980, began his missile career working on a targeting and alignment field team.

37. Personal accounts from missile combat crew members include Leon Hojegian, interview with the author, October 15, 2014; Ronald J. Bishop Jr., letter to the author, April 1, 2014; and Robert Wycoff, interview with the author, October 17, 2014. Hojegian served four years as a lieutenant working with the Atlas missiles in Plattsburgh AFB, New York, in the early 1960s. He left the service after his stint in missiles, believing he had no chance at promotion because he was not a flyer. Bishop, who entered missiles in 1958, retired in 1982 after serving as the commander of the 308th Strategic Missile Wing at Little Rock AFB, Arkansas. Wycoff's story is particularly interesting as he received his bachelor's degree in English, but the Air Force shortened the designator to "ENG" on his personnel records, which the personnel officers took to mean engineering. He was mistakenly selected as a missileer and when the Air Force discovered their mistake, they let him continue to the assignment.

38. Tarleton, email to the author, October 17, 2014. Tarleton served as a deputy missile combat crew commander.

39. Hojegian, interview with the author, October 15, 2014.

40. In addition to Anderson's article "Officers and Missiles," several Air Force officers produced Air University theses on the topic. Some of these include Bray, "The Role of the Rated Group in the Missile and Space Era"; Roger G. Conant, "The Use of Rated Officers in the Minuteman Missile System" (research study no. 0295-70, Air University, Maxwell AFB, AL, 1970); David E. Freeman, "An Analysis of the Need for Rated Officers in Missile Operations" (research study no. 0505-70, Air University, Maxwell AFB, AL, 1970); and John Bacs, "Missile Unit Commanders: Rated Versus Nonrated Officers" (master's thesis, Air Command and Staff College, Maxwell AFB, AL, 1972). Designating missiles a "rated" field is not as unlikely as it may seem. Lawrence Spinetta, in an email to the

author, March 7, 2015, acknowledged that the Air Force later designated unmanned aerial vehicles as a rated field, requiring pilots to operate them. Spinetta entered the Air Force in 1993 and has worked with unmanned aerial vehicle units since 2008, first commanding a Predator squadron and later commanding the 69th Reconnaissance Group.

41. Floyd Wikstrom, email to author, May 26, 2014. Colonel Wikstrom was the first commander of the 90th Strategic Missile Wing, responsible for Minuteman missiles. He commanded the unit from 1963 to 1965.

42. William R. Brooksher and Jimmy F. Scott, "A Study of the Intercontinental Ballistic Missile Operations Career Field" (master's thesis, National War College, Washington, DC, 1973), 61. Brooksher and Scott's findings are supported by the "United States Air Force Statistical Digest," table 121, which revealed that nonrated general officers were extremely rare. The older digests have been digitized and can be found at https://www.afhistory.af.mil/USAF-STATISTICS/.

43. These enlisted missileers include Frank Dlugas, Joe Andrew, and Bruce Raleigh.

44. The U.S. serviceman held a second launch key to ensure the British did not launch without the approval of the United States, but Bill Young, a squadron leader in command of the missile launch pads in Shepherd's Grove, Sussex, contended that the British quickly discovered that they could launch the missile without the second key. Young, "Silent Sentinals," *Fly Past*, no. 225 (April 2000), 36. Therefore, the SAC personnel assigned with the Thor squadrons really never held any value except to soothe national pride.

45. Jerry Page, "Tooling Up for the Ballistic Missiles Training Program," *Air University Quarterly Review* 10, no. 4 (Winter 1958–59): 17. When he wrote the article, General Page was the deputy chief of staff, plans and operations, Headquarters Air Training Command, and, as such, was also the project officer for ballistic missiles training.

46. Merriman's unnamed instructor is quoted in Baar and Howard, *Combat Missileman*, 62.

47. James L. Brewer, *Mules, Missiles and Men: An Autobiography* (Grant, AL: Brewco, 1988), 347–48.

48. Brewer, 348–49. To provide a better understanding of the magnitude of the effort required, Brig. Gen. Jerry Page documented that "223 separate courses must be conducted for these three [Atlas, Titan, and Thor] weapon systems alone." See Page, "Tooling Up," 16.

49. Page, 354–55.

50. Page, 359.

51. Lawrence Hasbrouck, email to the author, May 21, 2014.

52. Grimwood and Stroud, *History of the Jupiter Missile System*, 87, 91–92. See also Office of the Assistant to the Secretary of Defense (Atomic Energy), *History of the Custody and Deployment of Nuclear Weapons (U) July 1945 through September 1977*, February 1978, http://nautilus.org/wp -content/uploads/2015/04/306.pdf, p. 74.

53. Glantz, email to the author, May 2, 2014. Because the technical orders were written before the missiles were finalized, they were incomplete and, in many cases, incorrect.

54. Bishop, letter to the author, April 1, 2014. Bishop served as a maintenance officer on early Bomarc missiles and aeronautical missiles, and then as a missile combat crew commander at Whiteman AFB, Missouri. He retired as a colonel after commanding the Titan missile wing at Little Rock AFB.

55. William Kurtz and Blanche Johnson, "The History of the 706th Strategic Missile Wing (ICBM-Atlas), Francis E. Warren AFB, Wyoming, June 1958," Call #K-WG-706-HI, IRIS #00459751, in the USAF Collection, AFHRA, pp. 8–9. The fourth additional missile was required because it was assumed at one of every ten Atlas missiles would be undergoing maintenance at any time. In a 2002 interview, Lt. Col. Roy Ferguson, who designed the missile configuration, admitted that his decision to base the missiles in a two by three configuration was "purely arbitrary" but was designed that way so that the missileers could launch the missiles in fifteen minutes. By placing two guidance systems back to back, each could launch a missile every five minutes, and they could provide a backup to the other. Roy Ferguson, interview with Neil Sheehan, April 26, 2002, 12–14, Box 15 of 21, Sheehan Papers (accession 23821), Manuscripts Division, LOC.

56. Charles McCorkle, "Command and Control of Ballistic Missiles," *Air University Quarterly Review* 9, no. 3 (Summer 1957): 74–76. McCorkle's article was incorporated as chapter 3 of Gantz, ed., *Report on the Ballistic Missile*, 71–80.

57. William Kurtz and Blanche Johnson, "The History of the 706th Strategic Missile Wing (ICBM-Atlas) and 389th Air Base Group, July through September 1958," 2, Call #K-WG-706-HI V. 1, IRIS #00459752, AFHRA.

58. Baar and Howard, *Combat Missilemen*, 131–32. In a March 15, 1961, briefing to Congress, Gen. Thomas Gerritty, Commander, Ballistic Systems Division, remarked on "the rapid evolution of the ATLAS configuration. The first squadron is a 3 by 2, radio inertial guidance, and two additional squadrons with 3 by 3, radio guidance, but the primary force, three squadrons, coffin configuration, 25 p.s.i. hardened, and

six squadrons of the silo configuration. . . . These are the highlights of development milestones for 1961." Secret transcript [excised portions restored], "Missile Procurement, Air Force," 522, Item #NH00728, Digital National Security Archives. See also Convair (Astronautics) Division, General Dynamics Corporation, *Atlas Base Activation*, 7. This pamphlet is from the personal collection of Charles Simpson, executive director of the Association of Air Force Missileers.

59. Goldsworthy, "ICBM Site Activation," 159.
60. Jim Widlar, telephone interview with the author, January 30, 2015.
61. Goldsworthy, 155–57. Goldsworthy, one of the SATAF commanders himself, observed that all of the SATAF commanders were "pilots who had spent their careers with combat aircraft units. They were entering alien territory, and their immediate reaction was one of bewilderment over the magnitude and complexity of the job." See also "AMC Picks Missile Site Commanders," *Air Force Times*, August 6, 1960, 18.
62. LeMay quoted in Kohn and Harahan, *Strategic Air Warfare*, 101–2.
63. Concerns with the bombers are discussed in Peter J. Roman, "American Strategic Nuclear Force Planning, 1957–1960: The Interaction of Politics and Military Planning" (PhD dissertation, University of Wisconsin–Madison, 1989), 249 and 312. For Kistiakowsky's concern, see George Kistiakowsky to Eisenhower, memorandum dated February 12, 1960, Subject: Problems of the B-70 Project, Folder: Kistiakowsky (2), Administration series, ACW file, Eisenhower Library.
64. Andrew Goodpaster, Memorandum of Conference with the President, November 18, 1959, Augusta, Papers as President of the United States, 1953–1961 (Ann Whitman File), DDE Diaries, Box 45, Staff Notes, November 1959 (2), Eisenhower Presidential Library.

Chapter 5. An International Crisis Foments Change

1. John F. Kennedy, "Speech to Wood County, West Virginia Democratic Committee" as quoted in the *Parkersburg Sentinel*, October 10, 1958, accessed February 16, 2015 at *West Virginia Division of Culture and History*, West Virginia Archives and History, Battleground West Virginia: Electing the President in 1960, http://www.wvculture.org/history/1960pr esidentialcampaign/newspapers/19581010parkersburgsentinel.html.
2. Kennedy.
3. "Democratic Party Platform of 1960," July 11, 1960, accessed February 18, 2015 at *The American Presidency Project*, ed. Gerhard Peters and John T. Woolley, https://www.presidency.ucsb.edu/documents/1960-democratic -party-platform.

4. The Air Force designed the proposed B-70 bomber to fly at Mach 3 for short distances and to cruise at altitudes of over 70,000 feet so that it could overcome the Soviet Union's new antiaircraft defenses, but it was plagued by many problems. See Peter Roman, "Strategic Bombers over the Missile Horizon, 1957–1963," *Journal of Strategic Studies* 18, no. 1 (March 1995), 204. The Polaris missile was a two-stage solid fueled missile designed by the Navy to be fired from a submarine. The missile provided a protected second-strike capability, deterring attacks by remaining a hidden target, prepared to launch a follow-on attack if needed.

5. Flexible Response was a direct reaction to Eisenhower's "New Look" approach. Kennedy believed that Eisenhower's budget-conscious military options forced him into an all-or-nothing stance, so he devised Flexible Response to provide flexibility in nuclear responses and an increased conventional capability to deal with threats that did not require a nuclear response. However, Francis J. Gavin argued that the two strategies were much closer than the rhetoric would suggest. Gavin, "The Myth of Flexible Response: American Strategy in Europe during the 1960s," *International History Review* 23, no. 4 (December 2001), 847–75. The name of the strategy came from Taylor, *Uncertain Trumpet*, 6, where Taylor remarked, "The strategic doctrine which I propose to replace Massive Retaliation is called herein the Strategy of Flexible Response." He then explained that "this name suggests the need for a capability to react across the entire spectrum of possible challenge, for coping with anything from general atomic war to infiltrations and aggressions such as threaten Laos and Berlin in 1959."

6. Dwight Eisenhower, "Annual Message to the Congress on the State of the Union, January 9, 1959," accessed February 17, 2015, https://www .eisenhowerlibrary.gov/sites/default/files/file/1959_state_of_the_union .pdf.

7. After Kennedy revealed that the missile gap did not exist, Rep. Frank Osmers Jr. (R-N.J.) condemned Kennedy, saying that "the Eisenhower administration had been derelict in permitting a missile gap to develop between Russia and the United States . . . was probably the greatest single factor in his winning the election by a few thousand votes." U.S. Congress, House, *Congressional Record*, March 21, 1962, 4701. Kennedy appears to have believed the topic was important to the election as well because he warned in his inaugural address that "we dare not tempt [the nations who would make themselves our adversary] with weakness. For only when our arms are sufficient beyond doubt can we be certain beyond doubt that they will never be employed." John Fitzgerald Kennedy, "Inaugural

Address," January 20, 1961, *American Presidency Project*, accessed June 18, 2015, at https://www.presidency.ucsb.edu/documents/inaugural -address-2.

8. During this time, each missile could carry one nuclear warhead. There was also a Snark missile wing with thirty aeronautic intercontinental missiles that could carry a nuclear warhead 6,325 miles, although one of Kennedy's first actions related to defense was to "immediate[ly] phase out . . . the subsonic Snark . . . , which is now considered obsolete and of marginal military value." John F. Kennedy, "Special Message to the Congress on the Defense Budget. March 28, 1961," *Public Papers of the Presidents of the United States: John F. Kennedy. Containing the Public Messages, Speeches, and Statements of the President January 10 to December 31, 1961* (Washington, D.C.: U.S. Government Printing Office, 1962), 238. The mobile Minuteman missiles would not be placed in a silo but would be transported around the country by train, making them harder to locate and destroy. Numbers for the American intercontinental missiles, including the Snark, were found in J. C. Hopkins and Sheldon Goldberg, *The Development of the Strategic Air Command, 1946–1986* (Offutt AFB, NE: Office of the Historian, HQ, Strategic Air Command, 1986), 89, 94. The number of Thors and Jupiters is discussed in Philip Nash, *The Other Missiles of October: Eisenhower, Kennedy, and the Jupiters, 1957–1963* (Chapel Hill: University of North Carolina Press, 1997), 68. Zaloga, *The Kremlin's Nuclear Sword*, 64, provides the number of Soviet missiles for comparison. However, no one in the United States was aware of the Soviet capability number at the time.

9. Robert McNamara, *In Retrospect: The Tragedy and Lessons of Vietnam*, with Brian VanDeMark (New York: Random House, 1995), 20.

10. Desmond Ball, *Politics and Force Structure: The Strategic Missile Program of the Kennedy Administration* (Berkeley: University of California Press, 1980), 34–38.

11. McNamara, *In Retrospect*, 20. Jack Raymond's "Memo from Jack Raymond on the McNamara backgrounder" reveals that, in response to a question on the missile gap, McNamara replied, "We should not talk about missile gaps, but destruction gap[s]. 'There's no missile gap.' Wait a minute, a reporter said, the missile gap is a reference to the numbers of missiles we have compared with the number they could have produced. . . . 'There's no missile gap today even in the narrow sense of the term,' Mr. McNamara said." For Raymond's published article, see Jack Raymond, "Kennedy Defense Study Finds No Evidence of a 'Missile Gap,'" *New York Times*, February 7, 1961, 1, 21. For more on the interview that led to Raymond's story, see Christopher A. Preble, *Kennedy and the Missile*

Gap (DeKalb, IL: Northern Illinois University Press, 2004), 154–59. Although Preble admits that McGeorge Bundy and Adam Yarmolinsky both "claimed that Kennedy was not seriously upset by the gaffe," Preble argues that "Kennedy allegedly blasted McNamara over the phone." In a phone call with the author, Preble explained that his argument is based on Richard Reeves' biography, *President Kennedy: Profile of Power* (New York: Simon and Schuster, 1993), 58–59, and from Raymond's notes of a later conversation. In these notes, Raymond alludes to a hostile reaction when he later "suggested that Mr. McNamara be shown the President's recommendation of renewed backgrounders, and a public relations man observed, 'Listen, when your eyes are bloody, it's a little hard to see the flowers on your desk.'"

12. John F. Kennedy, "Annual Message to the Congress on the State of the Union," January 30, 1961, *Public Papers of the Presidents: John F. Kennedy: Containing the Public Messages, Speeches, and Statements of the President* (Washington, DC: Government Printing Office, 1962–64), 25. However, Jerome Wiesner, Kennedy's science advisor, informed historian Gregg Herken in a February 1982 interview that he had briefed Kennedy that there was no missile gap in early February. For further information on the Wiesner and McNamara interviews, see Preble, *Kennedy and the Missile Gap*, 153–54, 157, 215–16.

13. U.S. Congress, House, Committee on Appropriations, *Hearings on Department of Defense Appropriation for 1962*, 87th Congress, 1st Session, part 3, April 7, 1961, 59–60. However, McNamara told Christopher Preble in an April 10, 2003, interview that it was obvious that there was no missile gap in early February 1961.

14. Kennedy, "Special Message to the Congress on the Defense Budget," March 28, 1961, in *Public Papers of the Presidents*, 238. See also Ball, *Politics and Force Levels*, 122–23. Kaplan and colleagues contend that the money saved from the last two Titan squadrons could pay for "approximately 100 Minuteman missiles dispersed and hardened." Lawrence Kaplan, Ronald Landa, and Edward Drea, *The McNamara Ascendancy, 1961–1965*, vol. V, *History of the Office of the Secretary of Defense* (Washington, DC: Historical Office, Office of the Secretary of Defense, 2006), 59. The production of the Polaris missiles and associated submarines was later speeded up and some were ready by the Cuban Missile Crisis.

15. Following the Allied victory over Germany, the United States, France, England, and the Soviet Union jointly occupied the defeated nation, including the capital, Berlin. They divided the nation up into occupation zones with England, France, and the United States planning for the nation

to be reunified after resolving the concerns caused by the war. However, the Soviet Union, which controlled the section containing Berlin, wanted to retain control of the section it occupied indefinitely, either leaving the nation divided or dominating the entire country after the other Allies left. The occupied city of Berlin infuriated the Soviets because it allowed the other nations access to the eastern portion of the country and because it allowed the Germans from the eastern section to escape to the west as conditions worsened in the east.

16. Roswell Gilpatric, "Address before the Business Council at the Homestead, Hot Springs, Virginia," Press Release, October 21, 1961, *Digital National Security Archives*, Collection: Berlin Crisis, Item #BC02573 and #CC00115, accessed February 20, 2015, http://nsarchive.chadwyck.com.

17. During the Eisenhower administration, the CIA had devised a plan to help anti-Castro Cubans invade Cuba with the goal of overthrowing Castro and creating a government friendly to the United States. After his election, Kennedy authorized the plan, but several factors not only ensured that the invasion was a complete failure but also embarrassed the new Kennedy administration and the United States. Recalling the event, Khrushchev revealed, "We had to think up some way of confronting America with more than words. We had to establish a tangible and effective deterrent to American interference in the Caribbean. But what exactly? The logical answer was missiles." Khrushchev, *Khrushchev Remembers*, 493. Khrushchev tied the U.S. threats to Cuba with his threats to Berlin. Charles S. Sampson, ed., *Foreign Relations of the United States, 1961–1963*, vol. 6, *Kennedy-Khrushchev Exchanges* (Washington, DC: Government Printing Office, 1996), Document 56, "Message from Chairman Khrushchev to President Kennedy," 159. John Lewis Gaddis provides an alternate interpretation of events, arguing in *The Cold War* (75) that the real reason for the deployment was "to spread revolution throughout Latin America."

18. Robert Kipp, Lynn Peake, and Herman Wolk, *Strategic Air Command Operations in the Cuban Missile Crisis of 1962* (Historical Study No. 90), vol. 1 (Offutt AFB, NE: HQ, Strategic Air Command, 1963), 1, 7, 11. This study noted that "during the crisis a member of the SAC historical staff was on duty in the operations war room 24 hours a day, seven days a week. There he was able to follow events through the displays, briefings, informal discussions with battle staff personnel, and by examination of hundreds of messages which flowed in and out of the combat reports center. On a daily basis he was responsible for compiling a chronology of events for the Chief of Staff." Although much of volume 1, the narrative history,

has been declassified through Freedom of Information Act requests, the volumes containing the original documentation behind the narrative remain classified. For more information on the Soviets' placement of the missiles and the responding U.S. intelligence collection, see Lawrence Freedman, *Kennedy's Wars: Berlin, Cuba, Laos, and Vietnam* (New York: Oxford University Press, 2000), 169.

19. Declassified CIA map in "The World on the Brink: John F. Kennedy and the Cuban Missile Crisis," John F. Kennedy Presidential Library and Museum, accessed May 30, 2015, http://microsites.jfklibrary.org/cmc/oct16/. Nikita Khrushchev stated that "we had installed enough missiles already to destroy New York, Chicago, and the other huge industrial cities, not to mention a little village like Washington." Khrushchev, *Khrushchev Remembers*, 496.

20. For further information on the crisis, see Dobbs, *One Minute to Midnight*; and Coleman, *The Fourteenth Day*. Although both provide astonishing details of the crisis, neither deals with the actions of the missileers during the crisis.

21. Curtis LeMay to Maxwell Taylor, letter dated October 22, 1962, Subject: Additional Decisions, Taylor File, Box 6, October 1962, *Digital National Security Archives*, accessed February 20, 2015, http://www2.gwu.edu/~nsarchiv/NSAEBB/NSAEBB397/docs/doc%206%2010-22-62%20LeMay%20memo%20on%20SAC%20readiness.pdf. According to van Dijk and colleagues,

> The "DEFense CONdition" (DEFCON) alert system of the United States was formulated by the U.S. Joint Chiefs of Staff . . . at the height of the Cold War in November 1959 and is used to coordinate the readiness level of U.S. military and intelligence forces. . . . The DEFCON system is a series of gradated alert levels designed to harmonize the response of the U.S. to a variety of threats. There are five levels starting with DEFCON 5, the lowest level of alert, to DEFCON 1, the highest level of alert. While the DEFCON system has been raised as high as DEFCON 2 (during the Cuban Missile Crisis), it has never been raised to DEFCON 1, despite being in existence during periods of incredibly high military tension both during and after the Cold War.

Ruud van Dijk, William Glenn Gray, Svetlana Savranskaya, Jeremi Suri, and Qiang Zhai, eds., *Encyclopedia of the Cold War* (New York: Routledge, 2008), 237.

22. Simpson quoted in David Bath, ed., *Air Force Missileers and the Cuban Missile Crisis: A Collection of Personal Reminiscences from Missileers and*

Others Who Experienced the Cuban Missile Crisis of 1962 (Breckenridge, CO: Association of Air Force Missileers, 2012), 7, 88–89.

23. Kelchner quoted in Bath, 64.

24. Bath, 64. The targeting team was a three-man team that loaded the classified targeting information into nuclear missiles. The teams consisted of a missile systems analyst certified in electronics, a missile mechanic certified in the mechanical workings of the missile, and a junior officer required to control the classified targeting material. The classified targeting tapes were the best technology at the time to place the targeting data into the early computers that were on the missiles. Gary Hoselton, in an email to the author dated November 14, 2014, explained that "targets came on reels of punched mylar tape, which was read into the Univac Athena guidance computer and then stored in a safe." Anytime the crews carried this targeting material, they were required to carry weapons to protect the critical targeting data. Since Vandenberg AFB was primarily a training base by this time, the crews were used to working with training missiles that would be launched into the Pacific Ocean without a live nuclear warhead. This time, however, the missileers worked with a live "reentry vehicle" containing a nuclear warhead and "real" guidance and control data targeting a location on the potential enemy's soil rather than a designated location in the Pacific. Hoselton worked with the Titan I missile at Mountain Home AFB, Idaho, from 1962 to 1965.

25. Stanley quoted in Bath, *Air Force Missileers*, 90–91.

26. Bath, 76.

27. Kenderes quoted in Bath, 66–67. The missile field refers to the large area that contains all of the missiles and launch control centers for a single wing. It often covers hundreds of miles and is away from the supporting Air Force base.

28. Kipp, Peake, and Wolk, *Strategic Air Command Operations*, 62.

29. Kipp, Peake, and Wolk, 97.

30. McLaughlin quoted in Bath, ed., *Air Force Missileers*, 74.

31. Patrick Spellman, email to author dated November 20, 2014.

32. Morgan quoted in Bath, ed., *Air Force Missileers*, 78.

33. Gordon quoted in Bath, 44.

34. Power's announcement is quoted in Bath, 8. Kipp and colleagues provide even greater clarity, documenting that SAC ordered missileers "to deviate from normal technical data procedures in bringing ICBMs to rapid readiness configuration. Units would not check out systems or verify readiness, except when needed for personnel or equipment safety." This guidance "was rescinded three days later," mainly "because

of safety considerations." Kipp, Peake, and Wolk, *Strategic Air Command Operations*, 63.

35. Kipp, Peake, and Wolk, *Strategic Air Command Operations*, 64–66.

36. Bath, ed., *Air Force Missileers*, 84.

37. Ed Gill provides more information on the process of reorienting the missiles. Gill quoted in Bath, 40.

38. Rodolfo Armenta quoted in Bath, 16–17.

39. Bath, 16–17. Wyatt Earp is an American gunslinger and lawman best known for a gunfight at the O.K. Corral in Tombstone, Arizona, in 1881. The allusion along with the term "notches on his gun" are meant to suggest that the lieutenant may have been more willing to shoot the two technicians than Armenta would have liked.

40. Melvin Driskill, email to author, February 8, 2015. The official history, Kipp, Peake, and Wolk, *Strategic Air Command Operations*, contends that there were only two missiles originally, with twenty-two combat-ready crews (including the crews that were granted waivers) to operate the missiles on October 22. (The history does not address the number of crews that did not require a waiver.) However, on October 28, the squadron had seven ICBMs and only twenty-three crews, a significant increase in responsibility.

41. Melvin Driskill, email to author, February 8, 2015.

42. Combat-ready crews were fully trained and certified to work on and launch the missiles. According to the official history, the instructor crew was not used for "normal alert tours" but was used "as needed to cover maintenance problems," which the waivered crews were not allowed to do, and to provide training to the untrained crews. The four combat-ready crews returned to their normal duty stations on November 18, after the height of the crisis, but the instructor crew did not return to Vandenberg AFB "until relaxation of DEFCON 2." Kipp, Peake, and Wolk, *Strategic Air Command Operations*, 74–75.

43. Information from Sam Goodwin in Bath, *Air Force Missileers*, 42. Goodwin was a captain during the Cuban Missile Crisis. He retired from the Air Force as a colonel.

44. Christopher S. Adams, *Ideologies in Conflict: A Cold War Docu-Story* (Bloomington, IN: iUniverse, 2001), 427.

45. The evaluation process is discussed in Kipp, Peake, and Wolk, *Strategic Air Command Operations*, 74. For Goodwin's account, see Bath, *Air Force Missileers*, 42. He mentioned that his "crew was the first to be combat ready in the 12th SMS."

46. Liquid oxygen mixed with RP-1, or Rocket Propellant-1, provided the thrust to send the rockets to their designated targets.

47. Kipp, Peake, and Wolk, *Strategic Air Command Operations*, 64. The history specifically names the three field petroleum offices in St. Louis, Missouri; Houston, Texas; and Maywood, California; as well as the Middletown Air Matériel Area logistics facility in Pennsylvania as organizations that helped provide the liquid oxygen.

48. For the numbers of missiles, see Kipp, Peake, and Wolk, *Strategic Air Command Operations*, 66. For the contents of the Khrushchev letter, see "Letter from Chairman Khrushchev to President Kennedy, October 28, 1962," in "The World on the Brink: John F. Kennedy and the Cuban Missile Crisis," John F. Kennedy Presidential Library and Museum Reading List, October 28, 1962, accessed February 25, 2015, http://microsites.jfkli brary.org/cmc/oct28/doc1.html.

49. Kipp, Peake, and Wolk, *Strategic Air Command Operations*, 66, 71, 58. Information on the Navy submarines is from Robert S. Norris, "The Cuban Missile Crisis: A Nuclear Order of Battle October/November 1962." https://www.wilsoncenter.org/sites/default/files/2012_10_24_ Norris_Cuban_Missile_Crisis_Nuclear_Order_of_Battle.pdf.

50. Coleman, *The Fourteenth Day*, 167, 165–66. See also John F. Kennedy, *Kennedy Presidential Press Conferences* (New York: Earl M. Coleman Enterprises, 1965), 401–2.

51. The sources do not agree on the date that the command returned to DEFCON 4. Joseph Angell contends it occurred three days after November 21, making it November 24. Joseph W. Angell Jr., ed., *The Air Force Response to the Cuban Missile Crisis* (Redacted) (Washington, DC: USAF Historical Division Liaison Office, 1963), 11. But Kipp and colleagues assert that it was on November 27 (Kipp et al., *Strategic Air Command Operations*), 71. Charlie Simpson (in Bath, *Air Force Missileers*, 89) provides a plausible explanation for the difference, noting that command leadership "was concerned that if they let us all off for a long holiday weekend, they might lose a few of us in auto accidents" so retained the higher alert level until after the weekend was over.

52. Kipp, Peake, and Wolk, *Strategic Air Command Operations*, 77, 71, 62.

53. Doug Turner, email to author, November 21, 2014.

54. Jim Peck, interview with the author, March 3, 2015. Peck entered the Air Force in 1951 and retired in 1979 as a colonel.

55. LeMay and Zuckert quoted in Senate Hearings before the Subcommittee on DoD and the Committee on Armed Services, 88th Congress, 2nd session, *DoD Appropriations, 1965*, pt. 1, 307, 753–54, 722.

Although LeMay's memoirs and biographies are mostly silent about missiles, Thomas Coffey reveals a second LeMay quote that is similar to that in the text. When asked if he approved of any program reducing manned bombers, LeMay responded, "I think it is fair to say, however, that for some time to come, the bulk of the combat potential is in the manned system rather than in the missile system. . . . [The missiles] are not as good as we were hoping for." Coffey, *Iron Eagle: The Turbulent Life of General Curtis LeMay* (New York: Crown, 1986), 358–59.

56. Roger Hilsman, *The Cuban Missile Crisis: The Struggle Over Policy* (Westport, CT: Praeger, 1996), 151–52. Hilsman revealed that, in the aftermath of the Cuban Missile Crisis, "what President Kennedy really wanted was to use the crisis as a stepping-stone to a lessening of tensions in the world and a detente with the Soviet Union" (137). Hilsman postulated further, "Quite clearly, he was already thinking of what became his great American University speech that proposed a nuclear test ban treaty— which he hoped would be only the first step toward worldwide nuclear disarmament" (137).

57. Eisenhower quoted in Andrew Goodpaster, "Memorandum of Conference with the President," November 18, 1959—Augusta, Papers as President of the United States, 1953–1961 (Ann Whitman File), DDE Diaries, Box 45, Staff Notes, Nov. 1959 (2), Eisenhower Presidential Library. See also Lawrence Freedman, *The Evolution of Nuclear Strategy* (New York: St. Martin's Press, 1981), 230.

58. Hollywood Independent Citizens' Committee of the Arts, Sciences and Professions, "Statement of the Federation of Atomic Scientists," 1945, Published Papers and Official Documents, Linus Pauling and the International Peace Movement, accessed June 25, 2015, http://scarc.library .oregonstate.edu/coll/pauling/peace/papers/peace4.012.7-statement .html.

59. Nina Tannenwald, *The Nuclear Taboo: The United States and the Non-Use of Nuclear Weapons Since 1945* (New York: Cambridge University Press, 2007), 181–82. Her figures come from Thomas Graham, *American Public Opinion on NATO, Extended Deterrence and the Use of Nuclear Weapons: Future Fission?* CSIA Occasional Paper No. 4 (Center for Science and International Affairs, Harvard University, 1989), 70.

60. Daniel Ellsberg, *Secrets: A Memoir of Vietnam and the Pentagon Papers* (New York: Penguin, 2002), 57–60. Ellsberg acknowledged that the 1961 conversation had no impact on U.S. nuclear policy and even admits that "after we left McNamara's office, Adam [Yarmolinksy, McNamara's

assistant] took me into his small adjoining room and said, 'You must tell no one outside this room what Secretary McNamara has told you.'" (60).

61. Lawrence Wittner, *Resisting the Bomb: A History of the World Nuclear Disarmament Movement, 1954–1970* (Stanford, CA: Stanford University Press, 1997), 359.

62. Schlesinger quoted in Wittner, 377.

63. Kennedy, "Special Message to the Congress on the Defense Budget," March 28, 1961, in *Public Papers of the Presidents*, 232. Admittedly, Kennedy was no advocate of nuclear war. Just a month and a half earlier, he argued, "Now, if someone thinks we should have a nuclear war in order to win [against the Soviets], I can inform them that there will not be winners in the next nuclear war, if there is one, and this country and other countries will suffer heavy blows." Kennedy, "The President's News Conference of February 14, 1962," in *Public Papers of the Presidents*, 141.

64. U.S. Congress, Senate, Committee on Armed Services, *Congressional Record*, August 9, 1962, Citation: HRG-1962-SAS-0020, 4. Maxwell Taylor had served as Army chief of staff under President Eisenhower. However, he disagreed with Eisenhower's reliance on nuclear weapons and retired, authoring a book that aligned closely with Kennedy's thoughts on defense. Therefore, after the Bay of Pigs invasion of Cuba failed, Kennedy asked Taylor to determine what happened. During this time, Kennedy and Taylor became friends. Kennedy recalled Taylor to active duty to serve as his military representative, then appointed Taylor as chairman of the Joint Chiefs of Staff.

65. The address is printed in Robert McNamara, "Defense Arrangements of the North Atlantic Community," *Department of State Bulletin* 47, no. 1202 (July 9, 1962): 67.

66. Nitze quote from Paul Nitze, *From Hiroshima to Glasnost: At the Center of Decision*, with Ann Smith and Steven Reardon (New York City: Grove Weidenfeld, 1989), 248. Nitze helped draft the Gaither report, which criticized Eisenhower for allowing a "missile gap." He then advised Kennedy on national security affairs during the 1960 presidential campaign. Following Kennedy's election, Nitze became the assistant secretary of defense for international security affairs.

67. McNamara, "Defense Arrangements of the North Atlantic Community," 64–69. See also Freedman, "The First Two Generations of Nuclear Strategists," 767. For a detailed discussion of McNamara's counterforce strategy, see Gerard H. Clarfield and William M. Wiecek, *Nuclear America: Military and Civilian Nuclear Power in the United States, 1940–1980* (New York: Harper and Row, 1984), 245–54. The Kennedy administration asked

SIOP 63 planners to provide "a broad spectrum of attack options which the President may elect to execute in a careful, deliberate, controlled attack, presumably allowing for pauses to negotiate with the enemy for terms on which to end the war." *History of the Directorate of Plans, Deputy Chief of Staff, Plans and Programs, HQ USAF*, vol. 22, 1 July 1961–31 December 1961, 117, Item #CC 00127, Digital National Security Archives.

68. David Ormsby-Gore, Lord Harlech, in recorded interview by Jean Stein, April 30, 1970, 11, Stein Papers, as quoted in Arthur M. Schlesinger, *Robert Kennedy and His Times* (Boston: Houghton Mifflin, 1978), 530. Lord Harlech became friends with John Kennedy when Kennedy was a student at the London School of Economics and Kennedy's father, Joseph, served as the American ambassador to Great Britain. Aware of the close relationship, the British prime minister named Ormsby-Gore the British ambassador to the United States in 1961.

69. McNamara quoted in Gregg Herken, *Counsels of War* (New York: Knopf, 1985), 167.

70. Hilsman, *The Cuban Missile Crisis*, 151–52.

71. Clark Clifford, *Counsel to the President: A Memoir*, with Richard Holbrooke (New York: Random House, 1991), 380. Clifford first served in government as a naval aide to President Harry Truman. After guiding Truman's reelection, Clifford was named general counsel to the president. In this position, he helped author the National Security Act. During the Eisenhower administration, Clifford advised Stuart Symington and John Kennedy. When Kennedy was elected, Clifford acted as Kennedy's liaison with the Eisenhower administration and then served on Kennedy's Foreign Intelligence Advisory Board.

72. Clifford, 380.

73. McGeorge Bundy, *Danger and Survival: Choices about the Bomb in the First Fifty Years* (New York: Random House, 1988), 462. Bundy, who considered himself a Republican, grew disillusioned with Richard Nixon, so he supported Kennedy during the 1960 election campaign. He was appointed special assistant to the president for national security.

74. Henry Rowan, "The Evolution of Strategic Doctrine," in *Strategic Thought in the Nuclear Age*, ed. Lawrence Martin (Baltimore: Johns Hopkins University Press, 1979), 135. Clarfield and Wiecek use the interview between McNamara and journalist Stewart Alsop to "suggest that dramatic changes were taking place inside the Department of Defense. For more than a year, McNamara and his aides had devoted themselves to developing the capability to wage nuclear warfare. But the events of 1962 had forced them to reconsider their purposes." Clarfield and Wiecek, *Nuclear America*, 257.

75. Robert McNamara, *Blundering into Disaster: Surviving the First Century of the Nuclear Age* (New York: Pantheon Books, 1986), 139. See also Robert McNamara, "The Military Role of Nuclear Weapons: Perceptions and Misperceptions," *Foreign Affairs* 62, no. 1 (Fall 1983), 79. See also McNamara's quote in Errol Morris' film, *The Fog of War*: "The major lesson of the Cuban missile crisis is this: the indefinite combination of human fallibility and nuclear weapons will destroy nations. Is it right and proper that today there are 7500 strategic offensive nuclear weapons, of which 2500 are on 15 minute alert, to be launched by the decision of one human being?" Transcript accessed April 15, 2015, at http://www.errolmorris.com/film/fow_transcript.html.

76. Nitze, *From Hiroshima to Glasnost*, 249.

77. Wenger, *Living with Peril*, 311.

78. McNamara, *Blundering into Disaster*, 46–47.

79. Robert McNamara, "Mutual Deterrence Speech," San Francisco, September 18, 1967, accessed March 3, 2015, http://astro.temple.edu/~rimmerma/mutual_deterrence.htm.

80. Arnold Wolfers, "The Atomic Bomb in Soviet-American Relations," in *The Absolute Weapon: Atomic Power and World Order*, ed. Bernard Brodie (New York: Harcourt, Brace, 1946), 134–35.

81. Bernard Brodie, "Implications for Military Policy," in *The Absolute Weapon: Atomic Power and World Order*, ed. Bernard Brodie (New York: Harcourt, Brace, 1946), 74.

82. Clarfield and Wiecek, *Nuclear America*, 259–60.

83. Khrushchev quoted in Wittner, *Resisting the Bomb*, 416.

84. Snell Putney and Russell Middleton, "Some Factors Associated with Student Acceptance or Rejection of War," *American Sociological Review* 27 (October 1, 1962), 658, table 1.

85. Alice George, *Awaiting Armageddon: How Americans Faced the Cuban Missile Crisis* (Chapel Hill: University of North Carolina Press, 2003), 5.

86. USAIPO1963 0668, taken in February 1963, revealed the concerns about nuclear war, while USAIPO1964 0695, taken in July 1964, revealed the responses to the most important problem facing the country today. USIISR1964 633POS, taken in September 1964, revealed responses to Russia's willingness to launch a nuclear war. According to a Gallup poll, 52 percent disagreed while 19 percent said they did not know. Gallup poll details from the Roper Center, http://www.ropercenter.uconn.edu. See also Tom W. Smith, "Trends: The Cuban Missile Crisis and U.S. Public Opinion," *Public Opinion Quarterly* 67, no. 2 (Summer 2003), 268.

87. Lyndon Johnson, "Remarks in Seattle on the Control of Nuclear Weapons," *The American Presidency Project*, accessed April 7, 2015, https://www.presidency.ucsb.edu/documents/remarks-seattle-the-control-nuclear-weapons.
88. Bundy, *Danger and Survival*, 538.
89. Nina Tannenwald, "Nuclear Weapons and the Vietnam War," *Journal of Strategic Studies* 29, no. 4 (August 2006), 675–77.

Chapter 6. Freefall

1. Arguably, the Jupiter missiles should not be included in this discussion as they were traded away during the Cuban Missile Crisis. Freedman, in *Kennedy's Wars* (222), contends that Kennedy wanted to remove the obsolete missiles prior to the crisis but had been prevented by Turkish resistance. Numerous Kennedy officials testify to this as well, including McNamara, *In Retrospect*, 97; Ted Sorensen, *Counselor: A Life at the Edge of History* (New York: HarperCollins, 2008), 302; Nitze, *From Hiroshima to Glasnost*, 219–20; and Hilsman, *The Cuban Missile Crisis*, 129–30. McGeorge Bundy makes the argument that not even President Dwight Eisenhower wanted the Jupiter missiles in Turkey, but that he too was pressured by NATO concerns. Bundy, *Danger and Survival*, 428. For a more detailed understanding of the background of the trade, see Barton Bernstein, "The Cuban Missile Crisis: Trading the Jupiters in Turkey?" *Political Science Quarterly* 95, no. 1 (Spring 1980): 98.
2. Charles Donnelly, Document 155, "Compilation of Material Relating to U.S. Defense Policies in 1962," in 88th Congress, 1st Session (January 9–December 30, 1963), *House Documents*, vol. 3, *Miscellaneous* (Washington, DC: U.S. Government Printing Office, 1963–64), 30.
3. *Congressional Record*, Committee on Armed Services, House of Representatives, "Hearings on Military Posture and H.R. 2440, to authorize appropriations during Fiscal Year 1964, for Procurement, Research, Development, Test, and Evaluation of Aircraft, Missiles, and Navy Vessels for the Armed Forces, and for other purposes," January 30, 1963, HRG-1963-ASH-0009, 282.
4. L. Parker Temple III and Peter L. Portanova, "Project Emily and Thor IRBM Readiness in the United Kingdom, 1955–1960," *Air Power History* 56, no. 3 (Fall 2009): 45, table 1; and *Statistical Abstract of the United States, 1968* (Washington, DC: U.S. Department of Commerce, Bureau of the Census, 1968), 255, table 370.
5. Although unknown to almost everyone in the nation at the time, including many members of the Kennedy administration, the removal of the Jupiter

missiles in Turkey were also part of a quid pro quo to remove the Soviet missiles in Cuba. Gaddis, *The Cold War*, 78.

6. *Congressional Record*, Senate Committee on Armed Services, *Military Procurement Authorization FY64*, February 21, 1963, HRG-1963-SAS-0002, 313. Herbert York, a contemporary American physicist who worked on the Manhattan Project, contended that the Jupiter should never have been built. Herbert York, *Race to Oblivion: A Participant's View of the Arms Race* (New York: Simon and Schuster, 1970), 99–101. At the time (1963–64), nothing was said about Khrushchev's request to remove the missiles in Cuba in exchange for removing the missiles in Turkey or Kennedy's agreement to remove the Jupiters after the Cuban Missile Crisis was over. Even as late as 2008, senior Kennedy aides such as Ted Sorensen continued to downplay the agreement. See Sorensen, *Counselor*, 302–4. Intriguingly, LeMay, in his book *America Is in Danger*, contended that he "did not accept the explanation that the missiles had become obsolete so quickly, nor did any other military man [he knew]." Curtis LeMay and Dale Smith, *America Is in Danger* (New York: Funk and Wagnalls, 1968), 140.

7. Charlie Simpson, "LOX and RP-1—Fire Waiting to Happen," *AAFM [Association of Air Force Missileers]* 14, no. 3 (September 2006): 1–6.

8. During the retrofit, the Air Force incorporated many new technologies and parts that were not available when the missiles were first built in order to improve efficiency, reliability, and safety. George M. Watson Jr. reveals that "early Atlas missiles had an 18 percent reliability factor." Watson, *The Office of the Secretary of the Air Force, 1947–1965* (Washington, DC: Center for Air Force History, 1993), 198.

9. The Minuteman missiles' explosive capability was much smaller than either the Atlas or the Titan I missiles that they replaced. According to the Nuclear Weapon Archive (nuclearweaponarchive.org), the total of explosive yield in U.S. nuclear weapons has *dropped* since its height in 1960, when it was estimated at 20,491 megatons. Congress had authorized 800 Minuteman missiles by 1963, and the 1964 budget (created in 1962) had authorized another 150 Minuteman missiles. The missiles being added to the Air Force in 1963 and 1964 were authorized well before this time. At the same time that McNamara disposed of the Atlas and Titan missiles, he *reduced* the proposed Minuteman force from 1,200 to 1,000. Thus, the temporary continued growth in numbers of ballistic missiles should not be taken as a sign that McNamara's perspective on nuclear conflict had not changed after the Cuban Missile Crisis.

10. Bernard C. Nalty, *USAF Ballistic Missile Programs, 1962–1964*, U.S. Air Force Historical Division Liaison Office, April 1966, Top Secret, Excised Copy, National Security Archives, accessed November 6, 2013, http://www2.gwu.edu/~nsarchiv/nukevault/ebb249/doc03.pdf, 29; John Arnold, "A Revised Training and Evaluation Program for SAC Minuteman Missile Combat Crew Members" (Research study, Air Command and Staff College, Maxwell AFB, AL, 1971), 14; John Finney, "Less For Defense: Four-Year Expansion of Military Services Is Leveling Off," *New York Times*, January 26, 1965, A1; and Neufeld, *The Development of Ballistic Missiles*, 237–38. See also "SAC Will Bear Brunt of Defense Cutbacks," *Air Force Times* (December 2, 1964), A22.

11. "Operation 'High Train' Disclosed, 5000 Missile Men Transferred," *Air Force Times* (July 21, 1965), 7; and History extract, Strategic Air Command History, January–June 1964, 430–37, per Donald Koser, Air Force Global Strike Command historian. The history remains classified Top Secret.

12. Tannenwald, *Nuclear Taboo*, 206–7. In a September 7, 1964, speech, Johnson proclaimed, "For 19 peril-filled years no nation has loosed the atom against another. To do so now is a political decision of the highest order. And it would lead us down an uncertain path of blows and counterblows whose outcome none may know. No President of the United States can divest himself of the responsibility for such a decision." Lyndon Johnson, "Remarks in Cadillac Square, Detroit," *Public Papers of the Presidents: Lyndon B. Johnson, 1963–64*, vol. 1 (Washington, DC: Government Printing Office, 1965).

13. Harry Williams, "ICBM Career Management: The Impact of Advancement" (master's thesis, Air Command and Staff College, 1972), 46; and Vance O. Mitchell, *Air Force Officers: Personnel Policy Development, 1944–1974* (Washington, DC, Air Force History and Museums Program, 1996), 242–43, 247–48. (The Air Force records do not show how many were transferred from missiles.)

14. Mitchell, *Air Force Officers*, 249; see also Williams, "ICBM Career Management," 46.

15. Donovan Bowe, "Retention of Junior Officers in the Minuteman Missile Crew Force" (research report no. 3722, Air University, Maxwell AFB, AL, 1969), 9–10, 38. See also Spires, *On Alert*, 83.

16. Anderson, "Organizing and Manning Missile Units," 85. Anderson was the director of personnel for the 1st Strategic Air Division in 1957.

17. Arthur Engell, "The Morale of the Missileer: A Study of the Minuteman Launch Control Officer" (master's thesis, Air Command and Staff College, Maxwell AFB, AL, 1964), 2.

18. Pierce Smith, "Motivation of Minuteman Missile Crews" (master's thesis, Air Command and Staff College, Maxwell AFB, AL, 1965), 5.

19. Thomas Gilkeson, "Missile Crewmember—His Needs and Job Satisfaction" (master's thesis, Air Command and Staff College, Maxwell AFB, AL, 1972), 13.

20. Smith, "Motivation of Minuteman Missile Crews," 18.

21. Donald Sherman, "Boredom and Monotony: Their Effect on Titan II Crew Morale" (research study no. 1136-69, Air Command and Staff College, Maxwell AFB, AL, 1969), 30–31.

22. Williams, "ICBM Career Management," 19, quotes Air Force Technical Order 21M-LGM25C-1 "Model LGM-25C Missile Weapon System Operations" (Washington, DC: Department of the Air Force, 1967), 7-1.

23. Sherman, "Boredom and Monotony," 30–31.

24. Colonel Henney is quoted in Murray Morgan, "The Loneliness of the Missile Attendant," *Esquire*, July 1964, 50.

25. Baar and Howard, *Combat Missileman*, 165. See also Kenneth Holden, "A Study of Motivational Behavior of Missile Combat Crews" (master's thesis, Air Command and Staff College, Maxwell AFB, AL, 1966), 22. Captain Holden cited Harold W. Dietz, *Human Problems in Missile Launching* (Vandenberg AFB, CA: 392nd Aerospace Medical Group), 1963, reporting that 20 percent of missileers suffered from "stress" diseases, although this author has been unable to obtain a copy of Dietz's study.

26. Conant, "Use of Rated Officers," 6; Robert S. Luckett, "People Problems in the SAC Missile Force and What Is Being Done to Correct These Problems" (master's thesis, Air Command and Staff College, Maxwell AFB, AL, 1972), 34; and Holden, "A Study of Motivational Behavior," 95. Holden reviewed official RCS:10-T12 Reports from 1962–64 to determine the unit manning strength.

27. Bowe, "Retention of Junior Officers," 3; and E. S. Ewart, "A Survey of Potential Morale, Motivation, and Retention Problems at Ballistic Missile Sites" (Wright-Patterson AFB, OH: Air Research and Development Command, 1958); copy found at AFHRA. Spires revealed that "in May 1971, . . . questionnaires from 625 captains and lieutenants assigned to missile duty at five bases revealed that the same irritants present when the Atlas and Titan I first went on alert continued to trouble missile officers a decade later." Spires, *On Alert*, 81–82.

28. Robert Rodwell, "Morale in a Missile Force," *Aeronautics* 38, no. 1 (March 1958), 66.

29. Rodwell, 66. See also Spires, *On Alert*, 82, 124–25.

30. Hopkins and Goldberg, *The Development of Strategic Air Command*, 96. Joseph Andrew, email to author dated October 20, 2014. Airman Andrew entered the missile career field, and the Air Force, in 1959 and served as a launch crew member with the Matador missiles before transitioning into Minuteman missile maintenance in 1962.

31. John Richard McCone, "The Manned Bomber and the Ballistic Missile: Problems of Strategy and Politics" (master's thesis, University of Pittsburgh, 1962), 42; Extract from Annual Report of the Secretary of the Air Force, July 1, 1962, to June 30, 1963, 246–47, Item #CC03198, Digital National Security Archives; and Melvin Deaile, "The SAC Mentality: The Origins of Organizational Culture in Strategic Air Command, 1946–1962" (PhD dissertation, University of North Carolina at Chapel Hill, 2007), 296–97.

32. Joseph Andrew, email to author dated October 20, 2014.

33. Mike Worden, *Rise of the Fighter Generals: The Problem of Air Force Leadership, 1945–1982* (Maxwell AFB, AL: Air University Press, 1998), 125. Air Force Instruction 38-101, "Air Force Organization," March 16, 2011, defines a wing as having "a distinct mission with significant scope. A wing is usually composed of a primary mission group (e.g., operations, training) and the necessary supporting groups. By pulling together the mission and support elements, a wing provides a significant capability under a single commander. . . . Wings will have a minimum adjusted population of at least 1000."

34. Halberstam, *The Best and the Brightest* (New York: Random House, 1972), 72. James M. Lindsay also contends in his book that McNamara continued to build one thousand Minuteman missiles "because he believed it was the smallest number that Congress would accept." Lindsay, *Congress and Nuclear Weapons* (Baltimore: Johns Hopkins University Press, 1991), 148. The B-17 Flying Fortress and B-29 Superfortress were four-engine bombers used extensively in World War II, while the B-47 Stratojet was a six-engine bomber built in 1951. All three were retired in the late 1950s and 1960s.

35. David W. Mabon, ed., *Foreign Relations of the United States, 1961–1963*, vol. 8, *National Security Policy*, Document 115 (Washington: Government Printing Office, 1996), "Draft Memorandum from Secretary of Defense McNamara to President Kennedy" dated December 3, 1962; and Worden, *Rise of the Fighter Generals*, 139–40.

36. Bowe, "Retention of Junior Officers," 9–10, 38. See also Gilkeson, "Missile Crewmember," 14.

37. Luckett, "People Problems in the SAC Missile Force," 14. One of the first missile commanders, Col. Bill Erlenbusch, was nonrated. However, Colonel Erlenbusch was placed in command of the Jupiter squadron just after Secretary of Defense Neil McElroy moved the missile from Army control to the Air Force and the squadron was still assigned to the Army's Redstone Arsenal. A newspaper article of the time described Erlenbusch as an Air Force Trojan horse and Erlenbusch admitted that he and his family were "apprehensive" about moving "into this center of antagonism to the Air Force." Although Erlenbusch appears to have done a great job with the unit under trying circumstances, the Jupiters were never operationalized under U.S. command, so he never actually commanded an operational missile unit.

38. Lloyd Brauer, "Chairborne Minutemen," *Air University Quarterly Review* 9, no. 1 (Winter 1956–57): 70. When he wrote the article, Colonel Brauer was serving as a member of the Air War College faculty. He was a pilot who flew in both World War II and Korea. In the article, he was not recommending that the same standard hold true for missileers. Air Force Regulation 35-54, "Rank, Precedence, and Command" (Washington, DC: Department of the Air Force, 1970), 8.1, directed that all personnel who command or direct flying activities were required to be rated (on flying status).

39. Deaile, "The SAC Mentality," 308.

40. Worden reminded his readers that "investment in ICBM procurement . . . never exceeded money spent on aircraft. But money spent on ICBMs fielded many weapons systems quickly, with high alert rates at relatively low cost." Worden, *Rise of the Fighter Generals*, 124. Worden notes that while McNamara stopped funding bombers, he increased the number of fighter wings from sixteen to twenty-one (139).

41. Williams, "ICBM Career Management," 44.

42. Spires, *On Alert*, 82, provides information from Strategic Air Command, *History of the Strategic Air Command*, 30 July 1971–30 June 1972, Historical Study no. 121, vol. 1, 630–32. The historical study itself was downgraded from Top Secret to Secret on February 7, 1984, but remains classified.

43. Brooksher and Scott, "Study of the Intercontinental Ballistic Missile Operations Career Field," 83. Emphasis in original. Although the authors do not say when the survey was conducted because the survey was used in their thesis, it seems very likely that the survey would have been conducted during the year they were in the National War College, 1972–73.

44. Brooksher and Scott, 63, 125.
45. Brooksher and Scott, 83.
46. Leon Hojegian, personal interview with the author on October 14, 2014.
47. Greg Ogletree asserts that the "US military aviators added a distinctive aviation badge to their uniforms the same year the first US tactical aviation unit was organized (1913)." Ogletree, *The Missile Badge: A Not So Brief History* (Breckenridge, CO: Association of Air Force Missileers, 2002), 1.
48. Ogletree asserts that missileers had discussed the need for a specific designator to recognize missileers from the early 1950s, although the earliest written record was a two-page memo dated September 25, 1956. Ogletree, 1. A memorandum responding to a request for a new Air Policeman's Badge, dated June 6, 1958, reveals the abhorrence that senior Air Force leaders, all pilots, had toward allowing any insignia other than aeronautical wings. Memorandum for Assistant Vice Chief of Staff, Subject: Air Policeman's Badge, dated June 6, 1958, Record Group 341, UD-UP Military Personnel, 1948–1959, Box 2 HQ USAF/AFPDP, Entry 63 A1531, Folder A.4.10 Awards and Decorations, NARA-MD.
49. Air Force Regulation 35-5, "Guided Missile Insignia" (Washington, DC: Department of the Air Force, July 18, 1960), 1, RG 341, UD-UP 80, Box 3, NARA-MD.
50. Ogletree, *Missile Badge*, 2; and Luckett, "People Problems," 32–33.
51. Colonel Henney is quoted in Morgan, "Loneliness of the Missile Attendant," 110.
52. Edward A. Osborne, "An Analysis of the Morale of the Titan II Missile Combat Crews" (master's thesis, Air Command and Staff College, Maxwell AFB, AL, 1967), 24. See also "Special Pay for Officers Holding Positions of Unusual Responsibility," *Military Compensation Background Papers* (Washington, DC: Undersecretary of Defense for Personnel and Readiness, 2005), 279. See also Spires, *On Alert*, 82, who revealed that a Missile Management Working Group, established by Gen. Bruce Holloway, the commander in chief of SAC in 1971, determined that "incentive pay would be a major factor in retaining missile officers and that the predicted number of officers retained would offset the cost of the bonus." The Air Force never seriously considered paying additional money to missileers until Secretary of the Air Force Deborah Lee James authorized the special-duty pay for nuclear career fields on October 1, 2014, but the missileers' request for pay under the Military Pay Act of 1958 would not have helped much, as it did not apply to lieutenants, the vast majority of the missile crew force. By comparison, see Watson,

Office of the Secretary of the Air Force, 199, revealing "the Air Force's extreme reluctance [in July 1960] to accept any reduction in its number of rated officers. . . . General [Thomas] White had made it clear . . . that the grounding of a large number of rated officers would cause severe morale problems by denying the right to fly to many who wanted it."

53. Brooksher and Scott, "Study of the Intercontinental Ballistic Missile Operations Career Field," 63. Peter Pringle and William Arkin explain the "Single Integrated Operations Plan—single because it is the only contingency plan that accounts for the nuclear weapons of all three branches of the United States military, and integrated because it embraces all the nuclear contingency plans of the United States' regional commands in the Pacific, the Atlantic, and Europe, plus the lesser forces of America's closest and only real nuclear ally, Britain." Pringle and Arkin, *SIOP: The Secret U.S. Plan for Nuclear War* (New York: Norton, 1983), 11.

54. Howard Tarleton, email to author dated October 17, 2014.

55. Wolfe's quote is in the preface for Jack Broughton, *Going Downtown: The War against Hanoi and Washington* (New York: Orion, 1988), x, which he wrote. Wolfe is also quoted in Worden, *Rise of the Fighter Generals*, 186.

56. Donald MacKenzie contends that, in late 1973, the Air Force started the advanced development of a new land-based missile capable of carrying ten nuclear warheads, the MX or Peacekeeper missile, but Congress defunded the program in 1976. Restarted under President Jimmy Carter in 1979, the MX missiles struggled to gain political support and only fifty were deployed, beginning in 1986. The Defense Department retired the Peacekeeper missiles in 2005, leaving the Minuteman as the only ballistic missile in the Air Force inventory. By then, Minuteman had been operational for forty-four years. MacKenzie, *Inventing Accuracy*, 225–26.

57. McCorkle, "Command and Control of Ballistic Missiles," 70.

Conclusions

1. Robert T. Finney, *History of the Air Corps Tactical School* (Washington, DC: Air Force History and Museums Program, 1998), 56–57.

2. For the influence of nuclear bombs on bombing primacy, see Karl P. Mueller, "Strategic Airpower and Nuclear Strategy: New Theory for a Not-Quite-So-New Apocalypse," in *Paths of Heaven: The Evolution of Airpower Theory,* ed. Phillip Meilinger, 279–320 (Maxwell AFB, AL: Air University Press, 1997), 282; and Phillip Meilinger, *Bomber: The Formation and Early Years of Strategic Air Command* (Maxwell AFB, AL: Air University Press, 2012), xv–xvi. Dudley Sharp, secretary of the Air Force under Eisenhower,

revealed more of the Eisenhower administration's thought process in a 1961 interview, contending, "We had to put all our technical resources and monetary resources that we could get our hands on to do the number one thing which was to defend us against an attack by the Soviets either on us or—either against us or against our ally. And if we hadn't put this much emphasis on it we might have lost that race." Dudley C. Sharp, Interview #790, with Arthur Marmor, May 29, 1961, USAF Oral History Program, Call #K239.0512-790, IRIS #01000352, AFHRA, Maxwell AFB, Alabama.

3. The systemic problems of missile duty were identified in Rodwell, "Morale in a Missile Force," 66; Ewart, "Survey of Potential Morale, Motivation, and Retention Problems"; and Engell, "Morale of the Missileer," 2; as well as several other contemporary studies.

4. Deaile, "The SAC Mentality," 281–82. Melvin Deaile reveals that part of the motivation behind this act was to ensure that missileers never vied for their own service, as the Air Corps had done while a part of the Army. Deaile ties SAC concerns with incorporating missiles to the Army's failure to assimilate pilots, contending, "When pilots were the subculture of the Army, they became a counterculture and sought their independence. . . . SAC took active measures to make sure this new SAC subculture espoused the same values and beliefs as the organization. Missileers would be indoctrinated into the 'SAC Mentality'" (244). See also the discussion of the SAC mindset in chapter 4.

5. James Holmes, *Report of Commander-Directed Investigation Prepared by Lt. Gen. James M. Holmes, Investigating Officer Concerning ICBM Test Compromise at Malmstrom Air Force Base, Montana & Assessment of Twentieth Air Force ICBM Training, Evaluation, and Testing Culture*, February 26, 2014, C-3. A former missileer contends, "Many missileers were bad test takers and thought to be bad missileers, but they were the best. . . . These tests are supposed to determine whether you're fit to be a leader, an instructor, or an evaluator, but it has nothing to do with real leadership." Quoted in Mark Thompson, "Are You Smarter than a Nuclear Launch Officer?," *Time* (February 13, 2014), accessed July 29, 2015, http://time.com/8530/are-you-smarter-than-a-nuclear-launch-officer/.

6. Daniel Sharp, interview with Leslie Stahl, transcript in "Who's Minding the Nukes?," *60 Minutes*, accessed July 29, 2015, http://www.cbsnews.com/news/whos-minding-the-nuclear-weapons/. See also Air Force investigation report, as provided to *Time* by Lt. Gen. Stephen Wilson, commander of AF Global Strike Command as quoted in Mark Thompson, "Air Force Applies a Band-Aid to a Sucking Chest Wound," *Time*

(March 27, 2014), accessed July 30, 2015, http://time.com/41088/air-force-cheating-scandal/.

7. Secretary James is quoted in Thompson, "Air Force Applies a Band-Aid."

8. Colonel Henney is quoted in Morgan, "Loneliness of the Missile Attendant," 50.

9. R. Jeffrey Smith, "Aiming High," *Slate*, April 14, 2014, http://www.slate.com/articles/news_and_politics/politics/2014/04/air_force_s_nuclear_missile_corps_is_struggling_millennial_missileers_suffer.html.

10. Smith, "Motivation of Minuteman Missile Crews," 4. See also Conant, "Use of Rated Officers," 6; and Donald Robb, "An Analysis of the Probable Effects of an Underground Environment Upon Men Assigned to Hardened Missile Sites" (special study, Air Command and Staff College, Maxwell AFB, AL, 1961), 25–26.

11. Worden, *Rise of the Fighter Generals*, 85, reveals that the fighter community only produced one new aircraft between 1955 and 1964. James Ruehrmund Jr. and Christopher Bowie appear to support Worden's contention, revealing that the F-5 was added to the Air Force inventory in 1963. Ruehrmund and Bowie, *Arsenal of Airpower: USAF Aircraft Inventory 1950–2009* (Washington, DC: Mitchell Institute Press, 2010). Worden further contends that "SAC had complete dominance in the selection of new technologies, and usually the best TAC [Tactical Air Command] could do was to accept SAC rejects." Worden, *Rise of the Fighter Generals*, 85. Worden quotes LeMay, then vice chief of staff of the Air Force, arguing that the United States "could no longer afford the luxury of devoting a substantial portion of our Air Force effort to support ground forces" (81).

12. For detailed examinations of this speculation, see William Bruce Danskine, "Fall of the Fighter Generals: The Future of USAF Leadership" (master's thesis, School of Advanced Airpower Studies, Air University, Maxwell AFB, AL, 2001); and Laura L. Lenderman, *The Rise of Air Mobility and Its Generals* (Maxwell AFB, AL: Air University Press, 2008). Danskine argues that the Delphic tribe, a group that he defines as those who "build the battlespace picture," should next take the lead of the Air Force, while Lenderman contends that the next group of leaders should come from the mobility airlifters. However, both acknowledge that changing the group that controls the Air Force is a challenging process fraught with difficulties.

13. Quoted in Rebecca Grant, preface to Thomas P. Ehrhard, *Air Force UAVs: The Secret History* (Arlington, VA: Mitchell Institute for Airpower Studies, 2010), 2.

14. Ehrhard, *Air Force UAVs*, 50.

15. Gates, to General Norton Schwartz, memorandum, Subject: Continued Growth of Unmanned Aircraft Systems, dated June 29, 2011, quoted in Lawrence Spinetta, "The Glass Ceiling for Remotely Piloted Aircraft," *Air & Space Power Journal* (July–August 2013), 102.

16. Bryan quoted in "A Drone Warrior's Torment: Ex-Air Force Pilot Brandon Bryan on His Trauma from Remote Killing," *Democracy Now* (October 25, 2013). See also Kate Brannen, "Air Force's Lack of Drone Pilots Reaching 'Crisis' Levels," *Foreign Policy*, January 15, 2015, accessed July 31, 2015, http://foreignpolicy.com/2015/01/15/air-forces-lack-of-drone-pilots-reaching-crisis-levels/, accessed July 31, 2015.

17. Charlie Simpson, "Missileers, Inspections, Morale," *AAFM [Association of Air Force Missileers]* 21, no. 2 (June 2013), 8. See also Joe Pappalardo, "A Disgraced Air Force General's Last Interview," *Popular Mechanics*, January 6, 2014, accessed July 30, 2015, http://www.popularmechanics.com/military/a9924/a-disgraced-air-force-generals-last-interview-16341301/. See also Noah Shachtman, "Bosses Nuked, Some Air Force Missileers Cheer," *Wired*, June 6, 2008, accessed August 4, 2015, http://www.wired.com/2008/06/defense-secreta-2/.

18. Quoted in Robert Burns, "'Just the Ticket' 4-Star Solution to Nuclear Air Force Ills," Associated Press, July 27, 2015.

19. Brooksher and Scott, "Study of the Intercontinental Ballistic Missile Operations Career Field," 61. Since 1957, the Air Force has promoted only two missileers to a fourth star. Lance Lord commanded Air Force Space Command from 2002 to 2006, and Robert Kehler commanded Air Force Space Command from 2007 to 2011 and U.S. Strategic Command from 2011 to 2014.

BIBLIOGRAPHY

Archival Materials
Air Force Global Strike Command History Office, Barksdale AFB, Louisiana
  History extract, Strategic Air Command History, January–June 1964
Air Force Historical Research Agency (AFHRA), Maxwell Air Force Base, AL
  USAF Collection
    Personal collection of General Henry H. Arnold, MICFILM 43804, IRIS # 01102996
Digital National Security Archives
  U.S. Nuclear History Collection
Dwight D. Eisenhower Presidential Library, Abilene, Kansas
  Dwight David Eisenhower Papers
  Bryce N. Harlow Papers
  C. D. Jackson Papers
  Records of the White House, Special Assistant to the President for National Security Affairs
  Ann Whitman Papers as President
Library of Congress (LOC), Washington, DC
  Bernard Schriever Papers
  Neil Sheehan Papers, Interview Notes
    Brig. Gen. Maurice A. "Chris" Cristadoro, USAF, Ret.
    Richard D. Curtin
    Lt. Col. Roy Ferguson, USAF, Ret.
    Col. Richard "Jake" Jacobson, USAF, Ret.
    Col. William R. Large Jr., USAF, Ret.
    Ray Soper
    Lt. Col. Jamie W. Wallace, USAF, Ret.

Lyndon Baines Johnson Presidential Library and Museum, Austin, Texas
  National Security File
Mudd Manuscript Library, Princeton University, Princeton, New Jersey
  Arthur Krock Papers
National Archives and Records Administration, College Park, Maryland
  (NARA-MD)
  Record Group 218—Records of the Joint Chiefs of Staff
  Record Group 330—Records of the Office of the Secretary of Defense
  Record Group 340—Records of the Office of the Secretary of the Air Force
  Record Group 341—Records of Headquarters U.S. Air Force (Air Staff)

Interviews and Oral Histories
Author Interviews
  Alkire, Gary. Personal interview. January 28, 2015.
  Andrew, Joseph. Email. October 20, 2014.
  Bishop, Ronald J. Letter. April 1, 2014.
  Brown, Joe. Telephone interview. August 23, 2014.
  Brown, Manning. Telephone interview. July 30, 2015.
  Dlugas, Frank. Telephone interview. March 2, 2014.
  Driskill, Melvin. Email. February 8, 2015.
  Glantz, Donald. Email. May 2, 2014, and May 4, 2014.
  Hasbrouck, Lawrence. Email, May 21, 2014; letter, June 28, 2014.
  Hojegian, Leon. Personal interview. October 14–15, 2014.
  Hoselton, Gary. Email. November 4, 2014.
  Keireck, John. Letter. October 16, 2014.
  Kelchner, Robert. Email. November 12, 2014; January 19, 2015.
  Koser, Donald. Email. December 14, 2015.
  Martin, Jerome. Phone call. December 12, 2014.
  Peck, Jim. Interview with the author. March 3, 2015.
  Raleigh, Bruce. Email. February 6, 2015.
  Spellman, Patrick "Jerry." Letter hand delivered to author on September 30,
    2014; email, November 20, 2014.
  Spinetta, Lawrence. Email. March 7, 2015.
  Tarleton, Howard. Email. October 17, 2014.
  Turner, Doug. Email. November 21, 2014.
  West, Duane. Email. September 10, 2014.
  Widlar, James. Email, October 23, 2014; telephone interview, January 30,
    2015.

Wikstrom, Floyd. Telephone interviews; email, May 26, 2014.

Wyckoff, Robert. Email. November 17, 2014.

Oral Histories

Air Force Historical Research Agency (AFHRA), Maxwell Air Force Base, AL

Bellis, Benjamin (Call #K239.0152-1629, IRIS #01070943). Transcripts.

Fleming, David (Call #K239.0512-2395, IRIS #01143416). Transcripts.

Glasser, Otto (Call #K239.0512-1566, IRIS #01105111). Transcripts.

LeMay, Curtis E. (Call #K239.0512-714, IRIS #00904841). Transcripts. (Image 1285-1290)

Putt, Donald L. (Call #K239.0512-724, IRIS #01001024, 01001025, 01001026, 01001027, 01001028, 01001029, and 01001030). Transcripts.

Sharp, Dudley C., SECAF (Call #K239.0512-790, IRIS #01000352). Transcripts. (Image 1256-1280)

Soper, Ray E. (Call #K239.0512-783, IRIS #01000339). Transcripts. (Image 1291-1302)

Stever, Guyford (Call #K239.0512-1752, IRIS #01095219). Transcripts.

Taylor, Maxwell (Call # K239.0512-1508, IRIS # 01053461). Transcripts.

Wilson, Roscoe C. (Call #K239.0512-774, IRIS # 01002224). Transcripts. (Image 1303-1316)

Columbia University, Oral History Collection, New York

Beebe, Eugene. "The Reminiscences of Eugene Beebe (1959–1960)."

Eaker, Ira. "The Reminiscences of Ira Eaker (1959–1960)."

Dwight D. Eisenhower Presidential Library, Abilene, Kansas

MacIntyre, Malcom A. Transcripts.

Interview notes from Christopher Preble

McNamara, Robert, notes from phone interview dated April 10, 2003.

Interview transcript from Leslie Stahl, 60 Minutes, April 27, 2014

Sharp, Daniel. "Who's Minding the Nukes?" *60 Minutes.*

John F. Kennedy Presidential Library, Boston, Massachusetts

Gilpatric, Roswell. (Digital Identifier: JFKOH-RLG-03). Transcripts.

Published Works

Adams, Christopher S. *Ideologies in Conflict: A Cold War Docu-Story.* Bloomington, IN: iUniverse, 2001.

Adams, Valerie L. *Eisenhower's Fine Group of Fellows: Crafting a National Security Policy to Uphold the Great Equation.* Lanham, MD: Rowman and Littlefield, 2006.

Air Force Instruction 38-101. "Air Force Organization." Washington, DC: Department of the Air Force, March 16, 2011.

Air Force Regulation 35-5. "Guided Missile Insignia." Washington, DC: Department of the Air Force, July 18, 1960.

Air Force Regulation 35-54. "Rank, Precedence, and Command." Washington, DC: Department of the Air Force, 1970.

Allgaier, William A. "Enhancing the Missileer's Image." Master's thesis, Air Command and Staff College, Maxwell AFB, AL, 1979.

Anderson, J. W., Jr. "What Reliability Means to SAC." In *Proceedings, 6th Joint Military-Industrial Guided Missile Reliability Symposium*, February 15–17, 1960. https://apps.dtic.mil/dtic/tr/fulltext/u2/454674.pdf.

Anderson, Terry. *The United States, Great Britain, and the Cold War, 1944–1947.* Columbia: University of Missouri Press, 1981.

Anderson, William L. "Officers and Missiles." *Air University Quarterly Review* 10, no. 1 (Spring 1958): 73–81.

———. "Organizing and Manning Ballistic Missile Units." *Air University Quarterly Review* 9, no. 3 (Summer 1957): 78–85.

Angell, Joseph W., Jr., ed. *The Air Force Response to the Cuban Missile Crisis* (Redacted). Washington, DC: USAF Historical Division Liaison Office, 1963.

Armacost, Michael. *The Politics of Weapons Innovation: The Thor-Jupiter Controversy.* New York: Columbia University Press, 1969.

Arnold, Henry H. *Global Mission.* New York: Harper, 1949.

Arnold, John. "A Revised Training and Evaluation Program for SAC Minuteman Missile Combat Crew Members." Research study, Air Command and Staff College, Maxwell AFB, AL, 1971.

Ashley, Garland O. "A Momentum of Nuclear Talk." *Air University Quarterly Review* 13, no. 4 (Summer 1962): 94–95.

Augenstein, Bruno. *A Revised Development Program for Ballistic Missiles of Intercontinental Range* (Special Memorandum #21). Santa Monica, CA: RAND, 1954. Accessed September 20, 2014, http://www.rand.org/pubs/special_memoranda/SM21.html.

Baar, James, and William Howard. *Combat Missileman.* New York: Harcourt, Brace and World, 1961.

Bacs, John. "Missile Unit Commanders: Rated Versus Nonrated Officers." Master's thesis, Air Command and Staff College, Maxwell AFB, AL, 1972.

Bair, Jeffrey A. "An Examination of Intercontinental Ballistic Missile Development within the United States from 1952 to 1965." Masters' thesis, Army Command and General Staff College, Ft. Leavenworth, Kansas, 2003.

Baldwin, Hanson W. "ICBM." *Collier's Weekly*, March 16, 1956, 23–25, 74–80.

Ball, Desmond. *Politics and Force Levels: The Strategic Missile Program of the Kennedy Administration*. Berkeley: University of California Press, 1980.

Barlow, Myron F., and Frank J. Vanasek. "Personnel Lag and the Air Force." *Air University Quarterly Review* 10, no. 4 (Winter 1958–59): 78–84.

Bartlett, Paul V., and Relf A. Finley. "The Case for a Manned Space Weapon System." *Air University Quarterly Review* 10, no. 4 (Winter 1958–59): 40–46.

Bath, David W., ed. *Air Force Missileers and the Cuban Missile Crisis: A Collection of Personal Reminiscences from Missileers and Others Who Experienced the Cuban Missile Crisis of 1962*. Breckenridge, CO: Association of Air Force Missileers, 2012.

Beard, Edmund. *Developing the ICBM: A Study in Bureaucratic Politics*. New York: Columbia University Press, 1976.

Bernstein, Barton. "The Cuban Missile Crisis: Trading the Jupiters in Turkey?" *Political Science Quarterly* 95, no. 1 (Spring 1980): 97–125.

Bishop, Ronald J. "Missile Crewmember Attitudes and Job Satisfaction in a Minuteman Organization." Master's thesis, Air Command and Staff College, Maxwell AFB, AL, 1967.

Blight, James, and Janet Lang. *The Fog of War: Lessons from the Life of Robert S. McNamara*. Lanham, MD: Rowman and Littlefield, 2005.

Blight, James, and David Welch. *On the Brink: Americans and Soviets Reexamine the Cuban Missile Crisis*. New York: Hill and Wang, 1989.

Boog, Horst, Gerhard Krebs, and Detlef Vogel, eds. *Germany and the Second World War*. Vol. 7, *The Strategic Air War in the West and East Asia, 1913–1944/5*, trans. ed. Derry Cook-Radmore. Oxford: Clarendon Press, 2006.

Bose, Meenekshi. *Shaping and Signaling Presidential Policy: The National Security Decision Making of Eisenhower and Kennedy*. College Station: Texas A&M University Press, 1998.

Bowe, Donovan K. "Retention of Junior Officers in the Minuteman Missile Crew Force." Research report no. 3722, Air University, Maxwell AFB, AL, 1969.

Bowers, Robert D. "Fundamental Equations of Force Survival." *Air University Quarterly Review* 10, no. 1 (Spring 1958): 82–92.

Boyne, Walter J. *A History of the U.S. Air Force, 1947–1997*. New York: St. Martin's Press, 1997.

Brands, H. W. "The Age of Invulnerability: Eisenhower and the National Insecurity State." *American Historical Review* 94, no. 4 (October 1989), 963–89.

Brannen, Kate. "Air Force's Lack of Drone Pilots Reaching 'Crisis' Levels." *Foreign Policy*, January 15, 2015. http://foreignpolicy.com/2015/01/15/air-forces-lack-of-drone-pilots-reaching-crisis-levels/.

Brauer, Lloyd. "Chairborne Minutemen." *Air University Quarterly Review* 9, no. 1 (Winter 1956–57), 66–75.

Bray, Leslie W., Jr. "The Role of the Rated Group in the Missile and Space Era." Master's thesis, Air War College, Montgomery, AL, 1959.

Brewer, James L. *Mules, Missiles and Men: An Autobiography*. Grant, AL: Brewco, 1988.

Briggs, James E. "Training the Aerospace Force." *Air University Quarterly Review* 7, no. 3–4 (Winter and Spring 1960–61): 186–94.

Brodie, Bernard. "The Anatomy of Deterrence." *World Politics* 11, no. 2 (January 1959): 173–91. http://www.jstor.org/stable/2009527.

———. "Implications for Military Policy." In *The Absolute Weapon: Atomic Power and World Order*, ed. Bernard Brodie, 71–107. New York: Harcourt, Brace, 1946.

———. *Military Implications of Nuclear Weapon Developments*. Santa Monica, CA: RAND, 1953.

———. *Strategy in the Missile Age*. Princeton, NJ: Princeton University Press, 1959.

Brooks, Robert O. "Surprise in the Missile Era." *Air University Quarterly Review* 11, no. 1 (Spring 1959): 76–83.

Brooksher, William R., and Jimmy F. Scott. "A Study of the Intercontinental Ballistic Missile Operations Career Field." Master's thesis, National War College, Washington, DC, 1973.

Broughton, Jack. *Going Downtown: The War against Hanoi and Washington*. New York: Orion, 1988.

Brown, Harold. "Planning Our Military Forces." *Foreign Affairs* 45, no. 2 (January 1967): 277–90. http://www.jstor.org/stable/20039232.

Brownlow, Cecil. "First RAF Thor Sites Nearly Operational." *Aviation Week*, July 13, 1959.

Bundy, McGeorge. *Danger and Survival: Choices about the Bomb in the First Fifty Years*. New York: Random House, 1988.

Burgess, Eric. *Long-Range Ballistic Missiles*. New York: Macmillan, 1961.

Burns, Arthur Lee. "From Balance to Deterrence: A Theoretical Analysis." *World Politics* 9, no. 4 (July 1957): 494–529. https://www.jstor.org/stable/2009422.

Burns, Robert. "'Just the Ticket' 4-Star Solution to Nuclear Air Force Ills." Associated Press, July 27, 2015.

Bush, Vannevar. *Modern Arms and Free Men: A Discussion of the Role of Science in Preserving Democracy.* New York: Simon and Schuster, 1949.

Bybee, Rodger W. "Achieving Technological Literacy: A National Imperative." *Technology Teacher* 60 (September 2000): 23–28.

Campbell, Craig, and Sergey S. Radchenko. *The Atomic Bomb and the Origins of the Cold War.* New Haven, CT: Yale University Press, 2008.

Chapman, John L. *Atlas: The Story of a Missile.* New York: Harper, 1960.

Chertok, Boris. *Rockets and People.* Vol. 2, *Creating a Rocket Industry.* Washington, DC: NASA, 2006.

Chun, Clayton K. S. *Thunder over the Horizon: From V-2 Rockets to Ballistic Missiles.* Westport, CT: Praeger, 2006.

Clarfield, Gerard H., and William M. Wiecek. *Nuclear America: Military and Civilian Nuclear Power in the United States, 1940–1980.* New York: Harper and Row, 1984.

Clark, Clifford. *Counsel to the President: A Memoir.* With Richard Holbrooke. New York: Random House, 1991.

Coffey, Thomas. *Iron Eagle: The Turbulent Life of General Curtis LeMay.* New York: Crown, 1986.

Coleman, David. *The Fourteenth Day: JFK and the Aftermath of the Cuban Missile Crisis.* New York: Norton, 2012.

Conant, Roger G. "The Use of Rated Officers in the Minuteman Missile System." Research Study no. 0295-70, Air Command and Staff College, Maxwell AFB, AL, 1970.

Converse, Elliot V., II. *Rearming for the Cold War, 1945–1960.* Washington, DC: Department of Defense Historical Office, 2011.

Cownie, J. R. "Britain Pioneers IRBM Deployment: Thor—First R.A.F. Strategic Missile." *Aeroplane,* May 22, 1959.

Cumbaa, Noel T. "Training and Training Facilities for Strategic Missile Forces." Master's thesis, Air War College, Maxwell AFB, AL, 1958.

Danskine, William Bruce. "Fall of the Fighter Generals: The Future of USAF Leadership." Master's thesis, School of Advanced Airpower Studies, Air University, Maxwell AFB, AL, 2001.

Daso, Dik A. *Hap Arnold and the Evolution of American Airpower.* Washington, DC: Smithsonian Institution Press, 2000.

Davis, W. A. "Ballistic Systems." *Air University Quarterly Review* 14, nos. 1–2 (Winter–Spring 1962–63): 126–44.

Deaile, Melvin. "The SAC Mentality: The Origins of Organizational Culture in Strategic Air Command, 1946–1962." PhD dissertation, University of North Carolina at Chapel Hill, 2007.

DeHaven, Ethel M. *Aerospace—The Evolution of USAF Weapons Acquisition Policy, 1945–1961.* Los Angeles: U.S. Air Force Systems Command, Historical Publication Series 62-24-6, 1962.

Del Papa, E. Michael, and Sheldon A. Goldberg. *Strategic Air Command Missile Chronology, 1939–1973.* Offutt AFB, NE: Office of the Historian, HQ Strategic Air Command, 1990.

Dick, James C. "The Strategic Arms Race, 1957–61: Who Opened a Missile Gap?" *Journal of Politics* 34, no. 4 (November 1972): 1062–1110. http://www.jstor.org/stable/2128929.

Dietz, Harold W. *Human Problems in Missile Launching.* Vandenberg AFB, CA: 392nd Aerospace Medical Group.

Dobbs, Michael. *One Minute to Midnight: Kennedy, Khrushchev, and Castro on the Brink of Nuclear War.* New York: Knopf, 2008.

Donnelly, Charles, ed. Document 155, "Compilation of Material Relating to U.S. Defense Policies in 1962," in 88th Congress, 1st Session (January 9–December 30, 1963), *House Documents.* Vol. 3, *Miscellaneous.* Washington, DC: U.S. Government Printing Office, 1963–64.

Dower, John W. *Cultures of War: Pearl Harbor/Hiroshima/9–11/Iraq.* New York: Norton, 2010.

Driscoll, David L. "Missile Combat Crew Morale: Its Impact on Officer Retention." Master's thesis, Air Command and Staff College, Maxwell AFB, AL, 1972.

Dungan, T. D. *V-2: A Combat History of the First Ballistic Missile.* Yardley, PA: Westholme, 2005.

Egan, John C. "Impact on Strategy of the ICBM." Individual Research Paper, National War College, 1958.

Ehrhard, Thomas P. *Air Force UAVs: The Secret History.* Arlington, VA: Mitchell Institute for Airpower Studies, 2010.

Elderfield, Matthew. "Rebuilding the Special Relationship: The 1957 Bermuda Talks." *Cambridge Review of International Affairs* 3, no. 1 (1989): 14–24.

Ellsberg, Daniel. *Secrets: A Memoir of Vietnam and the Pentagon Papers.* New York: Penguin, 2002.

Engell, Arthur. "The Morale of the Missileer: A Study of the Minuteman Launch Control Officer." Master's thesis, Air Command and Staff College, Maxwell AFB, AL, 1964.

Enthoven, Alain C., and K. Wayne Smith. *How Much Is Enough? Shaping the Defense Program, 1961–1969.* Santa Monica, CA: RAND, 1971.

Erdmann, Andrew. "'War No Longer Has Any Logic Whatever': Dwight D. Eisenhower and the Thermonuclear Revolution." In *Cold War Statesmen Confront the Bomb: Nuclear Diplomacy since 1945,* ed. John Lewis Gaddis,

Philip H. Gordon, Ernest R. May, and Jonathan Rosenberg, 87–119. New York: Oxford University Press, 1999.

Eula, Michael J. "Giulio Douhet and Strategic Air Force Operations: A Study in the Limitations of Theoretical Warfare." *Air University Review*, 37, no. 6 (September–October 1986): 94–99.

Ewart, E. S. *A Survey of Potential Morale, Motivation, and Retention Problems at Ballistic Missile Sites.* Wright-Patterson AFB, OH: Air Research and Development Command, 1958.

Faber, Peter R. "Interwar U.S. Army Aviation and the Air Corps Tactical School: Incubators of American Airpower." In *Paths of Heaven: The Evolution of Airpower Theory*, ed. Phillip Meilinger, 183–238. Maxwell AFB, AL: Air University Press, 1997.

Feis, Herbert. *From Trust to Terror: The Onset of the Cold War, 1945–1950.* New York: Norton, 1970.

Ferguson, James. "Manned Craft and the Ballistic Missile." *Air University Quarterly Review* 12, no. 3–4 (Winter–Spring 1960–61): 251–56.

Ferguson, Roy L. "The Ballistic Missile and Operational Capability." *Air University Quarterly Review* 9, no. 4 (Winter 1957–58): 55–61.

Fink, Carole. *Cold War: An International History.* Boulder, CO: Westview Press, 2014.

Finney, Robert T. *History of the Air Corps Tactical School.* Washington, DC: Air Force History and Museums Program, 1998.

Fish, Robert W. "The USAF Role in the Cold War." *Air University Quarterly Review* 13, no. 4 (Summer 1962): 75–83.

Fisher, Thomas L., II. "'Limited War'—What is It?" *Air University Quarterly Review* 9, no. 4 (Winter 1957–58): 127–42.

Fogle, James M. "Impact of Missiles and Space Vehicles on Air Force Organization by 1970." Master's thesis, Air War College, Montgomery, AL, 1960.

Foreign Relations of the United States. Vol. 14, *1955–1957.* Washington, DC: U.S. Government Printing Office, 1990.

Frank, Richard B. *Downfall: The End of the Imperial Japanese Empire.* New York: Random House, 1999.

Freedman, Lawrence. *The Evolution of Nuclear Strategy.* New York: St. Martin's Press, 1989.

———. "The First Two Generations of Nuclear Strategists." In *Makers of Modern Strategy from Machiavelli to the Nuclear Age*, ed. Peter Paret, 735–78. Princeton, NJ: Princeton University Press, 1986.

———. *Kennedy's Wars: Berlin, Cuba, Laos, and Vietnam.* New York: Oxford University Press, 2000.

Freeman, David E. "An Analysis of the Need for Rated Officers in Missile Operations." Research study no. 0505-70, Air University, Maxwell AFB, AL, 1970.

Friedman, Norman. *The Fifty-Year War: Conflict and Strategy in the Cold War.* Annapolis, MD: Naval Institute Press, 1999.

Futrell, Robert Frank. *Ideas, Concepts, Doctrine: Basic Thinking in the United States Air Force, 1907–1984.* 2 vols. Maxwell AFB, AL: Air University Press, 1989.

Gaddis, John Lewis. *The Cold War: A New History.* New York: Penguin Press, 2005.

Gaddis, John Lewis, Philip H. Gordon, Ernest R. May, and Jonathan Rosenberg, eds. *Cold War Statesmen Confront the Bomb: Nuclear Diplomacy since 1945.* New York: Oxford University Press, 1999.

Gainor, Christopher John. "The United States Air Force and the Emergence of the Intercontinental Ballistic Missile, 1945–1954." PhD dissertation, University of Alberta, Edmonton, 2011.

Gantz, Kenneth Franklin, ed. *The United States Air Force Report on the Ballistic Missile: Its Technology, Logistics, and Strategy.* Garden City, NY: Doubleday, 1958.

Garthoff, Raymond L. *Soviet Strategy in the Nuclear Age.* New York: Frederick A. Praeger, 1958.

Gavin, Francis J. "The Myth of Flexible Response: American Strategy in Europe during the 1960s." *International History Review* 23, no. 4 (December 2001): 847–75.

George, Alice. *Awaiting Armageddon: How Americans Faced the Cuban Missile Crisis.* Chapel Hill: University of North Carolina Press, 2003.

Giffin, S. F. "Relationships Among Military Forces." *Air University Quarterly Review* 9, No. 4 (Winter 1957–58): 31–45.

Gilkeson, Thomas A. "Missile Crewmember—His Needs and Job Satisfaction." Master's thesis, Air Command and Staff College, Maxwell AFB, AL, 1972.

Gill, Graeme, ed. *Routledge Handbook of Russian Politics and Society.* New York: Routledge, 2012.

Gilpatrick, Roswell L. "Our Defense Needs: The Long View." *Foreign Affairs* 42, no. 3 (April 1964): 366–78.

Goddard, Robert H. "A Method of Reaching Extreme Altitudes." *Smithsonian Miscellaneous Collections* 71, no. 2 (1919): 1–69. Accessed February 20, 2014, http://www.clarku.edu/research/archives/pdf/ext_altitudes.pdf.

Goldsworthy, Harry. "ICBM Site Activation." *Aerospace Historian* 29, no. 3 (Fall, September 1982): 154–61.

Gorn, Michael H. *Harnessing the Genie: Science and Technology Forecasting for the Air Force, 1944–1986.* Washington, DC: Office of Air Force History, 1988.

Gosling, F. G. *The Manhattan Project: Making the Atomic Bomb.* Washington, DC: Department of Energy, 2010.

Graham, Thomas. *American Public Opinion on NATO, Extended Deterrence and the Use of Nuclear Weapons: Future Fission?* CSIA Occasional Paper No. 4. Cambridge, MA: Center for Science and International Affairs, Harvard University, 1989.

Greene, Warren E. *The Development of the SM-68 Titan.* Andrews AFB, MD: Historical Office, Deputy Commander for Aerospace Systems, Air Force Systems Command, August 1962.

Grimwood, James M., and Frances Strowd. *History of the Jupiter Missile System.* Redstone Arsenal, AL: History and Reports Control Branch, Management Services Office, U.S. Army Ordnance Missile Command, 1962. http://heroicrelics.org/info/jupiter/jupiter-hist/History%20of%20 the%20Jupiter%20Missile%20System.pdf.

Groves, Leslie R. *Now It Can Be Told: The Story of the Manhattan Project.* New York: Harper and Brothers, 1962.

Halberstam, David. *The Best and the Brightest.* New York: Random House, 1972.

Halperin, Morton H. "The Gaither Committee and the Policy Process." *World Politics* 13, no. 3 (April 1961): 360–84. http://www.jstor.org/stable/2009480.

Herken, Gregg. *Counsels of War.* New York: Knopf, 1985.

Herring, George. *America's Longest War: The United States and Vietnam, 1950–1975*, 4th ed. New York: McGraw-Hill, 2001.

Hilsman, Roger. *The Cuban Missile Crisis: The Struggle Over Policy.* Westport, CT: Praeger, 1996.

———. *To Move a Nation: The Politics of Foreign Policy in the Administration of John F. Kennedy.* Garden City, NY: Doubleday, 1967.

Holden, Kenneth L. "A Study of the Motivational Behavior of Missile Combat Crews." Master's thesis, Air Command and Staff College, Maxwell AFB, AL, 1966.

Holloway, David. "Entering the Nuclear Arms Race: The Soviet Decision to Built the Atomic Bomb, 1939–1945." *Social Studies of Science* 11, no. 2 (May 1981): 183.

———. *Stalin and the Bomb: The Soviet Union and Atomic Energy, 1939–1956.* New Haven, CT: Yale University Press, 1994.

Holmes, James M. *Report of Commander-Directed Investigation Prepared by Lt. Gen. James M. Holmes, Investigating Officer Concerning ICBM Test Compromise at Malmstrom Air Force Base, Montana & Assessment of Twentieth Air Force ICBM Training, Evaluation, and Testing Culture.* February 26, 2014.

Hopkins, J. C., and Sheldon Goldberg. *The Development of the Strategic Air Command, 1946–1986.* Offutt AFB, NE: Office of the Historian, HQ, Strategic Air Command, 1986.

Hudson, John B. "The ICBM Race." Research paper, National War College, 1960.

Hunter, Robert E. "The Politics of U.S. Defense 1963: Manned Bombers versus Missiles." *World Today* 19, no. 3 (March 1963): 98–107.

Huntington, Samuel P. "Interservice Competition and the Political Roles of the Armed Services." *American Political Science Review* 55, no. 1 (March 1961): 40–52. http://www.jstor.org/stable/1976048.

Hurley, Alfred. *Billy Mitchell: Crusader for Air Power.* Bloomington: Indiana University Press, 1964.

Huston, John W., ed. *American Airpower Comes of Age: General Henry H. "Hap" Arnold's World War II Diaries.* 2 vols. Maxwell AFB, AL: Air University Press, 2002.

Ingersoll, George L. "Discipline and Morale of Missile Alert Forces." Master's thesis, Air War College, Maxwell AFB, AL, 1961.

Jacobsen, Annie. *Operation Paperclip: The Secret Intelligence Program that Brought Nazi Scientists to America.* New York: Little, Brown, 2014.

Johnpoll, Alexander C. "NATO Enters the ICBM Age." Individual Research Paper, National War College, Washington, DC, 1961.

Johns, Claude J., Jr. "The United States Air Force Intercontinental Ballistic Missile Program, 1954–1959: Technological Change and Organizational Innovation." PhD dissertation, University of North Carolina at Chapel Hill, 1964.

Johnson, Lyndon. "Remarks in Cadillac Square, Detroit." September 7, 1964. *Public Papers of the Presidents of the United States: Lyndon B. Johnson, 1963–64,* Book 2. Washington, DC: U.S. Government Printing Office, 1965.

Johnson, Stephen B. *The United States Air Force and the Culture of Innovation, 1945–1965.* Washington, DC: Air Force History Support Office, 2002.

Jordan, Amos, William Taylor Jr., and Lawrence Korb. *American National Security: Policy and Process*. Baltimore: Johns Hopkins University Press, 1981.

Kahn, Herman. *On Thermonuclear War*. Princeton, NJ: Princeton University Press, 1960.

Kaplan, Fred. "JFK's First Strike Plan." *Atlantic*, October 2001. http://www.theatlantic.com/magazine/archive/2001/10/jfks-first-strike-plan/376432/.

Kaplan, Lawrence, Ronald Landa, and Edward Drea. *The McNamara Ascendancy, 1961–1965*. Vol. 5, *History of the Office of the Secretary of Defense*. Washington, DC: Historical Office, Office of the Secretary of Defense, 2006.

Karnow, Stanley. *Vietnam: A History*. New York: Viking, 1983.

Keeney, L. Douglas. *15 Minutes: General Curtis LeMay and the Countdown to Nuclear Annihilation*. New York: St. Martin's, 2011.

Kennedy, Gregory P. *Vengeance Weapon 2: The V-2 Guided Missile*. Washington, DC: Smithsonian Institution Press, 1983.

Kennedy, John F. *The Kennedy Presidential Press Conferences*. New York: Earl M. Coleman Enterprises, 1965.

———. "Special Message to the Congress on the Defense Budget," March 28, 1961. *Public Papers of President John F. Kennedy 1961*. Washington, DC: U.S. Government Printing Office, 1964.

Kennedy, Robert. *Thirteen Days: A Memoir of the Cuban Missile Crisis*. New York: Norton, 1968.

Khrushchev, Nikita. *Khrushchev Remembers*. Edited by Strobe Talbott. Boston: Little, Brown, 1970.

Kieklak, Ronald J. "Motivation of Missile Combat Crew Members." Master's thesis, Air Command and Staff College, Maxwell AFB, AL, 1972.

Kipp, Robert, Lynn Peake, and Herman Wolk. *Strategic Air Command Operations in the Cuban Missile Crisis of 1962* (Historical Study No. 90), Vol. 1, Top Secret / Formerly Restricted Data / No Foreign Dissemination; declassified in part, 2008. Offutt AFB, NE: HQ, Strategic Air Command, 1963.

Kohn, Richard H., and Joseph P. Harahan, eds. *Strategic Air Warfare: An Interview with Generals Curtis E. LeMay, Leon W. Johnson, David A. Burchinal, and Jack J. Catton*. Washington, DC: Office of Air Force History, U.S. Air Force, 1988.

Kozak, Warren. *LeMay: The Life and Wars of General Curtis LeMay*. Washington, DC: Regnery, 2009.

Lake, Daniel E. "SAC Missile Duty Handbook." Master's thesis, Air Command and Staff College, Maxwell AFB, AL, 1978.

Laurence, Martin. *Strategic Thought in the Nuclear Age.* Baltimore: Johns Hopkins University Press, 1979.

Lebovic, James. *Flawed Logics: Strategic Nuclear Arms Control from Truman to Obama.* Baltimore: Johns Hopkins University Press, 2013.

Lee, John J. "Nation's First Ballistic Missile Base." *Air University Quarterly Review* 9, no. 4 (Winter 1957–58): 62–68.

Leighton, Richard M. *Strategy, Money, and the New Look, 1953–1956.* Vol. 3, *History of the Office of the Secretary of Defense.* Washington, DC: Historical Office, Office of the Secretary of Defense, 2012.

LeMay, Curtis E. "The Present Pattern." *Air University Quarterly Review* 12, no. 3–4 (Winter–Spring 1960–61): 25–39.

LeMay, Curtis E., and Dale Smith. *America Is in Danger.* New York: Funk and Wagnalls, 1968.

Lemmer, George F. *The Air Force and Strategic Deterrence, 1951–1960.* Washington, DC: USAF Historical Liaison Office, December 1967.

Lendermann, Laura L. "The Rise of Air Mobility and Its Generals." Maxwell AFB, AL: Air University Press, 2008.

Lepard, Donald G. "Missiles, Men, and Management: Do USAF Policies and Directives Insure Adequately Trained Personnel to Maintain and Operate the Missile Force?" Master's thesis, Air War College, Maxwell AFB, AL, 1963.

Lindahl, Carl O. "A Look at Missile Combat Crew Status and Prestige." Research study no. 1195-71, Air Command and Staff College, Maxwell AFB, AL, 1971.

Lindsay, James M. *Congress and Nuclear Weapons.* Baltimore: Johns Hopkins University Press, 1991.

Lonnquest, John C. "The Face of Atlas: General Bernard Schriever and the Development of the Atlas Intercontinental Ballistic Missile, 1953–1960." PhD dissertation, Duke University, Durham, NC, 1996.

Lowther, Adam. "A Year Later: Responding to Problems in the ICBM Force." *Bulletin of the Atomic Scientists*, February 12, 2015. http://thebulletin.org/year-later-responding-problems-icbm-force7984.

Luckett, Robert S. "People Problems in the SAC Missile Force and What Is Being Done to Correct These Problems." Master's thesis, Air Command and Staff College, Maxwell AFB, AL, 1972.

Mabon, David W., ed. *Foreign Relations of the United States, 1961–1963.* Vol. 8, *National Security Policy*, Document 115. Washington: Government Printing Office, 1996.

MacKenzie, Donald A. *Inventing Accuracy: A Historical Sociology of Nuclear Missile Guidance*. Cambridge, MA: MIT Press, 1990.

Maes, Vincent O. "Career Satisfaction: A Focus on Missile Launch Officer Retention." Research study no. 1235-71, Air University, Maxwell AFB, AL, 1971.

Makowski, Louis F. "Motivation . . . A Problem of the Minuteman I Launch Control Officer." Master's thesis, Air Command and Staff College, Maxwell AFB, AL, 1966.

Martin, Donald F. "Effective Aerospace Power—Counterforce." *Air University Quarterly Review* 12, no. 3–4 (Winter–Spring 1960–61): 152–60.

———. "Nuclear-Powered Deterrence." *Air University Quarterly Review* 12, no. 1 (Spring 1960): 102–8.

Martin, Lawrence, ed. *Strategic Thought in the Nuclear Age*. Baltimore: Johns Hopkins University Press, 1979.

McCone, John Richard. "The Manned Bomber and the Ballistic Missile: Problems of Strategy and Politics." Master's thesis, University of Pittsburgh, 1962.

McCorkle, Charles. "Command and Control of Ballistic Missiles." *Air University Quarterly Review* 9, no. 3 (Summer 1957): 69–77.

McDougall, Walter. *The Heavens and the Earth: A Political History of the Space Age*. New York: Basic Books, 1985.

McGehee, Thomas K. "The Case for a Separate USAF Guided Missiles Command." Master's thesis, Air War College, Montgomery, AL, 1955.

McNamara, Robert. "American ABM Deployment." *Survival: Global Politics and Strategy* 9, no. 11 (1967): 342–46.

———. *Blundering into Disaster: Surviving the First Century of the Nuclear Age*. New York: Pantheon, 1986.

———. "Defense Arrangements of the North Atlantic Community." *Department of State Bulletin* 48, no. 1202 (July 9, 1962): 64–69.

———. *In Retrospect: The Tragedy and Lessons of Vietnam*. With Brian VanDeMark. New York: Random House, 1995.

———. "The Military Role of Nuclear Weapons: Perceptions and Misperceptions." *Foreign Affairs* 62, no. 1 (Fall 1983).

McRae, Kenneth. *Nuclear Dawn: F. E. Simon and the Race for Atomic Weapons in World War II*. Oxford: Oxford University Press, 2014.

Meehan, Harry D. "Phase-Out of Manned Bombers—Will Missiles Suffice?" Master's thesis, Air Command and Staff College, Maxwell AFB, AL, 1965.

Meilinger, Phillip. *Bomber: The Formation and Early Years of Strategic Air Command*. Maxwell AFB, AL: Air University Press, 2012.

——, ed. *Paths of Heaven: The Evolution of Airpower Theory*. Maxwell AFB, AL: Air University Press, 1997.

Metz, Roman A. "Design, Construction, and Operation of Missile Facilities." *Air University Review* 19, no. 3 (March–April 1968): 66–72.

Mieczkowski, Yanek. *Eisenhower's Sputnik Moment: The Race for Space and World Prestige*. Ithaca, NY: Cornell University Press, 2013.

"Minuteman Gains a Year: A Quarterly Review Picture Brief." *Air University Quarterly Review* 12, no. 2 (Summer 1960): 22–27.

"Missiles vs. Bombers: Congressional Committees Express Some Doubt." *Science* 133, no. 3464 (May 19, 1961): 1585–86. doi:10.1126/science .133.3464.1585.

Mitchell, Vance O. *Air Force Officers: Personnel Policy Development, 1944–1974*. Washington, DC: Air Force History and Museums Program, 1996.

Mitchell, William. *Winged Defense: The Development and Possibilities of Modern Airpower—Economic and Military*. New York: G. P. Putnam and Sons, 1925.

Morgan, Murray. "The Loneliness of the Missile Attendant." *Esquire*, July 1964, 50–53, 110.

Mueller, John. *Atomic Obsession: Nuclear Alarmism from Hiroshima to al-Qaeda*. New York: Oxford University Press, 2010.

Mueller, Karl P. "Strategic Airpower and Nuclear Strategy: New Theory for a Not-Quite-So-New Apocalypse." in *Paths of Heaven: The Evolution of Airpower Theory*, ed. Phillip Meilinger, 279–320. Maxwell AFB, AL: Air University Press, 1997.

Nalty, Bernard C. *USAF Ballistic Missile Programs, 1962–1964*. U.S. Air Force Historical Division Liaison Office, April 1966, Top Secret, Excised Copy. National Security Archives. Accessed November 6, 2013. http://www2 .gwu.edu/~nsarchiv/nukevault/ebb249/doc03.pdf.

——, ed. *Winged Shield, Winged Sword: A History of the United States Air Force*. 2 vols. Washington, DC: Air Force History and Museums Program, 1997.

Narducci, Henry M., ed. *SAC Missile Chronology, 1939–1988*. Offutt AFB, NE: Office of the Historian, HQ Strategic Air Command, 1990.

Nash, Philip. *The Other Missiles of October: Eisenhower, Kennedy, and the Jupiters, 1957–1963*. Chapel Hill: University of North Carolina Press, 1997.

Neal, Roy. *Ace in the Hole*. Garden City, NY: Doubleday, 1962.

Neufeld, Jacob. *The Development of Ballistic Missiles in the United States Air Force, 1945–1960*. Washington, DC: Office of Air Force History, 1990.

Newton, Jim. *Eisenhower: The White House Years*. New York: Doubleday, 2011.

Nitze, Paul. *From Hiroshima to Glasnost: At the Center of Decision*. With Ann Smith and Steven Reardon. New York: Grove Weidenfeld, 1989.

Norris, Robert, Steven Kosiak, and Stephen Schwartz. "Deploying the Bomb." In *Atomic Audit: The Costs and Consequences of U.S. Nuclear Weapons Since 1940*, ed. Stephen Schwartz, 105–96. Washington, DC: Brookings Institution Press, 1998.

Office of the Assistant to the Secretary of Defense (Atomic Energy). *History of the Custody and Deployment of Nuclear Weapons (U) July 1945 through September 1977*, February 1978. http://nautilus.org/wp-content/uploads/2015/04/306.pdf.

Ogletree, Greg. *The Missile Badge: A Not So Brief History*. Breckenridge, CO: Association of Air Force Missileers, 2002.

Osborne, Edward W. "An Analysis of the Morale of Titan II Missile Combat Crews." Master's thesis, Air Command and Staff College, Maxwell AFB, AL, 1967.

Page, Jerry D. "Tooling Up for the Ballistic Missiles Training Program." *Air University Quarterly Review* 10, no. 4 (Winter 1958–59): 6–20.

Paolucci, John F. "Making Minuteman Missile Combat Crew Duty a Challenge—A Radical View." Master's thesis, Air Command and Staff College, Maxwell AFB, AL, 1977.

Pappalardo, Joe. "A Disgraced Air Force General's Last Interview." *Popular Mechanics*, January 6, 2014. http://www.popularmechanics.com/military/a9924/a-disgraced-air-force-generals-last-interview-16341301/.

Paret, Peter, ed. *Makers of Modern Strategy from Machiavelli to the Nuclear Age*. Princeton, NJ: Princeton University Press, 1986.

Parrish, Noel F. "Effective Aerospace Power—Deterrence: The Hard Questions." *Air University Quarterly Review* 12, no. 3–4 (Winter–Spring 1960–61): 148–51.

Pearl, Albert L. "The SAC Management Control System." *Air University Quarterly Review* 13, no. 4 (Summer 1962): 17–27.

Perry, Robert. "The Atlas, Thor, and Titan." *Technology and Culture* 4, no. 4 (Autumn 1963): 466–77. http://www.jstor.org/stable/3101380.

———. *The Ballistic Missile Decisions*. Paper #P-3686. Santa Monica, CA: RAND, 1967.

Peterson, Edward H. "Atlas Launch Crew Proficiency." *Air University Quarterly Review* 10, no. 3 (Fall 1958): 57–63.

Phillips, Thomas R. "The Growing Power of the Soviet Air Force." *Reporter* (June 30, 1955): 16–19.

Podvig, Pavel, ed. *Russian Strategic Nuclear Forces.* Cambridge, MA: MIT Press, 2001.

Polmar, Norman. *Strategic Air Command: People, Aircraft, and Missiles.* Mount Pleasant, SC: Nautical and Aviation Publishing Company of America, 1979.

Polmar, Norman, and Robert S. Morris. *The U.S. Nuclear Arsenal: A History of Weapons and Delivery Systems since 1945.* Annapolis, MD: Naval Institute Press, 2009.

Pomeroy, Steven. *Echoes That Never Were: American Mobile Intercontinental Ballistic Missiles, 1956–1983.* Wright-Patterson AFB, Fairborn, OH: USAF Air Force Institute of Technology, 2006.

Power, Thomas. *Design for Survival.* Toronto, Canada: Coward-McCann, 1965.

———. "SAC and the Ballistic Missile." *Air University Quarterly Review* 9, no. 4 (Winter 1957–58): 2–30.

Preble, Christopher A. *John F. Kennedy and the Missile Gap.* DeKalb, IL: Northern Illinois University Press, 2004.

———. "Who Ever Believed in the 'Missile Gap'? John F. Kennedy and the Politics of National Security." *Presidential Studies Quarterly* 33, no. 4 (December 2003): 801–26.

President's Air Policy Commission. *Survival in the Air Age.* Washington, DC: U.S. Government Printing Office, 1948.

Prichard, Gilbert L. "A Re-Evaluation of the Roles and Missions of the Armed Forces in Light of New Weapons Development." Individual Research Paper, National War College, 1957.

Pringle, Peter, and William Arkin. *SIOP: The Secret U.S. Plan for Nuclear War.* New York: Norton, 1983.

Putnam, Claude E. "Missiles in Perspective." *Air University Quarterly Review* 10, no. 1 (Spring 1958): 2–10.

Putney, Snell, and Middleton, Russell. "Some Factors Associated with Student Acceptance of or Rejection of War." *American Sociological Review* 27, no. 5 (October 1, 1962): 655–67.

Rearden, Steven L. *The Formative Years, 1947–1950.* Vol. 1, *History of the Office of the Secretary of Defense.* Washington, DC: Historical Office, Office of the Secretary of Defense, 2012.

Reed, George A. "U.S. Defense Policy, U.S. Air Force Doctrine and Strategic Nuclear Weapon Systems, 1958–1964: The Case of the Minuteman ICBM." PhD dissertation, Duke University, Durham, NC, 1986.

Reeves, Richard. *President Kennedy: Profile of Power.* New York: Simon and Schuster, 1993.

Richardson, Robert C., III. "In the Looking Glass." *Air University Quarterly Review* 9, no. 4 (Winter 1957–58): 46–54.

Robb, Donald S. "An Analysis of the Probable Effects of an Underground Environment upon Men Assigned to Hardened Missile Sites." Special study no. 1287-61. Air Command and Staff College, Maxwell AFB, AL, 1961.

Rockefeller Brothers Fund. *Prospect for America.* Garden City, NY: Doubleday, 1961.

Rodwell, Robert. "Morale in a Missile Force." *Aeronautics* 38, no. 1 (March 1958): 66.

Roman, Peter J. "American Strategic Nuclear Force Planning, 1957–1960: The Interaction of Politics and Military Planning." PhD dissertation, University of Wisconsin, Madison, WI, 1989.

———. *Eisenhower and the Missile Gap.* Ithaca, NY: Cornell University Press, 1996.

———. "Strategic Bombers over the Missile Horizon, 1957–1963." *Journal of Strategic Studies* 18, no. 1 (1995): 198–236.

Rosenberg, Max. *The Air Force and the National Guided Missile Program, 1944–1950.* Washington, DC: USAF Historical Division Liaison Office, 1964.

———. "USAF Ballistic Missiles, 1958–1959." USAF Historical Division Liaison Office, July 1960, Secret, Excised Copy. National Security Archives. Accessed November 6, 2013. https://nsarchive2.gwu.edu//nukevault/ebb249/doc01.pdf.

Rothstein, Stephen M. "Dead on Arrival? The Development of the Aerospace Concept, 1944–1958." Master's thesis, School of Advanced Airpower Studies, Montgomery, AL, 1999.

Rowan, Henry. "The Evolution of Strategic Doctrine." In *Strategic Thought in the Nuclear Age,* ed. Lawrence Martin, 131–56. Baltimore: Johns Hopkins University Press, 1979.

Ruehrmund, James, Jr., and Christopher Bowie. *Arsenal of Airpower: USAF Aircraft Inventory 1950–2009.* Washington, DC: Mitchell Institute Press, 2010.

Ruggiero, Francis X. "Missileers' Heritage." Master's thesis, Air Command and Staff College, Maxwell AFB, AL, 1981.

Russell, Kendall. "Strategic Missiles and Basing Concepts." *Air University Quarterly Review* 13, no. 3 (Spring 1962): 69–82.

Sampson, Charles S., ed. *Foreign Relations of the United States, 1961–1963.* Vol. 6, *Kennedy-Khrushchev Exchanges.* Washington, DC: Government Printing Office, 1996.

Schlesinger, Arthur M. *Robert Kennedy and His Times.* Boston: Houghton Mifflin, 1978.

Schlosser, Eric. *Command and Control: Nuclear Weapons, the Damascus Incident, and the Illusion of Safety.* New York: Penguin, 2013.

Schofield, Martin B. "Control of Outer Space." *Air University Quarterly Review* 10, no. 1 (Spring 1957–58): 99–101.

Scholin, Allan R. "Aerospace World." *Air Force and Space Digest* 50, no. 1 (December 1964): 24.

Schriever, Bernard A. "Forecast." *Air University Quarterly Review* 16, no. 3 (March–April 1965): 2–12.

———. "ICBM—A Step toward Space Conquest." Speech given at the Astronautics Symposium, San Diego, California, in February 1957, in *Selected Documents in Air Force Space History,* ed. David N. Spires, 20–26. Peterson AFB, CO: Air Force Space Command, 2004.

———. "The USAF Ballistic Missile Program." *Air University Quarterly Review* 9, no. 3 (Summer 1957): 5–21.

Schwartz, Stephen, ed. *Atomic Audit: The Costs and Consequences of U.S. Nuclear Weapons since 1940.* Washington, DC: Brookings Institution Press, 1998.

Schwiebert, Ernest G. *A History of the U.S. Air Force Ballistic Missiles.* New York: Praeger, 1965.

Segell, Glen, ed. *Nuclear Strategy: The Jim King Manuscripts.* London: Glen Segell, 2006.

Self, Mary R. *History of the Development of Guided Missiles, 1946–1950.* Wright-Patterson AFB, OH: Historical Office, Air Material Command, 1951.

Shachtman, Noah. "Bosses Nuked, Some Air Force Missileers Cheer." *Wired,* June 6, 2008. http://www.wired.com/2008/06/defense-secreta-2/.

Sheehan, Neil. *A Fiery Peace in a Cold War: Bernard Schriever and the Ultimate Weapon.* New York: Random House, 2009.

Sherman, Donald H. "Boredom and Monotony: Their Effect on Titan II Crew Morale." Research Study no. 1136-69, Air Command and Staff College, Maxwell AFB, AL, 1969.

Sherwood, John Darrell. *Officers in Flight Suits.* New York: New York University Press, 1996.

Siddiqi, Asif. *Challenge to Apollo: The Soviet Union and the Space Race, 1945–1974.* Washington, DC: NASA, 2000.

———. *The Red Rockets' Glare: Spaceflight and the Soviet Imagination, 1857–1957.* New York: Cambridge University Press, 2010.

Sights, Albert P., Jr. "We Can Win a Nuclear War." *Air University Review* 14, no. 4 (September–October 1963): 37–45.

Simpson, Charlie. "LOX and RP-1—Fire Waiting to Happen." *AAFM [Association of Air Force Missileers]* 14, no. 3 (September 2006): 1–6.

———. "Missileers, Inspections, Morale." *AAFM [Association of Air Force Missileers]* 21, no. 2 (June 2013): 6–9.

Smith, Frederic H., Jr. "Nuclear Weapons and Limited War." *Air University Quarterly Review* 12, no. 1 (Spring 1960): 3–27.

Smith, James S. "Who Will Lead Tomorrow's Air Force?" *Air University Quarterly Review* 9, no. 4 (Winter 1957–58): 69–79.

Smith, Kenneth A. "The Ballistic Missile and Its Elusive Targets." *Air University Quarterly Review* 10, no. 1 (Spring 1958): 61–72.

Smith, Pierce L. "Motivation of Minuteman Missile Crews." Master's thesis, Air Command and Staff College, Maxwell AFB, AL, 1965.

Smith, R. Jeffrey. "Aiming High." *Slate*, April 14, 2014. http://www.slate.com/articles/news_and_politics/politics/2014/04/air_force_s_nuclear_missile_corps_is_struggling_millennial_missileers_suffer.html.

Smith, Tom W. "Trends: The Cuban Missile Crisis and U.S. Public Opinion." *Public Opinion Quarterly* 67, no. 2 (Summer 2003): 265–93.

Snead, David. "Eisenhower and the Gaither Report: The Influence of a Committee of Experts on National Security Policy in the Late 1950s." PhD dissertation, University of Virginia, 1997.

Sorensen, Ted. *Counselor: Life at the Edge of History.* New York: Harper, 2008.

South, Oron P. "The Door to the Future." *Air University Quarterly Review* 9, no. 4 (Winter 1957–58): 110–26.

Spinetta, Lawrence. "The Glass Ceiling for Remotely Piloted Aircraft." *Air & Space Power Journal* 29, no. 5 (July–August 2013): 101–18.

———. "White vs. LeMay: The Battle over Ballistic Missiles." *Air Force Magazine* 96, no. 1 (January 2013): 56–60.

Spires, David. *On Alert: An Operational History of the United States Intercontinental Ballistic Missile Program, 1945–2011.* Colorado Springs, CO: U.S. Space Command, 2012.

Stenvick, Luther L. *The Agile Giant: A History of the Minuteman Production Board.* Seattle: Boeing Company, 1966.

Stephens, Allen W. "Missilemen—Present and Future." *Air University Quarterly Review* 10, no. 1 (Spring 1958): 11–19.

Stevenson, Jonathan. *Thinking beyond the Unthinkable: Harnessing Doom from the Cold War to the Age of Terror.* New York: Viking, 2008.

"The Stever Report: A Quarterly Review Staff Report." *Air University Quarterly Review* 10, no. 3 (Fall 1958): 43–56.

Stimson, Henry L., and McGeorge Bundy. *On Active Service in Peace and War.* New York: Harper, 1948.

Stumpf, David K. *Air Force Missileers.* Paducah, KY: Turner, 1998.

———. *Titan II: A History of a Cold War Missile Program.* Fayetteville: University of Arkansas Press, 2000.

Sugg, Lem Davis. "An Analysis of the Organization of the Atlas F Strategic Missile Squadron." Master's thesis (no. 1401–65), Air Command and Staff College, Maxwell AFB, AL, 1965.

Tannenwald, Nina. *The Nuclear Taboo: The United States and the Non-Use of Nuclear Weapons since 1945.* New York: Cambridge University Press, 2007.

———. "Nuclear Weapons and the Vietnam War." *Journal of Strategic Studies* 29, no. 4 (August 2006): 675–77.

Tate, James P. *The Army and Its Air Corps: Army Policy toward Aviation, 1919–1941.* Maxwell AFB, AL: Air University Press, 1998.

Taylor, Maxwell D. *The Uncertain Trumpet.* New York: Harper, 1959.

Thompson, Mark. "Air Force Applies a Band-Aid to a Sucking Chest Wound." *Time,* March 31, 2014. http://time.com/41088/air-force-cheating -scandal/.

———. "Are You Smarter than a Nuclear Launch Officer?" *Time,* February 13, 2014. http://time.com/8530/are-you-smarter-than-a-nuclear-launch -officer/.

Truman, Harry S. *Memoirs: Years of Trial and Hope,* vol. 2. Garden City, NY: Doubleday, 1956.

Tsiolkovsky, Konstantin. "Exploring Space with Reactive Devices." *Scientific Review* (in Cyrillic), 1903.

Ulanoff, Stanley. *Illustrated Guide to U.S. Missiles and Rockets.* New York: Doubleday, 1959.

"The USAF Reports to Congress: A Quarterly Review Staff Report." *Air University Quarterly Review* 10, no. 1 (Spring 1958): 30–60.

van Dijk, Ruud, William Gray, Svetlana Savranskaya, Jeremi Suri, and Qiang Zhai, eds. *Encyclopedia of the Cold War.* New York: Routledge, 2008.

Walin, William J. "Career: The Intercontinental Ballistic Missile Program." Research study no. 1345-69, Air Command and Staff College, Maxwell AFB, AL, 1969.

Walker, Chuck, and Joel Powell. *Atlas: The Ultimate Weapon by Those Who Built It*. Burlington, ON: Apogee, 2005.

Watson, George, Jr. *The Office of the Secretary of the Air Force, 1947–1965*. Washington, DC: Center for Air Force History, 1993.

Watson, Robert J. *History of the Office of the Secretary of Defense*. Vol. 4, *Into the Missile Age, 1956–1960*. Washington, DC: Historical Office, U.S. Department of Defense, 1997.

Wenger, Andreas. *Living with Peril: Eisenhower, Kennedy, and Nuclear Weapons*. Lanham, MD: Rowman and Littlefield, 1997.

Wheless, Hewitt T. "The Deterrent Offensive Force." *Air University Quarterly Review* 12, no. 3–4 (Winter–Spring 1960–61): 59–73.

White, Thomas D. "The Aerospace and Military Operations." *Air University Quarterly Review* 12, no. 3–4 (Winter–Spring 1960–61): 4–8.

———. "The Ballistic Missile: An Instrument of National Policy." *Air University Quarterly Review* 9, no. 3 (Summer 1957): 2–4.

———. "USAF's Ten Top Priorities." *Air Force Magazine* 43, no. 9 (September 1960).

Williams, Harry C. "ICBM Career Management: The Impact of Advancement." Master's thesis, Air Command and Staff College, Maxwell AFB, AL, 1972.

Williams, Robert C., and Philip L. Cantelon, eds. *The American Atom: A Documentary History of Nuclear Policies from the Discovery of Fission to the Present, 1939–1984*. Philadelphia: University of Pennsylvania Press, 1984.

Wilson, Gill Robb. "The Public View of the Air Force." *Air University Quarterly Review* 6, no. 4 (Winter 1953–54): 3–7.

Wittner, Lawrence. *Resisting the Bomb: A History of the World Nuclear Disarmament Movement, 1954–1970*. Stanford, CA: Stanford University Press, 1997.

Wohlstetter, Albert. "Delicate Balance of Terror." *Foreign Affairs* 37, no. 2 (January 1959): 211–34. http://www.jstor.org/stable/20029345.

Wolfers, Arnold. "The Atomic Bomb in Soviet-American Relations." In *The Absolute Weapon: Atomic Power and World Order*, ed. Bernard Brodie, 111–47. New York: Harcourt, Brace, 1946.

Wolk, Herman S. "Men Who Made the Air Force." *Air University Review*, September–October 1972. Accessed October 27, 2012. http://www.airpower.au.af.mil/airchronicles/aureview/1972/sep-oct/wolk.html.

Worden, Mike. *Rise of the Fighter Generals: The Problem of Air Force Leadership, 1945–1982*. Maxwell AFB, AL: Air University Press, 1998.

Yoder, Edwin M., Jr. *Joe Alsop's Cold War: A Study of Journalistic Influence and Intrigue*. Chapel Hill: University of North Carolina Press, 1995.

York, Herbert. *Race to Oblivion: A Participant's View of the Arms Race.* New York: Simon and Schuster, 1970.

Young, Bill. "Silent Sentinals." *Fly Past*, no. 225 (April 2000): 36–37.

Zaloga, Steven J. *The Kremlin's Nuclear Sword: The Rise and Fall of Russia's Strategic Nuclear Forces, 1945–2000.* Washington, DC: Smithsonian Institution Press, 2002.

———. *V-2 Ballistic Missile 1942–52.* Oxford: Osprey Publishing, 2003.

INDEX

ABOUT THE AUTHOR

David W. Bath teaches military history at Rogers State University in Oklahoma. He served as an Air Force missileer at the end of the Cold War and edited *Air Force Missileers and the Cuban Missile Crisis*, a collection of personal reminiscences of the crisis, for the Association of Air Force Missileers in 2012.

The **Naval Institute Press** is the book-publishing arm of the U.S. Naval Institute, a private, nonprofit, membership society for sea service professionals and others who share an interest in naval and maritime affairs. Established in 1873 at the U.S. Naval Academy in Annapolis, Maryland, where its offices remain today, the Naval Institute has members worldwide.

Members of the Naval Institute support the education programs of the society and receive the influential monthly magazine *Proceedings* or the colorful bimonthly magazine *Naval History* and discounts on fine nautical prints and on ship and aircraft photos. They also have access to the transcripts of the Institute's Oral History Program and get discounted admission to any of the Institute-sponsored seminars offered around the country.

The Naval Institute's book-publishing program, begun in 1898 with basic guides to naval practices, has broadened its scope to include books of more general interest. Now the Naval Institute Press publishes about seventy titles each year, ranging from how-to books on boating and navigation to battle histories, biographies, ship and aircraft guides, and novels. Institute members receive significant discounts on the Press' more than eight hundred books in print.

Full-time students are eligible for special half-price membership rates. Life memberships are also available.

For a free catalog describing Naval Institute Press books currently available, and for further information about joining the U.S. Naval Institute, please write to:

Member Services
U.S. Naval Institute
291 Wood Road
Annapolis, MD 21402-5034
Telephone: (800) 233-8764
Fax: (410) 571-1703
Web address: www.usni.org